MAKING IT IN

Public Relations

AN INSIDER'S GUIDE TO

CAREER OPPORTUNITIES

SECOND EDITION

Leonard Mogel

LAWRENCE ERLBAUM ASSOCIATES, PUBLISHERS

2002   Mahwah, New Jersey   London

Acquisitions Editor:	Linda Bathgate
Editorial Assistant:	Karin Bates
Cover Design:	Kathryn Houghtaling Lacey
Textbook Production Manager:	Paul Smolenski
Full-Service Compositor:	TechBooks
Text and Cover Printer:	Sheridan Books, Inc.

This book was typeset in 11/13 pt. Sabon, Italic, Bold, Bold Italic.
The heads were typeset in Optima Extra Black.

Lawrence Erlbaum Associates, Inc., Publishers
10 Industrial Avenue
Mahwah, New Jersey 07430

Library of Congress Cataloging-in-Publication Data

Mogel, Leonard.
Making it in public relations : an insider's guide to career
opportunities / Leonard Mogel.—2nd ed.
p.   cm.
Includes bibliographical references and index.
ISBN 0-8058-4021-4 (case : alk. paper)—ISBN 0-8058-4022-2 (pbk. : alk. paper)
1. Public relations—United States.   2. Public relations.   I. Title.
HM1221 .M64   2002
659.2   2001051226

Books published by Lawrence Erlbaum Associates are printed on
acid-free paper, and their bindings are chosen for strength and durability.

Printed in the United States of America
10 9 8 7 6 5 4 3 2 1

At first it was, "Do we need to write another book?" But then once we were into it, she thrust herself into every step—thinking, editing, organizing, correcting misjudgments, finding just the right word to clarify a concept. Her friendship and love guided the daily enterprise. This book is dedicated to Ann Mogel. It is as much hers as mine.

ACKNOWLEDGMENTS

We met Linda Bathgate of Erlbaum Associates at an Association for Education in Journalism and Mass Communication convention in Phoenix, and it didn't take more than a few weeks for Linda to convince her associates that they should publish a second edition of *Making It in Public Relations*. I am indebted to Linda for her professional excellence, guidance, and intelligent advice.

My special appreciation to Janice Handler of TechBooks for her consummate supervision of the copyediting and final stages of the book's preparation.

Thanks to Peter Pitts of Wired World for his contribution to the book.

I may miss a few names but my sincere gratitude for splendid cooperation goes to Erin Rice-Mills, Liza Olsen, and Mischelle Leathers of Burson-Marsteller; Mike Lynch of the American Medical Association; Howard J. Rubenstein of Howard J. Rubenstein Associates; Catherine A. Bolton, president and chief operating officer of PRSA; John Bomier, Maggi Heffler, and Kimberly Baldwin of the Public Relations Society of America; Fraser P. Seitel, editor of PRSA's *STRATEGIST*, and John Elsasser, editor of PRSA's *TACTICS*;

Richard W. Edelman, Dana Grossman, Mark Bennett, and Barbie Casasus of Edelman Public Relations Worldwide; Charles Fremes and Johanne Papa of Edelman Public Relations (Canada); Jack Bergen and Sarah Drennan of the Council of Public Relations Firms; Juliette Don of the Bank of America; Jim Sinkinson of *Bulldog Reporter*; Rick Kaufman of the Jefferson County Public Schools, Golden, Colorado; Steve Stromp of Bernard Haldane Associates; Hilary Phillips of *Washington Post/Newsweek Interactive*; Douglas G. Pinkham and Wes Pedersen of the Public Affairs Council; Steven Style of the Steven Style Group; Suzanne Laurita and Samantha Fearn of Hill & Knowlton; Charles Francis of IdeaBank, Inc.; Derek Creevey of Ogilvy Public Relations; John Figurski of *PRWEEK*; Michael Guiney of Weber Shandwick Worldwide; Carrie Fenton and Laura Bachrach of BSMG Worldwide.

Special thanks of Holland Cooke for his contribution to the job search chapter and to the late John West for his insight in the chapter on entertainment and public relations.

CONTENTS

INTRODUCTION

Then and now. I was a novice printing salesman canvassing the famous Brill Building in New York's Times Square district for prospective customers. The building's tenants were a mixed bag of song pluggers, song publishers, song writers, agents, and even a few bookies who somehow convinced the building's management that they were legit. I didn't care what they did as long as they needed letterheads, envelopes, and business cards, my specialty.

I would start my cold canvassing on the top floor and work my way down. On one of these sales calls I came upon the painted metal door of an office that had a half-dozen names listed, so I thought it had good business possibilities. Upon entering, I presented my card to the only person in the office, a slovenly character in his early thirties. He introduced himself as Richie Roberts (his name has been changed for the purpose of this book).

When I arrived, he was on his way out and asked me to join him for a drink. It was early in the day, but I figured this was a good way to become fast friends, especially if he paid. The drink turned out to be an egg cream, a New York delicacy made of carbonated water, chocolate syrup, and milk (no egg, no cream). He ordered two for himself and one for me, then walked directly across the street to another candy store where he repeated the order for himself.

Later, back in his office, Roberts told me that he was a press agent. I didn't know just what a press agent did, but I was nonetheless impressed. He went on to explain with pride that most of his clients were Broadway restaurants. His job was to get the names of the restaurants into the major syndicated newspaper gossip columns. To accomplish this, Roberts would "package" a press release that included a small joke attributed to a name comedian or actor who was dining at one of Roberts's client restaurants.

All parties benefited from this collaborative "public relations." Columnists were pleased because this kind of journalism required little effort on their part. The comedian got his name in print, and Roberts's restaurant assumed status as the home base of the celebrated.

Who could resist eating at Sardi's if Henny Youngman or Rodney Dangerfield might be at the next table telling brilliantly funny stories? For this press agentry, Roberts was paid a small amount of cash plus free meals at the restaurant on slow Monday nights.

Roberts's biggest public relations client was a matchmaking service owned by one Sarah Kane; her Roberts-created slogan: "Don't live in vain, see Sarah Kane." For $25 the client was guaranteed three introductions, usually from a roster of unemployed actors. If the client was an older woman, Roberts's father was invariably one of the introductions.

Roberts's career path eventually led him to dubious Hollywood fame as a successful producer and director of "B" movies.

His brand of PR bears only a remote resemblance to the profession as it exists in the 21st century.

Today's PR is a diversified medium involving more than thirty practice areas or components from advocacy to strategic corporate PR, and includes such high-impact elements as crisis communications, planning, management, and recovery.

Large multinational corporations have in-house staffs of 200 to 300 people and, in addition, engage outside PR firms with international branches. We discuss one giant corporation's PR activities in a later chapter.

Then there is the area of new media and Internet PR. Many PR firms receive assignments from technology startups for which they are required to have a thorough understanding of hardware, software, online content, satellite and wireless communications, channel marketing, and systems integration.

Twenty-first-century PR is on a roll. It is replacing advertising as a corporation's primary source for getting its message across because it is often more cost-effective than advertising in building brands and reaching customers and constituents.

The PR boom means more jobs, higher salaries, and opportunities across the broad spectrum. In this book we analyze the modern practice of PR and discuss how it serves a wide variety of institutions in our society.

CHAPTER 1

A Very Short History of Public Relations

Perhaps it's a bit of a stretch, but some say the practice of public relations goes back more than 2,000 years to the time of Julius Caesar. Old Julius may have been recording history when he wrote his commentaries, but as the leader of all the Romans and the coiner of the memorable *veni, vidi, vici,* he was using an early form of PR to persuade the citizenry that he was doing a great job.

PR in its most basic form developed in the United States in the early 1800s when newspapers ran friendly notices in news columns to reward advertisers with "free publicity."

Literary bureaus were developed to contrive such items, and by the early 20th century, publicity agents, often former journalists, abounded in New York and in other large cities. This activity was an important element in the evolution of public relations and continues in modern-day press agentry and the promotion of special events.

THE ROBBER BARONS, RAKING THE MUCK, AND BEYOND

The latter part of the 19th century saw the rise of the "robber barons," industrialists such as Cornelius Vanderbilt, Jay Gould, and James Fisk, whose acquisitive business practices had as their precept "the public be damned." To counter their negative image, robber barons hired skillful and often unscrupulous press agents.

The excesses of these businessmen were targeted by a group of writers known as "muckrakers": Lincoln Steffens, Upton Sinclair, and Ida Tarbell, among others. One of their prime targets was the oil magnate, John D. Rockefeller.

In 1906, Ivy Lee, a former newspaperman and the founder of modern PR, was hired as publicity adviser by a group of anthracite coalmine operators who had drawn the attention of the press by their haughty attitudes toward the miners and the press in labor disputes. At that time, it was not a common practice for industrialists such as the mine owners to answer questions from the press about their activities. Lee, reasoning that it was good business for the mine owners to be more open, sent out an announcement that the operators would supply the press with all possible information.

Later that year Lee was retained by the Pennsylvania Railroad and introduced a new practice to that industry—the supplying of full information to the press about railroad accidents. In this he was forging a major ingredient of what would later be called public relations.

Rockefeller was Ivy Lee's first major client. One of Lee's well-publicized stunts was John D.'s distribution of dimes to children.

Early in the 20th century, government agencies began hiring publicity experts in Great Britain and the United States. These specialists were called "directors of information."

After World War I, public relations came into wide use in business and industry as well as in government. Today, under various titles, all government agencies have public affairs or public relations departments. When an important announcement is made, or a press conference is called, it emanates from these departments.

Significant in the history of modern PR is the contribution of Edward L. Bernays, who was still pursuing an active career when he died in 1995 at the venerable age of 105. Bernays coined the phrase "counsel on public relations."

Pejoratively labeled a huckster, a self-serving self-publicist, and the "Father of Spin," others credit this visionary image maker as an important theorist who dreamed up the modern industry of public relations. He wrote the first book and taught the first university course on the subject. His stunts are legendary. When it was taboo for women in the 1920s to smoke cigarettes in public, Bernays had socialites light up "torches of freedom" on Fifth Avenue—and alerted the press.

During his lengthy career, Bernays counseled such clients as Thomas Edison, Henry Ford, and Eleanor Roosevelt. He also advised former presidents Woodrow Wilson, Calvin Coolidge, and Dwight D. Eisenhower. Bernays reportedly turned down Adolf Hitler as a client, claiming, "I wouldn't want it on my superego [Bernay's uncle was Sigmund Freud] that I did for money what I wouldn't do without money."

In the 1950s, Bernays represented the United Fruit Company. When a leftist government challenged his client's interests in Guatemala, he was instrumental in spinning a widespread press campaign that led to a CIA-sponsored coup.

PR enjoyed exponential growth in the 20th century. Large corporations employed in-house staffs of as many as 200 to 300 people engaged in various aspects of PR.

In the United States and abroad, federal and local governments retain extensive staffs of PR specialists to deal with the press, as well as with their constituents.

And in business, PR executives now perform on an equal basis with advertising personnel in shaping and executing a client's marketing objectives.

Public relations is a major industry today, employing a vast network of skilled communicators charged with the responsibility of interpreting the client to the public and vice versa.

As we show in this book, public relations' exponential growth in the 21st century will be further escalated by the challenges of the new media revolution.

CHAPTER 2

Public Relations: What It Is, What It Does

Hill & Knowlton, one of the world's premier public relations firms, is an arm of the giant WPP Group, an advertising and marketing organization with more than $5 billion in annual worldwide gross income. Hill & Knowlton's U.S. fee income exceeded $177 million in 2000. Some of its major PR activities have included providing communications counsel for the Three Mile Island nuclear reactor crisis, a disastrous earthquake in Mexico City, the largest bank insolvency in the world, and the largest industrial bankruptcy.

During the same period, Hill & Knowlton put its skills to work in communications management for Humana's artificial heart implants. It introduced a new antiobesity pharmaceutical in Europe and Mexico, and created communications platforms to support ongoing immunization messages for a full spectrum of vaccinations in Australia.

While all this was going on, the firm was involved in new-product launches for Crest toothpaste, NutraSweet artificial sweetener, and Discover credit card.

At this writing, Hill & Knowlton offers its experience and expertise to such heavyweights as Boeing, Motorola, New York Life, Continental Airlines, and E*TRADE.

We can already gain a sense of the widespread diversity of PR functions. Of course, only a large PR firm such as Hill & Knowlton with global offices and hundreds of personnel can tackle issues and assignments of this breadth.

Other public relations firms are making news for their clients in traditional media outlets, as well as in the new universe of online media and e-business marketing. So, for example, Ogilvy Public Relations, another top 10 firm owned by the WPP Group, pioneered the first web-based study for its client Harvard University's Center for Cancer Prevention. Its purpose was to assess the utility of new media in educating people to make lifestyle changes that reduce the risk of cancer.

Most large organizations have their own PR and communications departments, but engage the counsel of PR firms as well. In chapter 6, we examine the extensive in-house public relations and communications activity of the Bank of America, the largest U.S. bank.

WHAT IS PUBLIC RELATIONS?

The foregoing are examples of PR in action. We discuss many more in this book. But first, here are some general definitions, beginning with *public relations*. A simple definition we like comes from *Lesly's PR Handbook*.[1] PR can be defined as "helping an organization (or group) and its publics adapt mutually to each other."

What is a *public*. A public is an entity *whose attention is sought* by a business corporation, an individual, a performer or writer or artist, a government or governmental agency, a charitable institution, a religious body, or almost any person or organization. The publics may be as diverse as female voters of a particular political party or the shareholders of a public corporation. To the Merck pharmaceutical company marketing a new antidepressant drug, its publics are medical practitioners, consumer advocates, the Food and Drug Administration (FDA), and, of course, patients.

To the giant Dow Chemical Company with 121 manufacturing sites in 32 countries and customers in 168 countries, its publics are employees, retirees, investors, governments, nongovernmental organizations, human rights and environmental groups, and community leaders with different media, policies, and cultures.

The Concerns of Public Relations

PR deals with the subject entity, or client, and the publics involved. Acquainting the clients with public perceptions of that client is an important element of PR; so is affecting these perceptions by focusing, curtailing, amplifying, or augmenting information about the client as it is conveyed to the publics.

In its simplest form, PR is concerned with creating a favorable climate for marketing the client's products or services. This becomes less simple in a crisis when the client is, say, a public company that shows a large earnings loss for the year or an automobile company whose defective tires have caused highway deaths.

To a large extent, the job of PR is to make good news as effective as possible and to forestall bad news. When disaster strikes, the PR practitioner's job is to assess the situation and the damage quickly, to assemble all the facts and background information, and to offer these to the news media, along with answers to their questions. It is the responsibility of PR to organize the client's response, often involving complicated issues.

Crisis communications and crisis management are big-league games in PR practice, but worldwide public affairs, major new product introduction, investor relations, and more than a dozen other activities and practice areas are no less important. These responsibilities all fit under the umbrella of public relations. We show how it unfolds.

The Tools of Public Relations

In carrying out the PR function, the industry calls on many peripheral services. Among these are:

Press release services
Satellite message delivery systems
Video news release preparation
Media monitoring
Speaker's bureaus
Media directories
Clipping bureaus
Computer-aided research and media analysis
Satellite interview tours
Desktop publishing services
Public speaking training

Film and video productions
Databank services
Preparation of corporate advertising
Writing and editing publications
Design and writing annual reports
Staging events
Arranging press conferences and interviews
Planning and coordinating media tours
Ghostwriting op-ed and bylined articles
Coordinating electronic communication

The sophistication of public relations practice today demands the implementation of these tools in a field in which a PR professional may be called on to perform such diverse activities as producing a 30-minute promotional film for a client, targeting politicians and other key decision makers on an issue, organizing the investment community solicitation on behalf of an Internet startup company, and developing a crisis response program for a client's product recall.

The Size of the PR Work Force

According to the most recent report of the U.S. Bureau of Labor Statistics, there are more than 200,000 PR professionals in the United States. The Institute for PR Research and Education estimates that there are approximately 250,000 to 300,000 people employed in PR and public affairs. John Budd, a prominent executive with a PR firm, claims that there are "some half million people with PR of some sort in their job titles."[2] Whoever is right about the employment numbers, on the basis of the vast amount of money spent annually on PR alone we can conclude that it is a major communications area. It is also one with exciting job possibilities.

In the United States, public relations is a multi-billion-dollar business. It is one of the fastest growing industries, with a projected growth of 47% between 1994 and 2005.

At the governmental level, the Department of Defense employs about 1,000 communications specialists, and the U.S. Information Agency has 9,000 communications people on its staff. Communications personnel are also employed in large numbers at the state and municipal level.

Academically, the number of college students majoring in public relations has risen dramatically. In 1951, only 12 colleges offered major programs in PR, and that number did not increase by much in the 1960s. At this writing, more than 22,000 students at 300 colleges are either majoring in PR or taking a least one course in this subject. The Public Relations Student Society of America (PRSSA) has more than 6,500 student members at 209 U.S. colleges and universities. There are also 5,400 U.S. companies and 500 trade associations with PR departments.

In chapter 4 we focus on the 10 largest global PR firms. But in the United States there are also 5,400 other firms.

Salaries in PR are basically equivalent to those in other media and communications professions. Top communications executives at major PR firms and at corporations draw six-figure salaries.

Public Relations Publics

We have offered a brief definition of a public and noted that different types of organizations have different publics. In Fraser P. Seitel's definitive book, *The Practice of Public Relations*, the author lists 20 key publics of a typical multinational corporation. These are groups and organizations with whom the corporation is closely involved. The term *stakeholder* is also sometimes used instead of public. Here are a few of Seitel's examples[3]:

Stockholders
Investment community
Dealers/distributors
Customers
Federal, state, local legislators
Board of directors
Labor unions

It is important to understand the relationship of an organization to its publics. The subject of publics also deals with images, identity, and reputation. We again quote Seitel: "It takes a great deal of time to build a favorable image for a corporation but only one slip to create a negative public impression. In other words, the corporate image is a fragile commodity."[4]

Other publics are equally important to a corporation or large organization. Add to this list scientific, trade, and professional organizations, special-interest groups such as women and minorities, opinion leaders, and government authorities.

THE FUNCTIONS OF A PR SPECIALIST

Whether working for a corporation, an organization, or a PR counsel firm, one will find that various jobs and services are common to all. Following are just a few of the functions of a PR practitioner:

- Coordinates media relations for the organization and its divisions.
- Plans and implements the organization's PR, public service, and public interest programs.
- Writes speeches for executives.
- Writes press releases for the trade and consumer press.
- Arranges speakers, meetings, and events.
- Writes and edits house publications, newsletters, and employee communications.
- Acts as spokesperson for organizations in event of accident or disaster.
- Arranges press conferences.
- Supervises audiovisual materials for sales meetings and financial presentations.
- Accompanies CEO (chief executive officer) and top management on business tours to arrange conventions.
- Works with financial staff on presentation of annual and quarterly reports.
- Provides corporate reputation research and positioning.
- Offers philanthropic investment counsel and planning.
- Tracks electronic and print media opportunities for clients.
- Organizes major scientific and political congresses.
- Targets politicians and other key decision-makers on behalf of clients' public affairs objectives.
- Counsels clients on all phases of business launches.
- Assists clients in leveraging the Internet.
- Researches market intelligence.

PR Counsel Firms

The PR function is carried out at two levels. At a corporation, organization, trade association, or governmental agency, PR is the responsibility of a group of specialists. As we show in chapter 6, a large corporation such as the Bank of America has a staff of hundreds performing numerous PR and public affairs activities. In addition, many large corporations and organizations supplement their own efforts by retaining outside specialists, called PR counsel. In the industry, counsel organizations are also known as PR counsel firms, PR agencies, PR firms, and agencies.

New York City, the hub of the nation's PR business, is home to hundreds of PR counsel firms and the headquarters of many global PR organizations. Although these firms do not employ as many people as do advertising agencies, they are nonetheless important adjuncts to their client's PR programs in the areas of managing crises, establishing global communications, positioning products and brands, planning special events, and the other areas discussed in this chapter. We discuss these and other PR counsel firm pursuits in detail in chapter 4.

Of the New York-based global PR counsel firms, more than a dozen employ 400 or more people. One of these firms, Burson-Marsteller, a branch of the giant WPP Group advertising and marketing organization, employs more than 2,000 professionals in 35 countries to service hundreds of clients.

PR counsel firms usually bill their clients on monthly retainers at fees ranging from a low of $1,000 up to $50,000 or more. Occasionally, the firms perform prescribed services for an agreed-on fee but will undertake other assignments on a per-project basis. Account executives at these firms are trained to juggle a number of accounts at the same time.

A trend in recent years has been for advertising agencies to own PR counsel firms—in a sense, being responsible for a client's total communications package. These large organizations maintain offices in New York City, in other U.S. cities, and abroad.

THE DIFFERENCE BETWEEN ADVERTISING AND PR

Advertising and PR are related, but there are definite differences. Advertising involves the planning, creation, and placement of sales messages for products and services. PR is concerned with corporate, financial, and marketing communications; product publicity; and public affairs. An ad agency will create TV and print ads for Kraft margarine. Kraft's PR firm will publicize the results of a survey that indicates margarine's positive contribution to a healthful diet.

In this era of increasing specialization, there are firms that do only financial PR and many large firms that have financial departments.

PR counsel firms attract some of the best and brightest university graduates. Many firms conduct competitive training programs that have enabled them to recruit MBAs, PhDs, and people with degrees in journalism, philosophy, science, and other disciplines. Tough competition, but it's worth it when you get there.

PR: A TWO-WAY STREET

PR professionals spend a great deal of their time on placements—that is, arranging for their company's or client's releases and other information to appear in the media. However, as important as placements are for them, the journalists on the other side of the fence need a constant flow of news and feature material to satisfy the voracious appetites of print and broadcast media. This is especially the case in newspapers, where, it has been estimated that a substantial portion of the content comes from PR sources.

Particularly with the advent of the Internet, working journalists have ready access to key individuals at corporations and data about the operations of these organizations.

If, for example, a working journalist is doing an article on agriculture, there are numerous sources at the U.S. Department of Agriculture, as well as at more than a dozen environmental groups, that can be contacted or whose Web sites can be downloaded to obtain information. And if the journalist is writing a piece about the New York Stock Exchange, there are six press officers who can handle the request.

In the following chapters we analyze specifically the components of PR and how they work for different kinds of corporations and organizations.

DON'T CALL THEM "FLACKS": THE MANY NAMES OF PR PEOPLE

In the introduction I referred to Richie Roberts as a "press agent." Most PR professionals consider this a pejorative term. Yet in the theater and allied entertainment fields, it is still widely used. A *publicist*, a term that in most cases is synonymous with *press agent*, is a person who spends most of the time trying to get stories written or broadcast about his or her clients. On Broadway, there is even a press agents' union, so a running Broadway show is required to have a press agent who is paid a fixed amount to publicize that particular production.

A less flattering term is *flack*. The name is said to derive from Gene Flack, a one-time movie publicity agent. Columnists still use it as a disparaging term for press agents.

The title *spokesperson* is used frequently by the media to designate an organization's key PR representative. *PR News* describes the title as "disparaging, incorrect, and irritating," implying that the spokesperson is merely a mouthpiece, having nothing to do with formulating or implementing programs and policies. Nevertheless, the terms *spokesman* and *spokesperson* are widely used, particularly in government, governmental agencies, and large corporations.

At a corporation, the term *director of public relations* is a popular designation for that individual who directs the company's entire PR effort. This title is given as *director of corporate communications* in some organizations. A *media relations director* is the individual whose efforts are concentrated on placing stories and releases in the print and broadcast media.

In recent years, the terms *spin* and *spin doctors* have become popular in political circles. Spin doctors are those engaged in manipulating public perceptions. Spin has a slightly negative connotation from a PR standpoint because it implies "image fixing."

Other job titles used in PR are public affairs manager, communications specialist, public information officer, press secretary, information representative, director of community relations, issues communications director, and consumer affairs director. There are differences in these job functions. A public affairs manager deals primarily with legislative and regulatory activity. A press secretary works for a public official and acts as that individual's link to the media. A consumer affairs director is concerned with a corporation's relationship with environmental and public-policy groups. These are terms used primarily by corporations and other organizations. At PR counsel firms, the title *account executive* seems to prevail. We discuss specific job functions in a later chapter.

How PR Professionals Are Accredited

The Public Relations Society of America (PRSA) has almost 20,000 members in 114 national chapters. The organization has established a Universal Accreditation Program that includes eight public relations organizations. The program grants the designation Accredited in Public Relations (APR) to professionals who pass a written and oral examination.

The International Association of Business Communicators (IABC) grants an Accredited Business Communicator (ABC) designation that recipients are able to use after their names. The IABC has about 20,000 members worldwide.

More about these important organizations is given in chapter 20.

CHAPTER 3

The Components of Public Relations

I n this book we deal with 11 components, or practice areas, of public relations. We offer an overview of these components here and discuss them in greater detail in later chapters.

PR counsel firms divide their specializations into "practice areas." Although the firms operate outside a corporation's or organization's own PR department, they perform certain duties supplemental to the in-house department.

Not every corporation or other organization engages all these practice areas in-house. The American Medical Association, for example, has little need for in-house financial public relations, but IBM's structure includes a large department involved in this activity.

MEDIA RELATIONS

Media relations is one of the dominant functions of public relations. Its basic role is the origination of press information and the handling of requests from the media about their subject areas and activities.

One industry leader summed up the importance of media relations to a corporation by saying that media is the customer, and the product or service is the news.

At a multinational corporation like IBM, media relations is divided into two main divisions—Corporate Media Relations, and Marketing and Services Media Relations. Within this structure, IBM Corporate Media Relations is responsible for issues and financial matters that have an impact on IBM worldwide, whereas Marketing and Services is concerned with IBM's products and services in the United States.

Corporate Media Relations assignments include financial issues, technology issues and developments, world trade issues, and tax legislation.

Marketing and Services Media Relations include U.S. employee and community media relations and research communications media relations.

But few companies or organizations have the size and clout of an IBM, where almost every move it makes is covered avidly by the financial and general press.

The tools of today's media relations practice include press releases, media briefs and alerts, tele-press conferences, media drops, satellite media tours, and video news releases.

No matter the increased sophistication of the tools, the basic goal for the media relations professional is "getting the ink" or providing maximum press coverage for the client. These professionals accomplish this by perseverance and knowing how and where to submit each story.

EMPLOYEE COMMUNICATIONS, EMPLOYEE RELATIONS, AND PUBLICATIONS

In 1998, two world-leader aeronautical companies, Boeing and McDonnell Douglas, agreed to merge. The implications for the combined company's 220,000 employees and their families were enormous. Who would be excessed, who would be moved, what would happen to union agreements and pension plans, what management group would run the show, and whose CEO should break the news?

The issues in this merger were detailed in the 1998 Creativity in Public Relations Awards (Cipra) competition conducted by PR CENTRAL.[1]

Employee communications is a practice of PR that focuses on internal messages, motivations, behaviors, and systems relating to a corporation's or other organization's personnel. It encompasses targeted publications about these issues. And when there is bad news, the organization deals with it and attempts to minimize the damage.

SPEECHWRITING

Consider the last time you weren't bored by a speech. It may be a long time ago, especially if we've just been through a U.S. Presidential campaign. Yet good speech writing and presentation are essential skills in politics and business.

Many large corporations have a "chief executive speech writer" whose main responsibility is writing speeches for CEOs. Speech writers also write for other top executives. This component of PR is also carried out at organizations and government agencies. An adjunct of speech writing is ghostwriting bylined articles for top executives to be published in the trade and consumer press.

Some groups like The Executive Speaker train people in speech presentation skills and even include negotiation skills in their program.

PUBLIC AFFAIRS, LOBBYING, AND ISSUES MANAGEMENT

First, let's have a basic definition of this PR specialization. Public affairs PR helps an organization understand, influence, communicate with, and adapt to its various publics—local and federal governments, governmental agencies, shareholders, and special interest groups.

One major PR counsel firm, Burson-Marsteller, categorizes the strategy of its public affairs practice: "When we help our clients communicate, we do so with a clear idea of who we are attempting to reach, the 'hot buttons' [issues] that will cause this audience to act and the specific desired outcome our efforts will achieve."

In Washington, D.C., at one time, a couple of dozen Congressional bigwigs had the power to get things done. The top lobbyists could simply buttonhole these politicos, have dinner and a few drinks, and win their support for an issue.

Today's lobbyists are sophisticated practitioners who offer their corporate and other clients a melange of services that includes traditional lobbying, research, polling, and direct mail canvassing.

According to an article in *The New York Times*, public affairs and lobbying have become bonanzas for ten of the top Washington PR firms who have racked up billings of more than $200 million in this specialization.[2]

Lobbying involves interaction between an organization's representatives and governmental officials. Often it takes the form of influencing legislation or, in some cases, introducing new legislation affecting the organization's interest.

Issues communications and issues management fall under the purview of public affairs departments, primarily in corporations, but in other organizations as well. Issues management deals with matters affecting the corporation in the present and potentially affecting it in the future. An organization might support a particular candidate in a political race or run ads in newspapers and magazines regarding its position on social, environmental, and technical issues.

Other issues that a corporation may face are hazardous waste disposal, unfair labor practices in Third World countries, and minority employment policy.

PUBLIC INTEREST, PUBLIC SERVICE, IMAGE, AND REPUTATION MANAGEMENT

Image building is a significant component of PR. Its implementation is the function of specialists within a corporation or other organization and their PR counsel firms.

As an example of the use of image building by a large corporation, consider the following case. Some years ago, the Bristol-Myers Squibb Company received FDA approval for an AIDS treatment drug. Financial estimates placed the drug's revenues for the company at $100 million a year. Shortly after the approval, the company announced that it would provide this expensive drug free to those who could not afford to pay for it. The company's PR staff distributed a report to the media on its policy regarding the drug. Clearly, this is positive image building targeted to a number of Bristol-Myers Squibb's publics—shareholders, the medical community, AIDS patients, governmental agencies, consumer groups, and the general public.

Community relations refers to a corporation's or organization's activities in the local and national community. AT&T, for instance, assumes a broad-based role in the school reform process in Chicago's public schools. It is the job of the community relations staff to explore opportunities, secure the corporation's support, and then encourage the participation of employees. The community relations staff also publicizes these programs.

Many corporations include support for poverty and minority programs in their community relations agenda, as well as health care, cultural activities, and charitable contributions. The desired result is the molding of a positive corporate image.

The public's vastly increased concern over environmental and public health issues has spawned the organization of thousands of advocacy groups. Often these groups engage in battles with industry and government over the resolution of key issues.

In one recent election in California, five ballot initiatives were offered to voters involving such sensitive areas as timber harvesting, alcohol taxes, marine resources, pesticide regulations, and the use of prison inmate labor. Each was contested by advocacy groups on one side and business and labor unions on the other.

This component of PR has developed discrete techniques in the implementation of its programs. It presents a particular challenge for the advocacy groups, because they are almost always outspent by their opponents.

An ad in *The New Yorker*, sponsored by the Philip Morris Companies, doesn't mention the company's cigarettes or its Miller Beer brand. Instead, the ad promotes the cause of helping survivors of domestic violence. In 2000, the cigarette maker budgeted a $100-million TV advertising campaign aimed at the problems of hunger, domestic violence, and teen smoking.

Other corporations engage in similar public service programs and are active in the area of corporate contributions.

These roles fall within the organizational structure of the public affairs department. A contribution to public television to produce a particular series is an example of such corporate giving. Other examples might be the sponsorship of college scholarships or graduate fellowships, or of matching grants for cultural programs.

STRATEGIC CORPORATE PR
AND INTEGRATED COMMUNICATIONS

Strategic corporate PR and integrated communications seem to be the key buzz words in the PR field today. My old press agent friend Richie Roberts surely didn't know about strategic marketing and communications. His PR efforts were simple. You had a client whose name you got into the columns. Today, the results of PR campaigns can be measured and evaluated, and its practitioners are held accountable for results.

Strategic corporate PR is the identification of an objective— corporate staff downsizing, improved share price, greater productivity, more sales—and the implementation of an integrated program to achieve these objectives.

"In attaining these goals," says veteran senior PR executive Philip J. Webster, "the corporation cannot succeed without the assistance and alignment of the individuals and constituencies it relies on for support. In short, its publics or stakeholders, including employees, shareholders, the financial community, suppliers, plant communities, government, media, special interest groups, and the public at large."

Integrated communications relates to the use of PR along with advertising, direct marketing, promotion, and other tools to shape public opinion and deliver audience actions. In practice, its effectiveness depends on close cooperation between the corporation and its PR firm, and coordination through a single planning system of all the disparate elements.

INVESTOR RELATIONS AND FINANCIAL PR

The story appeared on page one of the October 17, 2000, issue of *The Wall Street Journal*. This influential business newspaper has a daily circulation of more than 1.7 million. The article dealt with the negative impact of corporate rumors and changes at the Coca-Cola Company. As it did that day, such a story can have a dramatic effect on the company's stock.

Coke's financial and investor relations people may have pitched the story exclusively to the *Journal*, but Coca-Cola, no doubt, heard from dozens of other people in the media about the issue.

The role of investor relations and financial PR includes the task of communicating with the press, the shareholders of a corporation, or members of an organization regarding its financial performance and objectives. This complex function involves preparing periodic and annual reports, arranging stockholders' meetings, writing press releases on earnings or the financial implications of new product development, and coordinating interviews between corporate or organization executives and security analysts.

The preparation of quarterly and annual reports falls into the domain of this component of PR. The annual report is an extremely important "selling piece" for the corporation, with wide distribution to stockholders, brokers, security analysts, institutional investors, and those individuals considering investing in the company. Annual reports are issued by nonprofit organizations as well as corporations. Investor relations and financial PR are demanding activities calling for a broad range of skills on the part of its practitioners. It is also a well-paid job classification.

ENTERTAINMENT AND PERSONAL PUBLIC RELATIONS

In the theater, particularly on Broadway, each running show must have its own publicist. Record companies have their own PR staffs, but their artists have personal publicists to promote their tours and concerts. In TV, the major networks publicize their shows, but often a show's production company will supplement this activity.

Although many movie actors have their own publicists, the studios maintain large PR staffs under the umbrella of ad/pub departments, combining the functions of advertising and publicity. For a movie featuring major stars, the PR team arranges interviews on major TV talk shows, as well as elaborate press tours. TV and stage luminaries also have their own publicity representation.

Entertainment PR may seem to be a glamorous field, and in some respects it is. However, it is very stressful and highly competitive.

During celebrity divorce proceedings, each participant often has a separate publicist. Every jab and counterpunch is trumpeted to the media for instant transmission to their gossip-hungry audience. If this seems to be overreacting personal PR, it is commonplace in Los Angeles, where one's publicist is as necessary as one's therapist.

In fact, in LA it's not just actors, rock stars, and athletes who have their own publicists. Plastic surgeons, dentists who specialize in smile reconstruction, dog groomers, exercise physiologists, and even high-priced landscapers—all retain PR specialists as well. It's as simple as this: Getting your name in the newspapers or on TV is good business, justifying the monthly publicist's fee of $2,000 to $10,000. Personal PR is a lucrative field employing thousands of publicists.

HEALTH CARE MARKETING AND COMMUNICATIONS

Drug companies spend vast amounts of research money developing new drugs. Then, once approved, the companies expend huge sums on marketing the drugs to the consumer.

In promoting new drugs, pharmaceutical companies face many options. Where should marketing and advertising be positioned? What sampling techniques should be used to bring the drugs to the attention of busy medical practitioners? How should campaigns be focused and should the drugs be marketed abroad?

Often, PR specialists are called in regarding strategic planning, market analysis, sampling, and advertising positioning.

Health care marketing is a high-paying, dynamic component of public relations, one that is generally not affected by adverse economic conditions.

CRISIS COMMUNICATIONS, CRISIS MANAGEMENT, CRISIS PLANNING, AND CRISIS RECOVERY

The area of crisis communications provides the high drama of public relations.

The 2001 World Trade Center suicide attack, Bhopal, Three Mile Island, Lockerbie, the *Exxon Valdez*, the Bridgestone/Firestone Ford recall—this is a litany of disasters no less infamous in the eyes of the public than the battle sites of war. In Bhopal, India, an explosion at a Union Carbide chemical plant caused the death of thousands. For years afterward, Union Carbide's image was marred.

Philip Morris was severely wounded by 1997's huge tobacco settlement. Firestone suffered an enormous image loss, as well as financial loss, in the year 2000 tire recall.

Incidents such as those alluded to here—air crashes, school shootings product recalls, strikes, major accidents, attacks by environmental or advocacy groups, bankruptcies, a killing at a community hospital, and other emergencies that threaten the existence of a corporation or institution—require sophisticated crisis communications and crisis management.

In a crisis, the corporation or organization and its PR firm enlist the services of many people—writers to issue press releases to the media, on-site personnel to work with local and national press, speechwriters for the organization's spokespersons, and contact people to make arrangements for meetings between the organization's executives and local officials.

In chapter 17 we devote considerable coverage to this vital component of PR. We discuss the proactive approach to crisis communications and management and examine an organization's crisis planning, its execution, and its evaluation of the results.

NEW MEDIA AND HIGH-TECH PUBLIC RELATIONS

Interactive strategies, emerging technologies, e-commerce, core solutions, Internet marketing—these are some of the challenges for today's public relations professionals in the ravenous arena of new media. Specialists have been at this new game for only a few years, yet there are already long lists of winners and losers.

New media public relations specialists are developing strategies to position a company or a brand from a country-centric to a global business model.

High-tech and new media have turned from a geeky business overrun with acronyms into a cool, cultural phenomenon.

OTHER COMPONENTS, SPECIALIZATIONS, AND PRACTICE AREAS

We list here some of the subareas in the burgeoning field of public relations and communications:

> Activists, dealing with
> Business-to-business ethics
> Change management
> Corporate art
> Divestitures
> Economic development
> Guerilla marketing
> Initial public offerings
> Labor relations
> Litigation communications

Marketing to gays and lesbians, minorities, seniors, youth, women
Nutrition
Philanthropy
Privacy
Recruitment
Regulatory affairs
Repositioning
Social marketing and social responsibility
Vision and values

CHAPTER 4

The Public Relations Counsel Firm: Profiles of the 10 Largest

M any corporations with large in-house advertising departments also employ ad agencies to prepare and place their
advertising. Similarly, a corporation or other organization
may have its own large public relations or corporate communications department, yet supplement its own efforts by retaining outside
specialists. These specialists are known as PR counsel firms or PR
agencies. PR firms function very much like advertising agencies. In
fact, many PR firms are owned by advertising companies. Three global
advertising leaders, the WPP Group, Omnicom, and the Interpublic
Group, own 7 of the top 10 PR firms.

Public relations counsel firms perform numerous services for a
variety of clients. Although some firms are small one- and two-person
operations, a few of the top firms employ a thousand or more people
in the United States.

The Council of Public Relations Firms prepares an annual industry
ranking. Here is a listing of the top 10 PR counsel firms, along with
their 2000 U.S. revenues, followed by a profile of each.

NUMBER	FIRM NAME	2000 U.S. REVENUE ($)	2000 TOTAL STAFF
1	Fleishman-Hillard	266,831,000	1,808
2	Weber Shandwick Worldwide	219,184,000	1,512
3	Burson-Marsteller	182,259,000	980
4	Hill & Knowlton	177,858,000	1,096
5	Edelman Public Relations Worldwide	168,430,000	1,259
6	BSMG Worldwide	147,380,000	843
7	Ketchum Public Relations	143,779,000	1,014
8	Porter Novelli International	135,888,000	1,004
9	Ogilvy Public Relations Worldwide	129,063,000	978
10	Golin/Harris International	107,905,000	670

On a worldwide basis, Burson-Marsteller is number 1 with revenues of more than $300 million. In recent years, the top 10 PR firms have seen their billings rise 20 to 25% a year.

The number 100 firm, by comparison, Brotman Winter Fried, employs 12 people and had 2000 revenues of $4.2 million, and the number 200 firm, Richmond Public Relations, billed $1.56 million.

The large firms we focus on make history every day. They advise, consult with, and counsel management of an organization on such disparate issues as a product recall, an unfriendly corporate takeover, the development of a new breakthrough drug, or restoring confidence in the safety of a tourist destination after a series of violent incidents. They are sought out by governments, corporations, associations, trade commissions, and even individuals.

Here is a partial list of award-winning campaigns of our top 10 firms:

Fleishman-Hillard with client SBC Communications: "Bringing Broadband to the Masses... Pronto."

Burson-Marsteller with client Tennessee American Water Company: "Stopping the Government Takeover of Tennessee American Water Company."

Shandwick with client Dimensions Healthcare Group: "Condition Critical: Killing at a Community Hospital."

Hill & Knowlton with client Ciena: "Ciena Defines Its Own Image."

Edelman with MTD Products: "Yard-Man Moves Across America."

Ketchum with Mattel, Inc.: "Celebrating 40 Years of Barbie Doll Dreams."

BSMG Worldwide with Campbell Soup Company: "Unveiling the New Campbell's Soup Label."

Porter Novelli with Florida Tobacco Pilot Program: "The 'Truth' Campaign."

Ogilvy with KNPQwest: "KPNQwest IPO, Raising One Billion Dollars @ The Speed of Light."

Other examples of award-winning campaigns by the top firms are:

- Search for the ultimate PokeMOM.
- Tell Americans they need a cholesterol checkup.
- Create an annual report for Nike with a sense of humor.
- Promote the responsible use of credit cards by college students.
- Conduct a campaign for the world's largest food manufacturer to end childhood hunger.
- Convince the various publics that a merger between Ameritech and SBC is in the public interest.
- Guide Tide's search for the "dirtiest kid in America."

These are also award-winners, but hundreds of others fit into the mold of excellence.

Let's take a closer look at the 10 largest PR firms.

FLEISHMAN-HILLARD

Fleishman-Hillard began as a single office in St. Louis, Missouri, more than 50 years ago. The founders, Al Fleishman and Bob Hillard, opened a second office in Kansas City, Missouri, growing the agency from a local business to a regional operation.

In 1974, John Graham became president and the firm was transformed once again, this time into a national and international agency. In 1980 there were fewer than 60 employees, and from 1980 to

1990, the number jumped to almost 600. And by 2000, the firm had 49 offices located in 16 countries on 5 continents.

In 1997, America Online (AOL), a Fleishman-Hillard client, created the AOL Foundation. Its primary purpose was to leverage the power of the Internet and online technology to benefit society, improve the lives of families and children, and empower the disadvantaged.

The AOL Foundation conducted research that determined a growing gap between those with access to the digital economy and the Internet and those without these advantages. Programs were created to deliver the benefits of the new medium to communities worldwide.

Initially, the "publics" were identified: AOL members; influentials in Washington, D.C.; the financial community; and industry analysts. Two primary objectives were determined: First, provide educators with the tools necessary to experiment with the technology in the classroom, and second, position the AOL Foundation as the leader in the philanthropic effort to build capacity in the nonprofit community to meet demand for online nonprofit activities.

Interactive education initiative grants were sought. Fleishman-Hillard promoted these grants and secured coverage in education trade publications.

The firm arranged for the AOL Foundation's participation in educational conferences to identify and promote its objectives.

A "super portal" called helping.org was established that was to be a clearinghouse of "charitable best practices." Internet policy leaders and decision makers were introduced and oriented to the new portal.

Fleishman-Hillard sought opportunities for the AOL Foundation to become a leader in the effort to improve technological literacy in the community. In just a few years, the AOL Foundation had become a nationally recognized and respected nonprofit organization. The number of interactive education initiative grants increased dramatically year to year.

The agency secured speaking engagements at many national educational conferences, where the AOL Foundation was exposed to more than 34,500 educators.

The portal helping.org, launched in October 1999, was favorably received by the media, the nonprofit industry, and consumers. Stories in the print media informed hundreds of thousands of readers about helping.org. The broadcast media also focused on the story.

In only its first month, helping.org raised donations of about $50,000 from 500 people. In less than a year, the site has received an average of 38,200 page views a day.

Fleishman-Hillard aligned the AOL Foundation with many national philanthropic conferences. Speaking engagements were arranged. More than 1,000 charities registered and received donations on helping.org.

For this campaign, the firm and America Online won a coveted Public Relations Society of America (PRSA) Silver Anvil Award 2000.

The essence of a PR firm's excellence is the quality of its work. Let's look at two other examples chosen from the Creativity in Public Relations Awards (Cipra).

In 1994, Fleishman-Hillard helped the Dell Computer Corporation introduce its Latitude family of portable "longest-life" computers. At one point, the firm set up a mobile press conference at New York's JFK airport where Dell CEO Michael Dell invited American Airlines passengers to "test fly" the new Latitude computers on a special coast-to-coast flight between New York and Los Angeles. Latitude computers were distributed to everyone aboard the flight, and six Dell technical experts rode along to help users navigate the new PCs enroute.

Media coverage of the event was extensive. *The Wall Street Journal* ran a story with a headline that read, "Dell's Notebook Keeps Going and Going," and called the Latitude the "Holy Grail" of portables.

In another notable campaign, the agency helped client Aviron maximize the successful clinical trial results of its nasal spray flu vaccine for children.

Want to hit home runs for Fleishman-Hillard? Forward your résumé to careers@fleishman.com or submit your résumé online to www.fleishman.com/careers.

WEBER SHANDWICK WORLDWIDE

In 1974, Peter Gummer, ennobled in 1996 as Lord Chadlington, founded Shandwick International. As the company grew, it expanded worldwide by acquiring industry-specific businesses such as Rogers & Cowan (entertainment) and Miller/Shandwick Technologies.

Shandwick International was itself acquired in 1998 by the Interpublic Group of Companies, an advertising and marketing conglomerate that employs more than 28,000 people in 120 countries worldwide. In 2000, Shandwick merged with Weber Public Relations Worldwide, another high-ranking PR firm.

Here's an example of the firm's handling of a crisis situation.

The Prince George's Hospital Center is a community hospital near some of the toughest neighborhoods of Washington, D.C. In 1999, a well-liked senior hospital administrator and mother of three was discovered murdered, bound to her chair and sexually assaulted in her family health center office. The hospital's management called in the firm to implement a crisis communications plan both groups had carefully developed.

In the aftermath, the skillful handling of the tragedy by the hospital's executives and the Shandwick team served as a model in crisis management.

A global PR firm such as this one steps up to the plate in situations as diverse as publicizing Scotch-Brite's high-performance cleaning cloth to winning a Cipra award for speechwriting for client General Motors.

In January 1998, Nick Morris was a Miller/Shandwick account manager in London. Morris's client, giant Compaq Computer Corporation, was there for an annual strategy update for the European media, when he was handed a note from the client informing him that it had just bought Digital Equipment Corporation for $9.6 billion, the then-largest acquisition in the history of the industry. It made a giant story, and Morris was in a position to influence how it was communicated.

Going to work for Weber Shandwick is a learning experience. In fact, the firm even has a Reputation Management University, conducted in each office in North America. RMU has no football team, but the student/employee participates by monitoring programs, using electronic learning tools, and attending brown-bag sessions and seminars.

Insight is an interactive learning site on the firm's Intranet that gives younger employees access to the experience and wisdom of veterans and allows for a continuous exchange of ideas among offices and with the firm's clients.

Here's an example of how the *Insight* site works:

> An assistant account executive travels to Arizona with a vice president for a spring-break promotional event for a client. When they land, the VP tells the AE, "Role reversal—you're in charge, tell me what to do. I'm here to backstop you and help, but this is your gig." It's a great

chance for the junior employee to grow and an excellent example of how to manage people by giving them opportunity, tools, and support. After the event, the "student" jumps on the electronic learning site, selects the Managing People category, and bangs out a quick 10-minute analysis of what she and her "tutor" learned from this experience of running an event and growing their capabilities. She might also report trends in what young people are doing during spring break. This decentralized learning from people who are out doing real work keeps the firm in touch with the world as it changes.

Weber Shandwick's PR services include reputation management; strategic communications planning; business, trade, and broadcast media relations; analyst relations; interactive communications; and special events planning.

A prime advantage here is the opportunity to be exposed to global clients, programs, projects, and experiences on a regular basis. Employees gain broad understanding and skills to counsel clients as they face the complex challenges of a competitive global marketplace.

Not all of its clients have the cachet of Compaq and Lotus Development, yet the firm is clearly focused on understanding the issues and problems of its smaller clients.

Check out Weber Shandwick International on the Web: www. webershandwick.com.

BURSON-MARSTELLER

In 1953, Harold Burson merged his public relations firm with the advertising agency headed by Bill Marsteller. They called the combined operation Burson-Marsteller, although Marsteller was the taller of the two partners.

In 1979, the firm became a part of the Young & Rubicam family of advertising agency companies. Young & Rubicam was purchased by the WPP Group in October 2000, creating the world's largest advertising and communications company. In the public relations sphere, WPP not only owns Burson-Marsteller, but also two other top 10 players, Hill & Knowlton and Ogilvy Public Relations Worldwide.

We illustrate here a situation in the area of public affairs and issues management.

In 1999, in Chattanooga, Tennessee, the City Council voted 9–0 to take over the control of the city's water utility, which had been operated for 130 years by the Tennessee Water Company. The company hired Burson-Marsteller to stop the takeover.

Burson-Marsteller devised a three-phase strategy to overturn the council's vote. First, it stressed the water company's 130 years of reliable service. Then, it pressed for a public vote on this sensitive issue, and last, it emphasized the risks of the takeover.

The implementation of this program was treated like a political campaign. The firm, working side by side with the water company's own team, brought in other specialists to handle research, advertising, and local political insight.

Many months and many dollars later, the vote was overturned by the council, and Burson-Marsteller's water company client retained its franchise. The case won a Cipra 2000 award in the category of Public Affairs.

If you work for this PR firm, you're part of a company with more than 2,000 professionals in 35 countries with revenues of $275 million.

On any given day, Burson-Marsteller teams may be conducting a medical symposium in Tokyo; targeting politicians and other key decision makers, as well as activist groups, policy research institutes, academics, business leaders, trade unions, and the general public; or even promoting the introduction of a new ballpark in Pittsburgh.

The firm serves a diverse body of clients ranging from multinational corporations, business organizations, and professional associations to governmental bodies and not-for-profit institutions.

Burson-Marsteller specializes in a number of key practice areas: public affairs, technology, media, marketing communications, corporate/financial, and health care.

What constitutes health care in today's marketplace? It can involve counseling an AIDS prevention campaign, a breakthrough disease treatment, or a financially troubled managed care hospital chain.

Burson-Marsteller can do little about a stock's price, but the firm can influence investor confidence, if, of course, this is justified. It accomplishes this with a panoply of services that include positioning and message development, investor relations program evaluations, financial community surveys, targeted news stories, and Web site development.

Media relations is at the heart of this PR firm's marketing practice. It's a sophisticated mixed bag that includes chat rooms on the Internet, media tours, major press events, satellite news conferences, and ongoing news bureau functions.

Your career path at Burson-Marsteller will introduce you to the techniques of today's top-level practice in a half-dozen major areas. You'll learn such nuances as how clients are trained to face the media and, in the firms's giant health care practice, you'll see how it helps clients navigate this new media, political, social, and economic landscape. The specialties within the health care practice area alone include pharmaceuticals, public education campaign, and medical technology.

Running a global operation such as Burson-Marsteller requires that offices and employees around the world be linked together electronically. Media practice specialists have instantaneous access to various databases from which they are able to:

- Track electronic and print media opportunities for clients.
- Track coverage of clients and client issues.
- Track ongoing and emerging media trends and theories.
- Access the firm's huge network of media contacts.

Burson-Marsteller places heavy emphasis on communications training not only for its own people, but also for its clients, particularly those who meet with the media regularly. The firm's trainers prepare clients for media interviews, speeches and presentations, expert testimony, and other forums using specialized training modules to implement these programs.

See chapter 22 for an interview with an account executive at the firm's New York headquarters and an interview with its human resources director.

Go to www.bm.com for information on jobs and more.

HILL & KNOWLTON

In 1927, when John Hill opened his shop in Cleveland, press agents typically served as advance men for circuses, sports events, movies, and theaters. They gained favor with newspaper reporters and editors by handing out "Annie Oakleys" (free passes). Most press agents were former reporters or moonlighting working reporters supplementing their meager paychecks.

In 1934, Hill landed his agency's first big business client, the American Iron and Steel Institute, giving him a new-found respectability he could grow on.

In one 48-hour period, today's Hill & Knowlton helped nine CEOs and managing directors establish business dialogues with officials of the U.S., Japanese, Chinese, and Australian governments and two different committees of the European Parliament. At the same time, Hill & Knowlton worked with marketing professionals in five countries on the introduction or revival of seven products, including computer software, a breakthrough health care treatment, a packaged food innovation, and a telecommunications system.

In the same two days, its staff introduced a leading U.S. financial institution to top professionals in Great Britain and Germany, prepared the Wall Street presentations of two Asian and three European corporations, and counseled four other companies involved in takeover battles on three continents.

The results: In those 48 hours the front pages of *The Wall Street Journal*, the *Financial Times* of London, the *International Herald-Tribune*, and the news broadcasts of independent and state-owned TV networks in seven countries carried stories on nine Hill & Knowlton clients. In a sense, its actions and innovations affected business around the world.

Hill & Knowlton maximizes its specialization by offering the expertise of subsidiary units, Blanc & Otus and Socket PR in technology and Banner McBride in employee communication.

The firm's social marketing unit has performed some impressive client programs, including:

- Health coverage enrollment for California's uninsured children.
- A Spanish-language public awareness program to combat drunk driving and underage drinking.
- A hepatitis B screening program targeted to adults in the Asian community.

Hill & Knowlton's sports practice has worked with stars like Wayne Gretzky, Shaquille O'Neal, and Mark McGwire on star-branding campaigns for clients Goodyear, Nike, and Adidas.

If you work in Hill & Knowlton's worldwide health and pharmaceutical practice, you may be assigned to Europe, Africa, the Middle East, Canada, the Asia/Pacific, or Latin America. And some of the issues you would deal with include introducing a new antiobesity pharmaceutical in Europe and Mexico or communicating to Canadians the value of a new antismoking aid, or you may be assigned to the practice of transnational issues management ranging from trade to human rights to telecommunications and transportation.

Check out Hill & Knowlton's Web site, www.hillandknowlton.com, where you can post your résumé and get information about career opportunities worldwide in the practice area that interests you.

EDELMAN PUBLIC RELATIONS WORLDWIDE

As we show in this chapter and throughout the book, many large public relations firms are owned by other communications organizations. Edelman is unique. It's the largest independent public relations agency, the only one among the top 10, and the fifth largest worldwide.

Founded in Chicago in 1952, Edelman opened in New York in 1960, Los Angeles in 1965, and started its first international office in London in 1967. Today, its network extends to offices in Sacramento, San Francisco, the Silicon Valley, São Paulo, Stockholm, Seoul, Shanghai, Singapore, and Sydney, with a total of 38 offices worldwide.

Procter & Gamble's Vidal Sassoon hair-styling products are global brands. Edelman introduced them into the Chinese market with a series of hair and fashion shows.

Edelman Financial Services helped Fidelity, the mutual fund and financial products firm, make its move in Germany and extended the reach of Charles Schwab's products and services to consumers and institutional investors.

The firm's clients in the financial area include Allstate, Cigna, New York Life, and the Deutsche Bank.

Healthcare public relations is a sensitive practice area, combining the exigencies of a product's approval stage, launch marketing, consumer education, global strategy, product contamination, and other crises. The stakes are huge, particularly with a new drug. It is not uncommon for a drug to have worldwide revenues of $1 billion. The firm has worked on such well-known brands as Maxim (flu pill), Claritin, Advil, and Viagra.

Edelman gets involved with startup clients early on, then steers them through the vicissitudes of the launch, a process that includes working with industry analysts, trade magazine editors, and information technology conference and event organizers. Technology represents more than 25% of Edelman's overall agency portfolio.

Only recently recognized as a public relations practice area by Edelman and other PR firms, diversity marketing is a new specialization for an old issue. Today, Edelman Diversity Marketing has a network of offices in Chicago, New York, Los Angeles, Washington, Atlanta, and Miami.

What is a typical assignment for this team? Reaching out to seasonal allergy sufferers in the Hispanic community earned both Schering-Plough and Edelman a coveted Silver Anvil award for the Claritin campaign.

Edelman has implemented employee engagement strategies in diverse situations. For ConAgra, a $24 billion food company with 80,000 employees worldwide, the agency developed a program enabling local communicators to share strategies and practical advice.

Most large corporations have in-house financial communications and investor relations staff. Edelman has been called in to supplement this activity in acquisitions, mergers, and listing on the New York Stock Exchange.

As shown in chapter 11, public affairs is a high-stakes practice. The firm concerns itself with creation of and implementation of strategic communications plans that influence public opinion, promote regulatory and legislative initiatives, support litigation, and manage issues.

All the giant PR firms in this chapter offer competitive compensation. They have to do this to attract talented people. Edelman has a comprehensive benefits plan, a 401(k) with company match, tuition reimbursement, Edelman University for continuous learning opportunities, and a fast-paced, dynamic environment.

Edelman's internship program is a full-time commitment. Each intern is assigned to a specific business area of expertise, based upon his or her interest and the availability within the group or business area. At some locations, interns work on an "Edel-Project" that enables them to work together to develop a comprehensive public relations program for a hypothetical client. At the end of the program, interns present their completed projects to an internal review committee.

Check out Edelman on the Web at www.edelman.com.

BSMG WORLDWIDE

To traverse its vast global territory, BSMG is broken up into eight separate units. Adamson/BSMG, based in Brussels, with offices in three other European cities, specializes in public and regulatory affairs and communications management. Then there's BSMG Worldwide,

Deutschland; BSMG Worldwide, UK; FRB/BSMG Worldwide, specializing in financial communication; KRC/BSMG Worldwide, specializing in research; SawyerMiller+Company, an issues advertising group; and Scotchbrook/BSMG Worldwide, a public relations consulting firm in Asia.

The parent company, BSMG Worldwide, calls itself a "communication" firm that integrates the key disciplines of strategic consulting, public relations, marketing communications, public affairs, investor relations' attitudinal research, and advocacy advertising. If all this sounds like MBA-speak, here's a case study of BSMG's work.

Dunkin' Donuts Rocket Man

Coffee is hotter than ever. From every other street corner to bookstores, specialty coffee shops are all over. But even though Dunkin' Donuts has been brewing a truly extraordinary cup of joe for nearly 50 years, it has encountered difficulty distinguishing itself in the midst of America's coffee obsession.

Sound like a job for a superhero? BSMG Worldwide thought so:

> We (BSMG Worldwide) needed a way to tell people and have them see for themselves—that Dunkin' Donuts coffee is rich, robust...leaps and bounds above the competition. We need to capitalize on Dunkin' Dounts' heritage, bringing the brand to life in a fun, attention-getting way. We needed Dunkin' Donuts Rocket Man—the first and only coffee superhero.

In *PRWEEK*'s "Thirty Under Thirty" selection for 2000, two 28-year-old BSMG staffers, Ilene Siemer and John Corey, made the list. In 6 years with the firm, Siemer had risen to head of the youth division, where her clients included the milk mustache campaign, Kraft, and Oscar Mayer. Corey was an assistant account executive at 23, and in 5 years became senior managing director in charge of the firm's Chicago operation. These success stories are a testimonial to the two "Under Thirties," but also to BSMG Worldwide for nurturing their talents. It is also a tribute to the firm's outstanding training program, Career Destinations.

What about BSMG's impressive client roster? Here's a representative list:

American Airlines	Microsoft
BP/Amoco	Minolta
Bristol-Myers Squibb	Oscar Mayer
GE Capital	Pfizer
Harley-Davidson	Philip Morris
Hewlett-Packard	Procter & Gamble
IBM	Prudential
Johnson & Johnson	RJR Nabisco
Kraft Foods	SmithKline Beecham

The exclusivity factor within an industry doesn't seem to be a factor in the top ranks of global PR. Within BSMG's client roster there are eight pharmaceutical companies.

You can find out about BSMG on the Web at www.bsmgworldwide.com.

KETCHUM PUBLIC RELATIONS

Ketchum, the seventh-largest U.S. firm, has been a top creative achiever in PR for many years. Today, it is owned by the Omnicom Group, which is also the parent of Fleishman-Hillard, Porter Novelli International, and the 16th-ranked U.S. public relations firm, Brodeur Worldwide.

It has all of the resources of a top 10 firm, more than 1,200 employees in offices worldwide, and big name clients. But Ketchum asks to be evaluated on its achievements.

For fifty years, the Public Relations Society of America (PRSA) has been awarding its Silver Anvils for outstanding achievement in various practice areas of the industry. In 2000, Ketchum was the recipient of nine Silver Anvils. One was in the category of special events for a joint project for clients Pfizer, Parke Davis, and the American Heart Association. The subject: The Cholesterol Low Down.

Here is an overview of the winning citation:

> America needed a cholesterol check-up. Almost 100 million Americans registered cholesterol levels above the desirable 200 mg/dl in late 1997, even though cholesterol education programs have been conducted for years. Worse, 90 percent of adults didn't know that controlling low-density lipoprotein cholesterol (LDL-C) or "bad" cholesterol is the

key to lowering cholesterol and reducing the risk of heart disease. If trends continue, by the year 2008 high cholesterol will put close to 110 million Americans at risk for developing heart disease—the leading cause of death. So, cholesterol-lowering pharmaceutical leaders Parke-Davis and Pfizer partnered with the American Heart Association to sponsor a multiyear series of special events called *The Cholesterol Low Down*. Held in cities across the country, the events offer free cholesterol screening, encourage Americans to know their cholesterol number and goal, and motivate "high screeners" to see their doctors and get to goal. Parke-Davis, Pfizer, and the American Heart Association held a Cholesterol Summit to develop the campaign's messages, encouraging participants to think of cholesterol as a "vital sign" of heart health. A behavior modification component was created to help drive consumers to see their doctors. The events have spurred over 16,000 cholesterol screenings in a year and a half. Over 105 million media impressions have spread *The Cholesterol Low Down*'s message. Three celebrity spokespeople—Regis Philbin, Debbie Allen, and Dick Clark—have been instrumental in measurably increasing cholesterol awareness and motivating consumers to seek help. A pre/post survey after the year revealed a 23% increase in cholesterol level awareness, and among those aware of *The Cholesterol Low Down*, nearly 30% said they planned to see a doctor about getting their cholesterol to healthy levels. Seventy-seven percent of *The Cholesterol Low Down* participants with high cholesterol have enrolled in the behavior modification program.

The complete citation goes on to detail the research conducted for the project: the planning, execution, and evaluation. Although Ketchum's campaign had a budget of $1,100,000, its results more than merited the investment from its participants.

For the year 2000, in addition to winning nine Silver Anvils, a notable achievement, the firm also garnered five Cipra 2000 winners.

Ketchum breaks out its practice areas into 11 specializations that include some of the basic ones such as crisis management, investor relations, and public affairs, and also include corporate social responsibility, Hispanic marketing, and African American markets group. But beyond the boundaries of awards, numbers, and offices from Chicago to Shanghai, there are people. Ketchum nurtures its people with professional development programs, Road Scholarships, sabbaticals, and all the tools of today's technology.

One such tool is MyKGN, a portal that lets Ketchum professionals, clients, and partners personalize the information that's right for them.

News feeds, Web searches, knowledge libraries, and financial information can be customized to provide only the information most essential to the individual user. According to Ketchum, MyKGN allows everyone to create his or her own highly relevant "digital dashboard."

Seek out Ketchum on the Internet at www.ketchum.com for an insight into the seventh-largest PR agency in the world.

PORTER NOVELLI INTERNATIONAL

Porter Novelli International is the world's third-largest public relations firm and the eighth-largest PR firm in the United States. The agency specializes in these practice areas:

Food and nutrition	Health care
Consumer	Technology
Public affairs	Corporate
Business to business	Financial services
Social marketing	

Porter Novelli defines social marketing as "the harnessing of the many disciplines of marketing to promote social change on behalf of the world's largest and most highly regarded NGO [nongovernmental organizations], corporations, professional bodies, and government agencies."

Porter Novelli was the International Public Relations Association (IPRA) Golden World Awards Grand Prix Winner and won the Cipra 2000 award in the social marketing category with the Florida "Truth" Campaign, an effort to stem the surging increase of teen smoking in that state, which by 1998 had risen to 35%.

The firm and its client, the Florida Tobacco Pilot Program, faced formidable opposition in the campaign. Although teens were aware of the health risks of tobacco, "industry manipulation" and peer pressure contributed to the rising use.

First, the campaign conducted baseline surveys with 23,000 students 12 to 17 years of age, with the purpose of deriving data on tobacco use, knowledge, attitudes, and behavior.

The objective of the campaign was to change youth attitudes and reduce tobacco use. Porter Novelli would do this by creating a heavily advertised and well-marketed *antitobacco brand* to rival the major tobacco brands.

Print, radio, and TV ads were used with the same edgy humor and high production values that the tobacco industry used to reach teens. Conferences, seminars, and a Teen Tobacco Summit were mounted. At the first summit, in 1998, a grass-roots organization, Students Working Against Tobacco (SWAT), was formed to launch the "truth" (about tobacco) advertising campaign.

SWAT enlisted 25 celebrities who were anti–teen smoking to sign a pledge for the accurate depiction of tobacco use, aimed at the movie industry. Magazines that carried tobacco ads were targeted. At one point, teens tore tobacco ads from magazines and sent them back to the tobacco companies with an orange neon "Rejected, Rebuffed, Returned!" sticker on them. The package of ads included a letter saying, "We want you to know we are sick of being targeted with manipulative messages that enlist sexy models, good friends, and good times to glamorize tobacco use."

Another series of events, "Big Tobacco on the Run," was conducted to spread the message to tobacco executives and magazines. This aggressive-grass roots campaign resulted in a sharp drop in the tobacco use among middle school students, and a somewhat smaller drop among high schoolers.

The agency's "truth" campaign achieved wide coverage in print and electronic media. It is an excellent example of the practice area of social marketing.

In January 2000, Copithorne & Bellows, the world's foremost PR agency focused on technology, merged with Porter Novelli International to create the Porter Novelli Convergence Group. The group has more than 400 employees in Europe, Asia/Pacific, and the Americas, and annual billings exceeding $50 million. Porter Novelli's Web site is www.porternovelli.com.

OGILVY PUBLIC RELATIONS WORLDWIDE

David Ogilvy was a legendary figure in advertising, known for such creative gems as the Hathaway man. Today, the brand he founded is an international force in public relations, as well as advertising.

By the end of 2000, Ogilvy Public Relations was a top 10 PR firm with 50 offices in 45 markets and employed more than 1,100 professionals worldwide. And year on year, it has held onto top clients like Glaxo Wellcome, IBM, Merck, Pfizer, and Automatic Data Processing.

Public relations agencies, like advertising agencies, have highs and lows. The addition of a few blue-chip clients can turn it around for an agency. And once the word gets out that an agency is hot, more new business flows its way. That's what happened to Ogilvy in 1999 and 2000. Let's take a closer look at this high achiever.

In the rarefied atmosphere of multi-million-dollar yearly PR fees, success depends on a number of factors, not least of which is momentum. Bob Seltzer, who came to the firm as CEO in 1997, made a number of important acquisitions that powered its PR engine. In 1998, the company made a strategic growth move by buying a hot technology practice, San Francisco-based Alexander Communications. Now this division is called Alexander Ogilvy Public Relations Worldwide.

In 1999, Ogilvy acquired Feinstein Kean Healthcare, a Cambridge, Massachusetts-based biotech public relations firm.

At this point, Ogilvy had a 70+ percentage gain in fees. It landed new business from such formidable clients as Motorola, Minute-Maid, Lucent, the pharmaceutical heavyweight Novartis, and a bunch of Internet-related accounts.

The agency had not established much of a reputation in entertainment PR until its recent acquisition of Baker, Winokur, Ryder, a firm with a 21-year background in that specialization.

Under Seltzer's reign, Ogilvy introduced a formal professional development program, PLATO (Partners in Learning and Training at Ogilvy), as well as a management training initiative.

Here are some highlights from Ogilvy's practice areas.

Public Affairs Practice

Ogilvy PR public affairs professionals are "world citizens." Their hats hang in Washington, Brussels, and Beijing. For a coalition of Internet companies called openNet, including America Online, Mindspring, and hundreds of local Internet service providers, the firm supplied a comprehensive media relations campaign that mobilized more than 900 local Internet service providers in order to influence state and local legislators, and resulted in the introduction of pro-access legislation in 26 states and municipalities.

Health and Medicine Practice

Another Ogilvy PR strength is social marketing. The company is well known for designing programs that succeed in promoting health-related behavior change and motivating community action. For more than a decade, it has provided communications support to the AIDS and HIV prevention campaigns of the U.S. Centers for Disease Control and Prevention (CDC). Ogilvy also helped women make difficult decisions about contraception, prepared young adults to face the facts about sexually transmitted diseases (STD) treatment, and guided communities in taking on the issue of preventing drug abuse. In addition, the firm supports national communications initiatives for the National Heart, Lung, and Blood Institute and the National Institute of Neurological Disorders and Stroke in such areas as hypertension, cholesterol, asthma, obesity, sleep disorders, stroke, and Parkinson's disease.

Ogilvy E-Brand

Traditional brands are developed over decades. For many Internet startups, the make-or-break period can be measured in months. That's why Ogilvy PR and Alexander Ogilvy developed Ogilvy e-brand. It's a suite of services that fast-tracks brand development and ensures that key activities, from the launch of a product or service to the corporate IPO, become branding opportunities.

Corporate Practice

For BP Amoco, the world's third-largest energy company, Ogilvy PR is an integral member of its 360-degree communications team, supporting a worldwide brand transformation. By developing brand strategy and communicating it to the company's more than 15,000 retail partners and 80,000 employees, the agency is helping guide BP Amoco through the launch of its new identity and the transition of the company.

Contact Ogilvy from their Web site: www.ogilvypr.com.

GOLIN/HARRIS INTERNATIONAL

Golin/Harris International, an arm of the Interpublic Group, along with Weber Shandwick Worldwide, has been in the PR business for almost 50 years. Headquartered in Chicago, the firm operates in North America, Europe, and Asia and represents more than 4,000 multinational, regional and local clients in 110 countries around the world. Its total billings exceed $108 million.

Golin/Harris boasts that its client list is smaller than most firms its size because its people work on fewer accounts. This approach also allows senior management to get more deeply involved with its clients, a group that includes Bayer, Daimler/Chrysler, Gerber, McDonald's, Nintendo, Owens Corning, and Texas Instruments.

Golin/Harris also owns several public relations and marketing communications firms that operate under different brand names. They include:

- The MWW Group, specializing in Internet and technology marketing, investor relations, and a half-dozen other practice areas.
- Mindstorm Communications, a full-service public relations and marketing communications firm focusing on e-business, telecommunications, and digital entertainment clients.
- TSI Communications Worldwide, concentrating on strategic marketing development in the practice areas of business-to-business, consumer, and Internet.
- Springpoint, another Golin/Harris subsidiary in London, a leading brand strategy and corporate identity design consultancy.

Golin/Harris offers paid internships. Link to its application page and follow the instructions on how to submit your résumé. Indicate which office location interests you.

A scan of the firm's job openings at the time of this writing yielded account executive and account manager jobs in places like Houston, Hong Kong, Chicago, London, and Frankfurt.

The Golin/Harris Web site is www.golinharris.com.

CONCLUSION

In focusing on the top 10 counsel firms, we should consider that public relations competes with advertising for talent because many of the job assignments are similar. And, of course, the issue is further complicated by the joint ownership of large ad agencies and public relations firms. As a result, the major PR firms are making very attractive offers to new people in terms of the working environment, benefits, training and development, and internships.

It is also important to understand that organizations need PR firms to furnish the marketing and communications expertise they cannot render economically within their own structures.

CHAPTER 5

Life on the Fast Track at a Small Public Relations Firm

W e've seen how the big guys operate—as many as a thousand employees per firm, Fortune 500 clients, offices in Silicon Valley, Shanghai, and other world capitals, and million-dollar-a-year fees.

But surely not all PR agencies fit into this firmament. According to the Council of Public Relations Firms 2000 industry ranking, only 44 firms had billings exceeding $10 million a year, whereas another 200 firms billed over $1 million.

Big or small, they all hustle, whether the situation calls for lobbying a client's interests in Washington, D.C., showing the brightest face in a litigation, or introducing a new hand-held computer at the annual Consumer Electronics Show.

Formed in 1996, Steven Style heads an aggressive, six-person New York-based PR firm that bears his name. Style's annual billings run about $1 million a year, derived from nine clients. Here's a look at staffing at the Steven Style Group:

Principal and president (Style)
Account supervisors (2)

Account executives (2)
Account coordinator (1)

From time-to-time, the agency employs interns. Style has more than 15 years in marketing, the two account supervisors 8 to 10 years in large PR agencies or on the client side of the business, and the account executives have similar backgrounds but less experience.

When Style needs new people, he searches online job boards such as hotjobs.com, as well as classified ads in *The New York Times*. Universities in the New York area are a dependable resource for internship candidates.

The salaries at top 10 firms are high. The Style Group pays competitive salaries plus fully paid benefits and perks, such as the use of the corporate apartment in chic South Beach, Miami, for vacations.

The question of new business is paramount in any discussion on PR agency management. Clients are not forever. Here, the big guys have an advantage. Many are part of advertising agency conglomerates and obviously share contacts. The giants also have multiple offices abroad for servicing global accounts. In the public affairs arena, for example, most of the 10 top firms have Washington, D.C., representation. They also commit large budgets for new business solicitation and retain staff who work only on developing new clients.

Which brings us back to small PR firms like the Steven Style Group: How does it attract and retain new clients? The vast majority of new business comes from client referrals. Then, too, press coverage in business and trade publications serves as a means for branding. Branding refers to promotion of the firm's name as an established entity in the business.

And, as shown throughout this book, PR is about reputation, an issue that dominates any discussion of the merits of an agency.

STEVEN STYLE'S CAREER PATH

Style received a bachelor's degree in graphic design from New York's School of Visual Arts. During the 1980s East Village/New York City art scene, he ran a postcontemporary art gallery and nightclub combined with a celebrity party promotion business. We don't know if he made money in these ventures, but he did gain great contacts when he was profiled in major media outlets including *Town & Country*, *The New York Times*, the *Washington Post*, and *Interview* magazine.

Later, Style parlayed his media relations skills into a job as a publicist at the progressive Brooklyn Academy of Music. From there, he went to a midsize PR agency where he remained for 8 years, rising to the post of senior vice-president. In 1996, he launched his own business, the Steven Style Group.

A LOOK AT THE STYLE GROUP'S ACCOUNT LIST

None of Style's accounts are in the Fortune 500 category, yet some are high-profile names in the new technology. Here's a brief rundown:

- Discovery Kids is a 24-hour digital network from the Discovery Channel. Some of its offshoots are the popular reality series "Outward Bound," "Croc Files," and "Lonely Planet."
- K'NEX, a leading toy manufacturer.
- Lincoln Logs, a building set that's been around since 1916.
- Sony Wonder, the children's and family division of Sony Music.
- Silver Dolphin Books, a major publisher of interactive and educational children's books.
- Escient, a company that develops products that merge Internet power with home entertainment devices.
- SpringBoard Music, a digital music company.

In addition to these retainer clients, the Style company offers services to others on an assignment or product basis.

What is the challenge for an operation such as the Style Group? Today's public relations involves marketing, as well as communications. Results are based not only on how many clips or "hits" a client receives, but an agency is also expected to deliver result-driven promotional programs using traditional and cyber marketing. This becomes particularly important when representing high-tech products or services.

Of course, when a client pays its PR firm fees of $8,000 to $10,000 a month or more, consideration is often made to bringing the function in-house, where one or two people devote full time to an assignment. The PR firm responds that a company's small in-house department cannot possibly have the breadth of media contacts that a public relations agency may have developed through the years in its own practice.

Meanwhile, accounts come and go, so the public relations firm hustles along, pitching new business to replace what it may lose. Small PR agencies can boost their business by gaining special expertise in certain areas and applying this knowledge to win new accounts. The Style Group, for example, has a number of youth-oriented clients. To gain maximum exposure for these accounts, it has cultivated many strong relationships in this media category.

It's advantageous, for example, to know the right people at a magazine like *Teen People*, with a circulation of 1.6 million, plus its substantial pass-along audience; or *Teen*, with 2 million subscribers; and *Fox Kids Magazine*, with a huge 3.5 million circulation.

For major clients, there's a clear advantage to dealing with the top firms. The large PR firms profiled in the previous chapter have offices in many U.S. cities and abroad. Yet a small firm like the Style Group, based in New York, must also reach out for clients in other cities to grow its business. Four of the firm's clients are located in Indianapolis, a city with a bustling economy and a burgeoning technology sector.

One reason, perhaps, that clients are drawn to a New York-based firm is its proximity to the national media. Style communicates with his Indianapolis accounts by phone, computer, and regular visits.

The Steven Style Group is a good example of a small public relations firm that has succeeded in this highly competitive field.

CHAPTER 6

An Inside Look at Corporate Affairs at the Bank of America

Take two big banks, mix them carefully together, and, with the right ingredients, create one giant. That single entity, the Bank of America, formed in 1998 with the merger of Charlotte, North Carolina-based Nation's Bank and San Francisco-based Bank of America, is, at this writing, the largest geographic retail banking franchise in the United States. The combined organization employs 140,000 associates (the bank's term for employees) and by 2000 had become the largest geographic retail banking franchise in the nation, doing business with more than one in three U.S. households in the 23 states in which it operates, and with more than 2 million U.S. businesses.

Internationally, the bank does business in 190 countries and has offices in 38 of these foreign locations.

The numbers are awesome, even for the banking business. In 2000, the Bank of America had operating earnings of $7.86 billion on revenues of more than $33 billion.

The bank is in seven financial service areas:

Consumer Products. Bank of America has 4,500 banking centers, 13,000 ATMs, 3 million online customers, and holds more than 400,000 mortgages.

Asset Management. The bank has almost $300 billion of assets under management and runs mutual funds with more than $100 billion in assets.

Card and Payment Services. The bank is a major player in the credit and debit card business. Much of this activity has migrated from paper to electronic channels.

Serving Small Businesses. The bank does business with 2 million of the 25 million small businesses in America and more than 30,000 middle market companies.

Internet and E-Commerce. The many customers who use the bank's electronic billing and payment service can virtually eliminate checks by going online.

Investment Banking. The bank holds more than $27 billion in prime brokerage custodial assets for 700 clients. Bank of America was ranked 10th among mergers and acquisition (M&A) advisors in 2000.

Serving Large Corporations and the Institutional Market. The bank's role in this high-profile arena is in integrating equity securities. It combines mergers and acquisitions with its debt capital-raising activities.

Now we deal with various aspects of conducting a corporate affairs program to serve the multifaceted needs of this global organization.

THE ROLE OF CORPORATE AFFAIRS AT THE BANK OF AMERICA

The 250-person corporate affairs team follows a prescribed series of business processes in carrying out its assignments:

- Identify business partner needs. In the bank's lexicon a *business partner* is a senior-level company executive in some division of the bank: that is, retail banking, credit cards, Internet and e-commerce, investment banking, charitable contributions, or government and public policy.
- Research and analyze the project or problem.
- Develop a strategy.
- Implement the strategy, budget it, and gain management approval.
- Measure the results.

The corporate affairs team has four centers of expertise. Here's what they do:

1. Relationship management—Helps the bank's senior-level business partners achieve various goals and objectives in the lines of business the bank supports. An example: Promote investment banking services in the Far East or come up with a program to reward retail customers for bringing in more of their business.
2. Public policy—Aids in the continuing role of developing the bank's public policy position and advocacy strategy. The scope of such a program may reach out to federal and state capitals, as well as overseas. Public policy efforts may call on the use of in-house and outside lobbyists.
3. Charitable contributions—With an annual budget of about $100 million, contributions at the Bank of America are higher than those of any other U.S. financial institution. The formidable assignment of administering this huge cash grant falls into the domain of the Bank of America Foundation.
4. Support services—Provides effective and efficient systems and administrative support; includes clearinghouse to assist business partners and associates with basic requests for products, services, and information.

Publications Produced by Corporate Affairs In-House

Corporate Affairs edits and produces three regular publications. We offer a look at each.

Bank of America World. This full-color, eight-page publication is an outstanding example of employee communications, a subject we cover in chapter 9. A recent issue dealt with these subjects:

Bank of America

world

November 6, 2000
Vol. 2 Issue 25

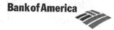
Bank of America

New check imaging company formed
Deal creates landmark customer service level

Bank of America, Chase Manhattan Bank and IBM will partner to form Viewpointe Archive Services, a new check imaging and archiving company. The deal, announced Nov. 1, will create the first environment in which banks can exchange check images with each other and ultimately will change the way customers interact with banks.

The formation of Viewpointe, which will begin operating later this year, jumpstarts the banking industry's conversion to a digital environment. The new company will enable banks to share digitized, or scanned, images electronically, eliminating the need to "touch" a check during processing — possibly reducing industry costs

see IMAGING page 7

Real estate group sees quick success

Bank of America's HomeFocus Services LLC has completed more than 35,000 title transactions in the past seven months, a milestone for the group that opened its doors on April 3.

HomeFocus

HomeFocus, a wholly owned Bank of America subsidiary, handles real estate loan title examination and closing services for families and individuals in 20 states and the District of Columbia. Given its performance to date, HomeFocus is on track to become the largest lender-owned real estate settlement service and vendor management company in the nation.

HomeFocus has 150 associates in its St. Louis headquarters focused on enhancing the customer experience and generating revenue. "We hope to be in all 50 states next

see HOMEFOCUS page 7

Bank ranks No. 1 in deposit accounts

Bank of America holds a larger share of consumer deposit accounts than any of its competitors. And, the bank has a strong lead over its three closest rivals — Wells Fargo, Washington Mutual and First Union — in the states where they compete.

These are the latest results from the Market Audit, an ongoing survey that

STRIDES TO THE SUMMIT

provides extensive data on consumer household use of all financial institutions. The findings collected by the Marketing Research department include customer and noncustomer survey data from the 22 states where the bank does business and the District of Columbia. Illinois usually is not included since the bank has a limited presence there.

Bank of America uses the Market Audit to track the number, location and balances of accounts by household, which

see ACCOUNTS page 7

FIGURE 6.1   (Courtesy Bank of America Corporate Affairs)

- A report on design of four Internet portals to help customers and clients do business with the bank online.
- The bank's top-ranking in a National Association for the Advancement of Colored People (NAACP) banking industry report card.
- An increase in the bank's quarterly stock dividend.
- The bank's rise to number one in deposit accounts.

Bank of America

leader
The information tool for leaders

Recipients: 24,000 leaders worldwide

Associate Banking launches in California

This month Bank of America will introduce Associate Banking in California. As part of the launch, Associate Banking representatives will conduct a series of expos throughout California. The expos, similar to mini-trade shows, are designed to show how this exclusive service benefits associates by providing confidential, quick and easy access to a variety of financial products and services. Associates can receive preferred pricing, as well as special rates and discounts, on deposit accounts, credit cards, home mortgages, investment certificates of deposit and more. Future communications will outline the dates and locations of the expos in your area.

Because associates are a valuable segment of the Bank of America customer base, we ask you to encourage your team to attend the expos and to take advantage of this valuable company benefit. Personal bankers are available through a dedicated toll-free number to assist associates with their financial questions. For added convenience, most transactions, including opening an account, applying for a loan or servicing an existing relationship, can be done over the phone or online. A 24-hour Automated Telephone Banking service is available as well.

For more information about Associate Banking, visit www.bankofamerica.com/associatebanking.

 ## procedural updates

Bank of America develops national temporary-staffing program

Bank of America has developed a national temporary-staffing program that provides clerical and accounting/financial associates for the bank. The goal of the program is to support the bank's temporary staffing needs with qualified associates in the most cost effective and efficient manner.

Adecco has been the preferred provider overseeing the temporary-staffing program since 1998. Accountants On Call (AOC), a subsidiary of Adecco, is the bank's preferred provider of accounting and other professional financial temporary staffing needs.

Adecco has dedicated staff across the country to assist

Bank of America associates. To request a temporary associate or for additional information about the program, call 1.888.741.8367 to speak to an Adecco representative. Job descriptions have been developed to help match a temporary associate with the skills required.

An electronic invoice will be submitted directly to the bank's Accounts Payable Department. Managers will receive biweekly reports to confirm Adecco charges to their company number and cost center. If managers are not satisfied with a temporary associate within the first eight hours of an assignment, they will not be responsible for paying for that time. Simply call 1.888.741.8367 and request the eight-hour guarantee.

Bank of America associate Todd Thacker, supplier relationship manager, is available at 1.704.387.5091 to support any daily issues related to the temporary-staffing program.

See Procedural Updates on page 2.

FIGURE 6.1 (*continued*)

Bank of America Leader. Twenty-four thousand of the bank's leaders worldwide receive this two-page publication as a printed copy and online. It deals with management issues such as temporary staffing, expense reports, and disability legislation.

Bank of America Associate. All of the bank's U.S. associates (employees) receive this benefits newsletter. Its content is nuts-and-bolts information about holiday pay, credit cards, and discounts.

Bank of America

associate

The benefits newsletter for U.S. associates

Bank of America

Associate Discount Web site makes its debut

Associates can now go online to obtain discounts on products and services offered by Bank of America and other leading companies through the new Associate Discount Web site.

The site serves as a central resource for the bank's current products and special discounts, providing links so associates can access Associate Banking products and theme park and other discount tickets previously offered through Team Bank of America. In addition it offers links to more than 150 brand-name companies offering special discounts to associates. "We're pleased to be able to leverage the bank's buying power to make the Associate Discount Web site available to associates," said Lisa Eversole, director of Procurement & Corporate Services, Charlotte. "The site will offer associates special discounts as well as the

convenience of one-stop shopping."

The Associate Discount Web site was developed by Bank of America Procurement & Corporate Services in conjunction with Abilizer, an Internet company that teams with companies to develop online shopping malls offering employees special discounts on brand-name products and services.

Current discounted products available through the site include apparel, automotive services, electronic equipment, flowers, office equipment and videos. New vendors are added to the site regularly. Associates will be able to personalize their Associate Discount Web site homepages so that they receive local weather, news, traffic and preferred vendor discount updates whenever they log on to the site.

Although Bank of America provides the platform for associates to receive

discounts, all purchases made through the site are personal transactions and must be purchased with a credit card directly from the vendor's Web site. Bank of America assumes no responsibility for purchases made

see DISCOUNT page 4

Associates get credit

It's now easier than ever for associates to obtain a Bank of America associate credit card. Beginning this month, Bank of America Card Services has established new special credit approval guidelines for associates who would like to obtain their first Bank of America associate credit card.

"Obtaining a credit card is an important step in establishing a good credit history," said Janet Peters, Card Services Relationship Strategy senior manager. "Any associate who meets the new guidelines is now not only pre-approved for a credit card, but will also receive a line of credit that recognizes his or her length of service with the bank."

Under the new guidelines, the line of credit available through the card will take into account both an associate's annual income and years of service with Bank of America. These changes, along with the new associate credit card eligibility guidelines, were developed based on feedback from associate focus groups that Bank of America Card Services held earlier this year, noted Richard Jennings, Card Services Relationship Strategy marketing manager.

The associate credit card includes special associate benefits such as no fees for cash advances and a reduced annual percentage rate (after introductory period) on both purchases and cash advance

balances. However, if an associate leaves the company, the fees and reduced rates will revert to the standard customer pricing.

To apply for a Bank of America associate credit card or obtain more information, associates in California, Idaho, Oregon and Washington should call 1.877.432.0824. Associates in all other states should call Associate Banking at 1.800.695.6262. After obtaining their new Bank of America associate credit cards, associates can take advantage of Bank of America's Photo Security feature by visiting their local banking centers to have their photographs taken. This service provides added security by placing the customer's photo and signature on the front of the card. The Photo Security feature is available free of charge on all personal Check Cards and credit cards (except for the US Airways Dividend Miles Visa).

FIGURE 6.1 (*continued*)

A CLOSER LOOK AT BANK OF AMERICA'S CHARITABLE PROGRAM

The subjects of public interest and public service are dealt with in chapter 12. This component of public relations embraces many sub-areas, such as support for the arts, corporate social responsibility, education, and community relations. When we analyze its budget of $100 million a year, we realize the broad challenge the foundation faces in the decision making and execution of this program.

Where does the money go? It is divided among the areas of education, health and human services, community development, and arts and culture. The emphasis in the foundation's program is serving the needs of local communities. Thus, a decentralized decision-making process prevails.

When awarding its grants, the foundation's consideration is based on community need, diversity, and equity and access to opportunity. This process also takes into account literacy rates, poverty levels, and other socioeconomic factors.

The work of distributing and managing the implementation of the largest financial services philanthropic foundation in the country is a group operation headed, at this writing, by Lynn Drury, a corporation affairs executive. She is also the president of the Bank of America Foundation.

Drury has a team of charitable contributions executives and specialists, grant analysts, and initiatives specialists. This group is charged with decision making on:

- Establishing corporate charitable contributions priorities.
- Evaluating and assessing charitable contributions needs.
- Allocating and managing charitable contributions budgets.
- Communicating with grant recipients.
- Overseeing implementation of tactical plans to communicate grants to target audiences.
- Measuring the impact of charitable contributions outcomes and reporting results.

Examples of Foundation Grants

One example in the education area is the Bank of America Abilities Scholarship Program, which receives up to $200,000 to provide students with disabilities equal access to higher education.

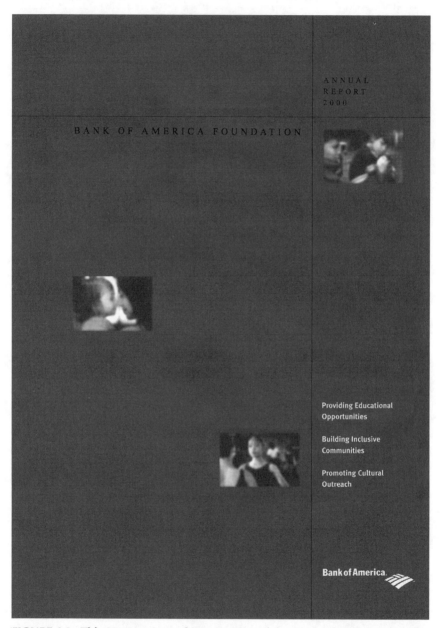

FIGURE 6.2 This 32-page Annual Report 2000 of the Bank of America Foundation affords a look at the bank's educational and cultural outreach programs. (Courtesy Bank of America Corporate Affairs)

Initiatives such as this foster not only personal growth, but also economic growth for the communities in which the bank does business.

In 2000, the foundation contributed $100,000 to the Yosemite Fund, a California initiative dedicated to preserving and protecting the park and enhancing visitors' experiences.

Another major foundation area, promoting cultural outreach, offers these examples:

- Purchase of the Hewitt Collection of 55 works by African American artists and touring the collection around the country. In 2000, the exhibition was seen by 750,000 people.
- Support for the Mexican Heritage Corporation's arts and cultural programs.
- A gift of $200,000 to the South Carolina Governor's School for the Arts and Humanities to fund teacher training and curriculum for the state's arts education programs, which are available to all students via a digital satellite system.

JOBS IN CORPORATE AFFAIRS AT THE BANK OF AMERICA

We have offered a brief look at the functions of the corporate affairs department. Many of the job assignments in this department fit under the same structure and definition as traditional public relations.

Salaries are comparable to those paid by other corporations, with larger salaries paid in major metropolitan centers.

The Corporate Affairs Leaders and Their Teams

The president of the Bank of America Foundation is also the principal executive of the corporate affairs department, with a staff of about 250 people. Six teams with discrete responsibilities report to this executive. Here is a breakdown on their departments:

Relationship Executives and Managers. Generally, relationship management refers to the connection between an organization and its key publics. As it is used at the bank, relationship executives and managers are assigned to each of its major business units: consumer/commercial, e-commerce, or asset management.

Most work is triggered when a need/risk is identified by a bank business executive who might be in federal government relations, charitable contributions, or communications. Relationship management helps business partners meet their objectives, develop strategies, and measure and report results.

Public Policy Executive. Helps business partners reach and influence internal and external audiences. Supervises a team of issues and outreach specialists and lobbyists.

Federal Government Relations Executive. Similar function to that of the public policy executive, but operates on the federal level, and supervises federal lobbyists.

Charitable Contributions Executive. Provides oversight and strategic counsel and develops and sets charitable contributions corporate strategy objectives. Runs a department of corporate affairs professionals that include charitable contributions specialists, grant analysts, and initiative specialists.

Communications Executive. Employs a large team of internal and external communications professionals, including media relations specialists, writers, graphic designers, Web publishers, project coordinators, editors, audiovisual specialists, and communications generalists.

Support Services Executive. Ensures that corporate affairs has effective systems and administrative support. Manages a team that includes process assessment manager, measurement specialists, database specialists, process analysts, tools and technology manager, and clearinghouse manager.

Technology Team. Offers a wide range of personal computing, telecommunication, technical project management, and technical consultation. The group not only has the ability to recommend the most viable technology-related tool, but also can implement a path to make the corporate affairs technology transition as simple as possible. The "tech" team supports all issues regarding hardware and software. Responsibilities also include providing clients with technical support and training, whether directly or by referral to a suitable internal or vendor-based source. The team furnishes clients with expert technical consultation based on available technology that falls within guidelines of the Bank of America Technology Services Unit and information security.

SUCCESS STORY

Juliet Don made it to a prominent spot at the Bank of America while still in her twenties. Today, she is vice-president and media relations specialist in corporate affairs at Bank of America, responsible for supporting proactive and reactive media relations efforts in California.

Don joined Bank of America in 1994, working in the San Francisco and Los Angeles offices as an intern reporting to the bank's corporate communications executive. In 1995, she became an associate commercial business public relations officer, and from 1996 to 1998 she was a corporate public relations officer, later becoming a business public relations officer. Don was promoted to assistant vice-president in 1999 until assuming her present post.

Don received a bachelor's degree in business administration from the University of Southern California in 1995. She is a member of the Public Relations Society of America.

CHAPTER 7

Public Relations for Diverse Organizations

W e have defined the role of the counsel firm and the way public relations works at the nation's largest bank. In this chapter we examine how PR is carried out at other organizations. Of course, no two organizations have the same objectives; therefore, their emphases vary greatly.

PR FOR AN INDUSTRY ASSOCIATION

Judith Burrell is the senior vice-president/communications at the Newspaper Association of America (NAA), the nonprofit membership organization of the $54-plus-billion newspaper industry. Its members publish 90% of the daily newspaper circulation in the United States.

In her role, Burrell is responsible for the NAA's editorial operations, including two magazines, seven newsletters, and a Web site; advertising sales for all publications, products, services, and conferences; creative services; the industry's online research service; and public relations.

One of the publications in Burrell's domain, *Presstime*, is published monthly for the NAA's membership and offers in-depth analyses of events, trends, and strategies. *TechNews*, another NAA publication, zeroes in on newspaper operations, developments, issues, and initiatives to improve day-to-day operations.

House and membership publications are a function of the communications and PR departments in many organizations.

The NAA also has an Information Resource Center to serve its member newspapers with a full range of information services including newspaper industry research, business and technical research, and online database services.

Government affairs and public policy are significant to the NAA's operation. The issues here include:

Telemarketing.
Database protection.
Newspaper/broadcast cross-ownership.
First Amendment issues.
Postal legislation.
OSHA ergonomics standard.

Many of the NAA's activities we list here are not public relations in a strict sense, yet in many organizations they fall under this umbrella.

PR FOR A PROFESSIONAL ORGANIZATION

Headquartered in Washington, D.C., the American Psychological Association (APA) is the largest scientific and professional organization representing psychology in the United States and is the world's largest association of psychologists. The APA membership includes more than 159,000 researchers, educators, clinicians, consultants, and students. We look at some of the APA activities through headlines of their recent press releases:

- Conference Explores How Interactive Technologies Influence Child Development.
- APA Supports Passage of Legislation for Office-Based Treatment of Heroin Addiction.
- Women's Worry About Being At Risk for Certain Cancers Not As High As Expected, Study Finds.

These releases emanated from the APA public affairs office and typically refer to articles written about the subject. Contact information is given for the lead author of a particular article.

The APA conducts a media referral service for the news media to reach experts in a wide variety of issues.

The organization is also active in the areas of public policy and advocacy. It implements these programs through the public interest arm of its public policy office. Some examples of their correspondence:

- Letter to Senators Grassley and Kennedy in support of the Family Opportunity Act of 2000.
- Letter to the House Commerce Committee on the use of buprenorphine in the treatment of heroin addiction.
- Letter of commendation to Surgeon General David Satcher for his report *Mental Health: A Report to the Nation.*
- Letter to the Centers for Disease Control National Center for Injury Prevention and Control, offering comments on the Draft Priorities for FY 2001 Injury Research.

The APA's Public Interest Directorate prepares programs that address issues related to aging; AIDS; children, youth, and families; disability; gays and lesbians; violence; and urban initiatives.

PR FOR AN EDUCATIONAL ASSOCIATION OR INSTITUTION

A national teachers' organization, a college or university, and a state or local school board have similar objectives: to present a favorable image of the group or institution and to deal with issues involving it with its publics. These may be legislatures, parents, alumni, or foundations.

Colleges and universities use PR extensively. At most institutions the press office deals with the functions of fundraising, giving awards, making policy changes, and publicizing appointments. Because sports are a prominent activity at most colleges, there is usually a sports information office apart from the school's primary press operation.

Here is an example of PR in action at a state educational association. Concerned with the problems of lower educational standards, a high dropout rate, and overcrowded classes, the State of Washington Education Association, primarily a teachers' group, embarked on a blitz campaign to increase public awareness of this condition. An outside PR counsel firm was engaged to supplement the efforts of the association's own PR staff.

The first step was to identify the publics—legislators, the business community, and the media—and then research the issue in depth. A press release was sent to 365 newspaper, radio, and TV outlets, along with a photograph of a typically crowded classroom. Accompanying the release was a can of sardines with a label reading, "Do our children deserve to be packed like this in school?" Ads in various media tied in to this theme.

Direct mail was used as a follow-up. More than 100 speeches were delivered by the group's leaders. Media coverage of the entire effort was extensive. The result: a 9% increase in public awareness of the problem and a large additional appropriation from the legislature for the state's education program.

PR FOR ADVOCACY GROUPS

There are thousands of advocacy groups, at least one for every possible interest. One well-known organization is the Sierra Club, with a membership of 600,000. Public relations is central to the group's primary role in protecting the environment. It achieves this objective by communication with the public and decision makers on such issues as:

> Stop sprawl: end runaway growth.
> Protect America's wildlands.
> End commercial logging in national forests.
> Protect water from factory farm pollution.
> Global warming.
> Human rights.
> Population stabilization.
> Responsible trade.

The Sierra Club also publishes the highly acclaimed *Sierra Magazine*.

Another example of an advocacy group is the Humane Farming Association, which seeks humane treatment for animals on large factory farms. It conducts an information program through advertising and direct-mail campaigns.

Earth Day Network is yet another advocacy group spreading the word through public relations on protecting the environment. Its initiatives led the way to the creation of the U.S. Environmental Protection Agency and the passage of the Clean Air Act, the Clean Water Act, and the Endangered Species Act.

With the aid of the Internet, the network has linked activists around the world to its program.

PR FOR RELIGIOUS GROUPS AND CHARITABLE ORGANIZATIONS

Many of the PR operations we have just discussed also apply to religious groups and charitable organizations. The Religious Communications Congress of PR Professionals, which serves all denominations, publishes the *Religious PR Handbook*. There are a number of suborganizations and publications in this field. Many PR people involved with religious groups are trained in theology.

A charitable organization deals with dozens of publics, including volunteers, donors, staff, clients members, the media, governmental agencies, legislators, community groups, related organizations, the headquarters office, affiliates and field offices, and foundations.

To get its message across, a charitable organization uses news and video releases, leaflets and brochures, newsletters, speeches, press conferences, meetings and conventions, opinion polls, exhibits and displays, legislative bulletins, special events, and, of course, the Internet.

According to Sunshine Janda, senior vice-president of United Way of America, charitable organizations need PR practitioners because of the "huge impact on these organizations of the new societal trends, and competition for limited resources and volunteers." She concludes that not-for-profit PR is big business with a lot at stake.[1]

PR IN A GOVERNMENT AGENCY

In chapter 11 we deal with public affairs and lobbying. These are primarily efforts of government intervention on behalf of corporations and other organizations. On the government side are the people whose concern is promoting and publicizing the activity of their federal, state, and local agency, all of whom use and practice PR. Practically every official above the rank of police lieutenant has a press spokesperson who sends out press releases, conducts interviews, and writes speeches for appointed officials. In addition, in the U.S. Congress, each senator and representative has a press aide.

If you read a big-city daily newspaper, consider its front page. Many of the news stories emanate from the press offices of various government agencies: federal, state, and local.

At times, a federal or local agency will join with a public relations firm on a particular assignment. An example from the Cipra 2000 competition is the campaign of the Washington, D.C., Department of Health, Administration for HIV/AIDS. For this program, the department contracted with Ogilvy Public Relations Worldwide, one of the top 10 PR firms we highlighted in chapter 4.

The Washington, D.C., area has one of the highest numbers of AIDS cases in the nation, with African American women leading the statistic. Previous efforts to reach this group effectively had failed.

The D.C. Department of Health and the Ogilvy firm came up with an ingenious "ConPact" that looked like a beauty compact but instead contained a condom and an educational insert. Ten thousand were distributed to beauty salons in the DC area.

The salons in the program were very cooperative and agreed to distribute refill condoms to their customers. Calls to an AIDS hotline increased 20% during the months of distribution, and safer sex dialogues at salons spurred the program's success.

Nearly 45 news stories broke about the unique program, and future coverage was planned. As a result of the publicity, calls came to the group from more than 50 health departments and nonprofit organizations eager to originate the program in their areas.

At the federal level, all agencies maintain large press offices to handle the demands of the media and the public for information on their activities. Most have Web sites to further expedite this process.

HOW OTHER ORGANIZATIONS PURSUE ACTIVE PR PROGRAMS

The American Institute of Architects is a national group representing the interests of 55,000 architects in the United States. Its PR arm provides information on architectural design and practice, housing and urban issues, and designing with environmentally safe products.

The National Association of Social Workers is a 130,000-member group that offers information on social work practices in the United States and abroad.

The Society of Professional Journalists is a national organization that disseminates comments on press matters, including referrals on libel and freedom-of-information issues.

Add to the list of organizations with PR departments many others in the nonprofit sector. It is estimated that there are 1.4 million non-profits in the United States. The majority are small in size, yet most maintain a public relations arm to promote their activities.

THE MANY FACES AND TITLES OF PR PEOPLE

When the Public Relations Society of America (PRSA) published the *Public Relations Journal*, it included a list of newly accredited members. Here is a random list of job titles taken from the October 1990 edition. Note the diversity of assignments for PR people not employed by PR counsel firms:

Public Affairs Manager
Automotive Components Group
Ford Motor Company

University Relations Director
Lehigh University

Director Community Relations
Catholic Social Services

Director Public Relations
University of Pittsburgh Medical Center

Director Communications and Marketing
Oregon Affiliate
American Heart Association

Director Marketing Publications and Editorial Services
Unisys Corporation

Manager Corporate Communications
Portland General Electric Corporation

Press Secretary Governor's Office
State of Oklahoma

Information Representative
IBM
Houston, Texas

Communications Director
National Shooting Sports Foundation

Director Public Relations
Society Expedition Cruises

Manager Public Relations
Capital Blue Cross

Public Relations Coordinator
Columbus (Ohio) Museum of Art

Looking for a job in PR? Consider all these options.

CHAPTER 8

Getting the Ink: Media Practice, Media Placement, and Media Relations

The news media is by far the most powerful delivery vehicle in the communications spectrum. A positive news story about a young tech company in the *The Wall Street Journal* can boost its stock 15 to 20% in a single day. An article about a new drug in a medical journal can generate follow-up stories in the consumer press and can also bring thousands of requests for samples from practitioners.

We offered a basic definition of media relations in chapter 3. Here, we tackle this singularly important component in greater detail.

Public relations veteran Howard R. Mitchell III summed up the essence of media relations.[1] Media relations programs should sell the editorial community on the informational value of a company (or organization), its people, and its products. As in any marketing effort, successful media relations depends on building an authentic rapport with the target audience (reporter and editors) while giving them something they can genuinely use.

Mitchell went on to list some of the typical tasks of a media relations program, which are to:

- Develop corporate or product positioning strategies for specific media outlets.
- Plan photo and editorial opportunities for use in the media and develop editorial ideas to fit a publication's or other medium's special promotions.
- Develop news and feature releases for print and electronic media.
- Gain favorable product reviews.
- Place articles: case histories, editorials, features, "how to" stories, first-person angles, and so on.
- Position client as an expert source for broad news and feature coverage.
- Execute media events, media tours, and promotions.
- Collect and analyze media coverage.

HOW MEDIA RELATIONS PROFESSIONALS BUILD RELATIONSHIPS TO DELIVERY THEIR MESSAGE

Each year, the PRSA holds its national conference. In the March 2001 conference, the organization conducted a one-day seminar on the fundamental subject of media relations. The primary role of the seminar was to present techniques to media relations professionals for working with both print and electronic media to help them develop media relationships. Some key subjects of the seminar were:

- The news media and its changing nature: competing for audiences; the new media in cyberspace, how reporters work to gather news.
- Developing the media/public relations relationship: initiating and scheduling communications, understanding media requirements.
- Elements of newsworthiness: making an event a story, building news value with themes and messages.
- Packaging and targeting your story: print versus electronic media, distribution outlets and decisions.
- Media interview and media events: setting objectives and allocating resources, preparing and executing the plan, managing the event and the message, evaluating the results, next steps.
- Earning credibility/respect from top management: supporting the company's objectives, proving program results.

From the subjects of this one seminar, we can readily see the so-phisticated nature of media relations, whether practiced within an organization or at a PR counsel firm.

Now we focus on some of the individual elements of media relations.

THE PRESS RELEASE OR NEWS RELEASE

The press or news release is at the heart of media relations.

The Wall Street Journal receives about 6,000 press releases a week. Many of these are two or three pages long. The Associated Press, the major news agency, receives about 1,000 releases a day. How can the staffs of these media sources possibly find time to read all this material? Experienced media relations people are well aware of this competition for placement of stories and strive to avoid the wastebasket with a number of techniques. One is brevity. A 200-word news story has a far better chance of being read by the editor and reporters beyond the lead paragraph. Another is the quality of the writing.

Today's press or news release is most likely transmitted electronically. The American Heart Association (AHA) is a leading health organization whose primary objective is fighting heart disease and stroke. A search of its Web site at the time of this writing yielded the subject headings of the organization's press releases for that year. Here are the titles of some releases the AHA issued in November 2000:

- Food in flight fights fainting spells and heart attacks.
- Three-minute skin test measures cholesterol levels.
- Low estrogen linked to heart attack in premenopausal women.
- Heavy meals may trigger heart attacks.
- High blood pressure gene also linked to obesity.

Let's look at the elements of one American Heart Association press release.

This report, delivered at an AHA meeting, makes news: the link of a gene to obesity, and the effect of the gene on White individuals with a sedentary lifestyle.

Press releases such as this one receive wide coverage because it is of interest to health, medical, and science editors in the print and broadcast media.

American Heart
Association

Fighting Heart Disease and Stroke

AHA News Releases

FOR RELEASE:
10:00 a.m. CT, Monday
Nov. 13, 2000
(Note: This will be part of
a news conference on Monday.)

CONTACT:
For information Nov. 12-15,
contact Darcy Spitz or
Carole Bullock at the
Ernest N. Morial Convention Center
(504) 670-4000

Abstract 4077

American Heart Association meeting report:

High blood pressure gene also linked to obesity

NEW ORLEANS, Nov. 13 - A natural gene variation that is already linked to high blood pressure may also predispose those who inherit it to obesity, according to a study reported today at the American Heart Association's Scientific Sessions 2000.

The discovery could lead to new approaches to prevent high blood pressure and obesity.

German researchers found that people who inherit two copies of the gene, one from each parent, have a high risk of obesity. However, exercising for two hours or more a week appears to block the genetic tendency.

"This underscores that obesity is not only a genetic disease, but that certain genes - in connection with environmental or behavioral factors - can increase the likelihood of obesity," says lead author Achim Gutersohn, M.D., of the University of Essen in Essen, Germany. "However, such inherited factors can be countered by a healthy lifestyle."

He notes that the gene variation, called the GNB3 825T allele, is a "thrifty genotype." He speculates that the once-beneficial gene arose early in human history, when a high level of physical activity was the norm, to help our ancestors in hunter-gatherer societies survive periods of low food supplies. But the gene variation now has become detrimental in industrialized countries where less physical activity is demanded.

The German team linked the 825T allele to obesity after studying 1,291 young, healthy, white volunteers - average age, 29.8 years. "We conducted this study to better understand why the GNB3 825T allele is associated with an increased cardiovascular risk," Gutersohn says.

Earlier studies had associated the gene variation with high blood pressure, particularly in people

FIGURE 8.1   This press release is a sure shot to be picked up by the media by virtue of its subject matter, the relationship of high blood pressure and obesity. It was issued by the American Heart Association at a press conference in New Orleans in November 2000, but was also distributed to health editors and the general press. (Courtesy American Heart Association)

with left ventricular hypertrophy, a thickening of the heart muscle that can be life threatening. Animal and laboratory cell studies have also shown that increased activation of G protein, a messenger system within cells, leads to a greater production of fat cells.

Gutersohn and his colleagues measured the height and weight of the 532 women and 759 men who took part in the study and gathered information on the participants' socioeconomic status, diets and physical activity. Examination of their DNA, obtained from blood samples, revealed whether or not a volunteer carried the 825T allele.

"One significant finding of our study is the strong effect of the gene in white individuals with a sedentary lifestyle," Gutersohn says. "Our findings show that individuals who have inherited two copies of the 825T allele have a high risk of obesity if they do not participate in regular physical activity."

Dr. Gutersohn and colleagues at the University of Essen also provided estimates of how often the 825T allele occurs in several racial groups by analyzing the genes of 1,153 anonymous individuals from five population groups - Australian aborigines, Japanese, Chinese, black Africans and black Americans. They found it was most common in black Africans and black Americans.

Combining the 825T allele data from these groups with that from the white volunteers allowed the team to estimate the frequency with which the gene variation occurs among different racial populations.

Gutersohn says the estimated frequency showed that at least one copy of the allele was carried by 71.4 to 87.8 percent of black Africans and black Americans; 43.1 to 49.0 percent of Asians; and 25.1 to 29.6 percent of Caucasians.

The researchers believe the 825T allele holds great potential as a genetic screening tool to identify people at risk of obesity-related diseases. This would allow physicians to initiate preventive treatments long before symptoms appeared.

Co-authors are Rainer Mueller, M.D., and Winfried Siffert, M.D.

NR00-1181 (SS2000/Gutersohn)

FIGURE 8.1 (*continued*)

We should note a few other things about this release. First, the contact names are listed at the top of the first page. Also listed are the names of the authors of the study, who may be reached for interviews through the AHA's media relations department.

The Elements of a Good Press Release

A good press release such as the one for the AHA should read the way a good news or feature story reads. The lead paragraph here is only

35 words long, yet it synthesizes the whole report. The busy editor or reporter needs to merely read it to know whether to go further.

The release should be just long enough to cover the subject. Short paragraphs make for easy reading. Here, the longest paragraph is only five lines. If an editor chooses to do a 100-word synopsis, it should be easily done from the release.

The release should be written in nontechnical language unless it is meant for technical or scientific journals. In this press release it is, of course, necessary to use such language as "allele" and "genotype."

A tailor-made or exclusive press release should be written to the needs and style of the reporter or editor who will use it. A press release must express a point of view that hasn't been widely expounded elsewhere. The recipient in the media must often make an instant decision on its value as news.

But Is It News, and Pitching to the Right Catcher

Many PR professionals have provided answers to the question, "When is a press release news?" Philip Lesly said it's news when it contains one or more of the major ingredients of human interest, such as when it:

- Is novel.
- Relates to famous persons.
- Is directly important to great numbers of people.
- Involves conflict.
- Involves mystery or crime.
- Is considered confidential.
- Pertains to the future.
- Is romantic or sexy.
- Is funny.[2]

To test these news qualifications, examine the front page of your daily newspaper. Many of the local and national political pieces reached that newspaper through press releases and press conferences. Also, many of the interviews in the paper were generated by media relations people who "pitched" the idea to the paper.

Those in the PR business call this practice "pitching stories." Stories, or news, are what media relations people have to sell to the media. The effective pitching of a story requires consummate skill.

If you're a Fortune 500 company and you have a dramatic financial turnaround, the job of placing that story is far easier than it might be if you represented a defense contractor cutting jobs.

A major financial story may be reported on by the Associated Press and distributed to all its newspapers and broadcast clients for release. The impact of such a story on the financial pages of a major newspaper or broadcast financial news service is far-reaching. It is read by stockholders, brokers, potential investors, customers, dealers, suppliers, employees, and competitors. The feature pages, as well, are typically developed from the pitches of media relations people.

The Exclusivity Factor and Other Woes

Very often it is the media relations person's judgment to "sell" an exclusive story to a newspaper, magazine, or broadcast or online source. He or she will make it clear on the release itself and in conversation with the reporter or editor that it is exclusive. The media may then elect to go with the story or reject it if its subject does not warrant coverage beyond a brief mention. In the latter case, the media relations person can submit it as an exclusive to another source or send it out to all the media.

Important newspapers such as *The Wall Street Journal*, *The New York Times*, and the *Washington Post* will often run exclusive pieces. Where a media relations person runs into trouble is when an "exclusive" is pitched to a number of different media sources. In the business that's called "double or triple planting." Most editors deplore it, but others don't care where and how they get their story ideas.

Joel Pomerantz, a veteran PR practitioner, airs the frustrations of media relations people. He decries the "disdainful attitudes" toward PR that some media people harbor.

Here are some cases in point:

- You suggest to a reporter a story idea involving your client, provide a great deal of background material, and give the writer many leads to flesh out the piece. The article appears without any mention of your client.
- You go to great lengths to make the CEO of an important client company available for an urgently solicited interview that consumes merely 45 minutes of his time. The piece runs, incorporating many of his thoughts, but completely without attribution.

- You propose a perishable story to an editor who expresses immediate interest. The editor sits on the proposal for weeks. Nothing
happens. Meanwhile, it's too late to pitch it to anyone else.
- You set up a requested interview with a client. She is quoted accurately, but totally out of context, resulting in a damaging, unin-
tended impression.[3]

We counter Pomerantz's plaint with the media person's point of
view. Most reliable journalists loathe PR-managed news—that is, the
piece with a positive twist or "spin." These writers prefer to originate
their own stories based on reportage and research. But of course, this is
not always possible because of budget and time considerations. Therefore, the relationship with PR people is often symbiotic—journalists
have difficulty working with PR people, yet they can't function without them.

THE TOOLS OF MEDIA RELATIONS

Media relations is sometimes called a tactic, an activity, a practice
area, or a component, and it uses all kinds of media tools to get its
message across.

The press release is perhaps the oldest tool of public relations. Its
use today is still widespread, even though it has been joined by many
other pieces of artillery in the media relations arsenal.

But first, let's define a number of these tools:

> *Backgrounder*—A briefing session or document that may be in
> the form of a fact sheet. Often it contains more information
> than a press release.
>
> *Biography*—A written account in biographical form of an indi-
> vidual's life and career, or of a corporation or other group's
> history.
>
> *Byliner*—A writer important enough to merit a byline. The writer
> is referred to as the byliner; the identification is the byline.
>
> *Case history*—All the relevant information or material gathered
> about an individual, group, or company.
>
> *Fact sheet*—A collection of data in long or short form that often
> accompanies a press release or press kit.
>
> *Media kit*—A packet of material containing information about
> an organization, publication, network, or even TV show.

News release—An article written by a public relations person that is sent to the media about an event, development, personality, or business organization.

Pitch letter—A public relations person's advance communication to an editor, print or broadcast, about a story or proposed publicity.

Position paper—A formal, usually detailed, written statement about a single issue, which articulates a position, viewpoint, or policy.

Round-up article—A summary or published list of items; an extended article or a radio or TV program bringing together a variety of sources.

B-Rolls and VNRs

Making their debut in the 1990s, B-rolls and VNRs are the new hot tickets in the media relations sweepstakes. Here are some basic definitions.

B-Roll. Used primarily in the broadcast medium but now also online, the B-roll is raw video footage, not scripted, about a new product, development, or even a competition. When TV stations or networks receive it, they must edit it and add the participation of the anchor.

B-rolls cost about $15,000 to make, plus the additional cost of shipping, sometimes by satellite.

VNR (Video News Release). Basically, a VNR is a news story with scenes, interviews and narration. The TV station receiving the VNR has the option of adding its own script for the station's reporter to read.

VNRs have been used to promote events like the opening of a super-plus new resort in Las Vegas, a breakthrough drug, or even a Victoria's Secret fashion show.

VNRs are most effective when they don't need too much editing. TV stations love them when they can be put right on the air.

Although VNRs have gained wide use in TV and online, there are pitfalls for media relations professionals. A story that is too commercial won't be used. A satellite feed of a VNR alone does not guarantee placement. It is still necessary to pitch the story to TV station news editors via fax and e-mail.

With more than 6,000 online news and consumer sites hungry for content, the Internet has become a new frontier for VNRs. The Web sites are eager for this kind of information. It improves their sites and makes them look like rich media providers.

E-Mail: A Powerhouse Media Relations Tool

Bye-bye faxes, messengers, and snail mail. Brian Ruberry, president of allhealth Public Relations in North Potomac, Maryland, now finds e-mail to be the most efficient and effective method of getting information to the media.

According to an article in PRSA's *TACTICS*, there are today more than 1,000 health care reporters who use the Internet for story ideas and pitches, and nearly three-fourths of journalists go online daily.

Ruberry has outlined a set of strategies he uses to make effective use of e-mail in media relations:

- Media list tailored to target only reporters who cover the topic.
- Place addressees in the bcc field.
- Place your address in the "to" field.
- Subject field is eye-catching and applicable to reporters' beats.
- The message captures the essence of the story without using more than one screen.
- Attach news release for reporters if requested.
- If manageable, personalize each message.
- Proofread the message.
- Preview the message by sending it to yourself first.
- Include your name, title, organization, and telephone number.[4]

How a Large PR Firm Tracks Media

At large public relations firms like Burson-Marsteller, media practice specialists have instantaneous access to various databases that:

- Track electronic and print media opportunities for clients.
- Track coverage of clients and client issues.
- Track ongoing and emerging media trends and theories.
- Access the firm's huge network of media contacts.

Case Histories in Media Relations

Ogilvy Public Relations, one of the top 10 PR firms, has adopted a Media Works program in dealing with the media. Its purpose is "to share important information with media, stakeholders and the marketplace in the most positive manner possible."

In the course of this program, Media Works offers

> Media analysis and research
> Message development
> Media kits
> Press conferences
> Media training
> Media surveys
> Research

Here is a case history of Ogilvy PR's Media Works 1997 campaign on behalf of client Ameritrade:

Ameritrade Holding Corporation sought to launch a new brand and company unit into the still embryonic deep discount online brokerage category. Although the company had a solid 23-year heritage in financial and brokerage services, Ameritrade was virtually unknown.

As part of an integrated marketing team, Ogilvy PR took the lead, announced the new company, and launched the Ameritrade brand in October 1997.

Ogilvy PR implemented an aggressive Media Works campaign to claim ownership of the online brokerage market, provide needed credibility for prospective customers, and help build a large customer base.

Key messages for media and industry analysis were developed, along with an in-depth press kit about Ameritrade and the burgeoning deep discount brokerage industry. Company spokespersons were media trained for national interviews.

On launch day, Ogilvy PR staged a massive media pitching effort from New York, Chicago, and Omaha to contact 200 national and regional business and personal finance media outlets. A CEO conference call was also set up with key analysts.

Following the launch, an aggressive Media Works campaign was maintained to help support and further build the Ameritrade brand.

The results?

- A virtually unrecognized name became a market leader; a brand was solidly established, partly through the power of Media Works.

- Nearly 1,100 media placements were generated, including feature profiles and coverage in *The Wall Street Journal*, *Time*, and *Kiplinger's*, and on CNN and CNBC, among many other top media.
- More than 350,000 new accounts were generated.
- Ameritrade's editorial "share of voice" nearly doubled its market share.
- Stock rose dramatically and hit a record high.
- Media recognized Ameritrade as a key player alongside its larger competitors, including Charles Schwab, Fidelity, Quick & Reilly, and Discover.

Note particularly some of the media relations elements Ogilvy used here:

- Key messages and an in-depth press kit were developed.
- Company spokespersons were media trained.
- A massive media pitching effort to media outlets was staged and a conference call with Ameritrade's CEO was set up with key stock analysis.
- More than 1,100 media placements were generated, including profiles and coverage in the influential *Wall Street Journal* and CNBC.
- And perhaps most important in the development of Ameritrade was its early recognition as a discount online brokerage brand.

Other Case Histories

When Hill & Knowlton represented a major U.S. telecommunications company that had opened offices in Europe and Asia, it was responsible for simultaneous press relations in seven target markets overseas. This required that Hill & Knowlton communicate in more than 17 languages, plus several dialects.

Sabre, a leader in the computer travel reservations field, maintains this position by an aggressive media relations program geared to reaching its publics: more than 440 airlines, more than 45,000 hotel properties, car rental companies, railroads, tour operators, in addition to 42,000 travel agencies and millions of travelers who make more than 400 million bookings each year.

Vollmer, Sabre's PR firm, used a variety of tactics to harness this vast audience. Vollmer's media relations mix included press releases, media briefs and alerts, tele-press conferences, media drops, interviews in target publications, and speaking opportunities for the company's executives.

For this effort, both Sabre and Vollmer won a Cipra 2000 award in the field of media relations.

Edelman PR, another of our top 10 PR firms, created a video package for client DuPont that involved motion picture and still photography shot on three continents and that contained video and brochures produced in six languages, and these packages were mailed to the 10,000 architects around the world.

The satellite media "tour," where a CEO or other spokesperson is interviewed in a single location by many TV and cable broadcasters, is today a common media relations practice.

Video news releases (VNRs) and public service announcements (PSAs) can have a total audience of 2 billion through network placement and repeated use on local and cable TV stations during a 1-year period.

Today, all major PR firms are involved in interactive media solutions as they relate to the Internet, e-commerce, and digital communications. The massive electronic dissemination of press materials at the click of a mouse is a reality.

Spreading the Words: Measuring the Effectiveness of Media Relations Campaigns

When I published magazines, we sold advertisers on the composition and demographics of our readers. We used total audience research to determine how many readers per copy we had. Then we promoted these numbers to show our magazine's efficiency compared to the competition. In retrospect, it's still not a very exacting measurement.

Broadcast uses a ratings system to tell advertisers the number of households watching a particular show. Ratings guide advertising agencies in buying TV time, and then help them evaluate the efficiency of their buys.

Public relations has its own market research techniques to measure the effectiveness of media relations campaigns. Many firms and organizations use database media monitoring systems to track and measure the reach and response of their messages. The sheer volume of clippings is not satisfactory media monitoring.

One firm, Ogilvy PR, analyzes the "favorability" of each clipping based on mutually agreed-on client criteria and recommended strategies. Their program even includes a competitor benchmark in their measurement of results.

Media relations monitoring and assessment now includes the Internet. Specialists search news and information sites, forums, and bulletin boards for clients' and competitors' mentions.

In placing messages and stories about a corporation or other organization, media relations professionals use online media such as affinity sites, webzines, activist sites, listservs, university sites, and online communities to directly reach target audiences.

When a campaign is completed, the PR firms gives its client an evaluation and its measure of success. The evaluation is often a game of numbers. For example, a PR firm represents a company that has developed a revolutionary new voice-driven word processor. The media relations campaign is targeted to print and broadcast media. When the campaign is completed, the PR firm delivers a report to the client detailing the number of "hits"—that is, the publications and broadcast media that actually carried the story about the new product.

The PR firm will highlight the story's appearance in such influential publications as *The New York Times*, *The Wall Street Journal*, *Fortune*, and *Business Week*. Also included are media placements in morning network talk shows and business news broadcast programs.

We should understand the comparison of a PR campaign to a paid advertising campaign. In PR, the client has to consider the PR firm's fee and the additional costs of delivering the message to the media. Advertising is more exact in the sense of finite media commitments. For example, if the manufacturer of a voice-driven word processor buys a black-and-white page ad in *Newsweek*, it will cost $99,450. That ad reaches a circulation of 3.1 million readers. When we add in the magazine's pass-along circulation (others reading a particular issue), the ad has a total audience of about 20 million. However, does every one of these "readers" read the ad?

Now, if the corporation and its PR firm are able to place a story (as opposed to an ad) in *Newsweek* about the word processor, there may be higher readership at no cost other than the PR firm's fee. It's often a difficult choice and one that depends on the product and the message.

Also, many situations don't lend themselves to treatment as advertising. Often in a product launch, the marketing plan calls for both advertising and PR.

STAGING PRESS CONFERENCES AND INTERVIEWS

When the U.S. President chooses to have a press conference, there's no problem guaranteeing that it will be attended. Dozens of domestic and foreign correspondents from broadcast and print media are assigned to the president. They're constantly receiving memoranda, advisories, and press releases from the president's press secretary. Also, a live press conference allows for direct questions to the chief executive.

Similarly, in November 2000, when General Electric, the world's largest corporation, appointed a new CEO to succeed its dynamic leader, Jack Welch, it called a press conference in the company's NBC studios in New York, and all the media came because of the worldwide importance of the move. Of course, the news was also disseminated to the media electronically.

Heads of corporations and organizations often desire to "meet the press." In this way, their comments and opinions will be transmitted to a wide audience. But press conferences aren't arranged spontaneously. Rather, according to *PR News*, a press conference is warranted only if:

- The news merits the busy reporters' time.
- The information cannot be communicated as effectively in writing or by telephone.
- It's necessary to tell the story to a number of the media at the same time.
- There's genuine interest in the news among a reasonable portion of the general public.
- A recognized, respected, and well-prepared spokesperson can be provided.
- The announcement can be tied to another timely and newsworthy issue or event.
- Interesting visual elements are available.
- It's required in order to meet competition from other breaking news, such as election coverage or other activities that command attention.

A CONVERSATION WITH HOWARD J. RUBENSTEIN

An article in *The New York Times* in September 1999 called Howard J. Rubenstein "image maker for those who move and shake," "a spinner with vast web of contacts," and "the dean of damage control."

The article went on to call him New York's number 1 public relations executive, who has spent "46 lucrative years in the art of manipulating the perceptions of powerful clients."

One British magazine gave him the title, "Superflak."

Rubenstein doesn't run a top 10 PR firm and doesn't have 1,000 employees, but insiders guess he makes $4 million to $7 million a year.

I first met Howard Rubenstein more than 30 years ago. He was handling PR for the fledgling Weight Watchers organization and I was publishing its magazine. Under his nurturing, Weight Watchers grew into a strong national organization that was later purchased by H. J. Heinz. Since then Rubenstein has become an influential force in New York PR and political affairs with a client list of the mighty and the celebrated, such as Rupert Murdoch, the New York Yankees, David Letterman, Michael Jackson, and the former Duchess of York, Sarah Ferguson. He also represents Rockefeller Center, Columbia University, the State of Israel, and Sony Music Entertainment.

Rubenstein linked up the duchess with his client Weight Watchers, where she became its spokesperson. Later, Ferguson performed similar services for Charles Schwab by appearing in its advertising.

I asked him a few questions about his practice and his profession.

According to a recent listing, your firm handles about 500 clients with a staff of about 175. Most other large firms have a higher ratio of employees to clients. How do you do it?

We are results oriented and bottom-line conscious. Our efforts are directed toward meeting the client's business goals. While we understand and highly value the importance of learning and listening, we do not waste time on unnecessary frills and meetings for the sake of meeting. Our objective is not to describe what we are going to do, but to do it—to break major stories in key media. We have a highly professional staff capable of honing a story, packaging it intelligently, and presenting it persuasively to the appropriate reporters.

All professional staff members have account responsibilities. No one simply manages others. We also utilize a team approach where appropriate for major, complex assignments. Each contributes what he or she does best in a dynamic, creative, and efficient mix.

In a magazine article, one PR professional said of you, "He won't call a press conference unless there's news; [he] has the best-attended press conferences in New York." How do you go about conducting a conference? Is it done with just a press release, or is there telephone follow-up to the media?

There are nine basic rules regarding press conferences:

1. Make sure you are making news—either because of what you're saying or who's saying it or both.
2. Don't schedule a conference unless there's a genuine interest in the news among a reasonable portion of the general public.
3. Don't schedule a press conference unless it's necessary to tell the story to a number of the media at the same time.
4. Have a powerful visual. Rarely rely on just talking heads, even if they're heads of state.
5. Provide a recognized, respected, and well-prepared spokesperson for the conference.
6. Hold the press conference in an accessible location at a realistic time. Make certain the room fits the event, for there is little worse than a low turnout in a vast space. Be flexible so that you can add (or remove) seats as needed.
7. Don't schedule your press conference for a time (or a day) when you know a major competing story will be breaking. Inform the press about the conference by releasing a "tip sheet," a catchy announcement—sent out a few days prior to the event—which is designed to entice but omits the hard news.
8. Follow up with phone calls and faxes the day before and morning of the press conference. After the press conference make sure you and your client are available to respond to further queries, as well as to arrange for "beeper" interviews. (The beeper allows the press to reach the PR person or interviewee any time following the press conference.)
9. Send the press kit to all appropriate media not present. It's also usually a good idea to have your own photographer there so you can service the wires [wire services], if they are interested, and the trades.

Howard Rubenstein Shares His Best Media Placement Secrets

So that the reader might benefit from the secrets of success of this renowned image-spinner, we reprint a portion of a column he wrote in the January 2001 premiere issue of *Bulldog Reporter's MEDIA RELATIONS INSIDER:*

> 1. *Don't begin a placement pitch until you're convinced the story has merit.* Before you can begin to place well, Rubenstein says, you have to understand what makes good news and future material. "You can't just be an order taker for your client," he says. "Too many beginners

in the field will listen to the client and say it's a great story. But unless you're convinced it's a good story the media will like and use, you should work on it and make it the best you can."

Three criteria determine whether a story will fly, according to Rubenstein: Is it new? Does it affect a lot of people? Will it interest most people? "If you are told to promote something that isn't news or at least isn't a dramatic feature story pegged around some kind of news, resist the temptation to prematurely pitch it."

Tip: Rubenstein advises publicists to look for the human element in a story. Start with one person's experience and then broaden the story out. Contrary to the traditional inverted pyramid story model, it is a technique that is being used more often by newspaper reporters. Rubenstein, like other high-profile PR pros, also learned a long time ago that the media loves stunts. "We've done 10,000 or more in all my days," says Rubenstein. That includes the spectacle he orchestrated in Times Square that attracted legions of reporters to witness magician David Blaine entombing himself in a block of ice.

2. *Resist the temptation to blanket the media with press releases.* Rubenstein says the best placement is achieved by giving a story to the right reporter and outlet. That requires reading everything about an area that concerns your client. "Don't be discouraged by rejection," advises Rubenstein. "Improve your pitch and go somewhere else. You can even go to a different department or another columnist or editor at the same paper. Just because you've been rejected one place doesn't mean you've been rejected at that outlet."

Tip: Keep media lists up-to-date. "We buy every list available in town," says Rubenstein. "We've got about 500,000 names and outlets worldwide in our database, but it would have no value if I didn't keep it up-to-date on a daily basis." He adds, though, that it is more valuable to intimately know five to ten reporters who cover your area than the names of 100 journalists.

3. *Exclusives—a help or a hindrance?* Some of Rubenstein's financial clients benefit when he gives an exclusive to *The Wall Street Journal* or *The New York Times.* Going to a powerful daily in advance of a major announcement and getting them interested in a story can be a major plus because most major newspapers don't like covering news conferences or just taking press releases and running with them. But favoring a daily newspaper too often angers other news media, he says.

4. *Get double the coverage by localizing your story.* Sometimes you're lucky to break a good national story, but then it tails off because reporters back off. "So we look for local angles and go to regional outlets in cities," says Rubenstein. "Sometimes, wire services will pick it up and shoot it back out over the country and it gets picked up all over the place again."

THE WORLD'S FASTEST PRESS CONFERENCE

Here's a unique approach Sprint Business took in 1997 to promote its campaign on the "50 Most Productive Cities in America" and an event titled "The World's Fastest Press Conference." The campaign won a Cipra 1998 award:

> Source: Cipra 1998.
> Organization: Sprint Business.
> Agency: Meltzer & Martin Public Relations.

For Sprint Business, the primary message platform for all marketing communications activities is the concept that Sprint's business services help companies improve their productivity. In 1997, Sprint delivered its "productivity" message to small businesses across the country, with a strategically focused video news release showcasing the "50 Most Productive Cities in America."

Research and Planning

As the telecommunications industry entered 1997, major players were faced with a host of competitors touting low prices to consumer and business audiences. Rather than play a price game, Sprint Business established a core message platform that focused on the promise to deliver productivity to companies.

For its part, Meltzer & Martin Public Relations was charged with developing a year-long campaign targeted to small business—typically companies with fewer than 100 employees and telecommunications billings of less than $5,000 per month. The agency crafted a plan with the ultimate goal of contributing to new customer acquisition for Sprint. As one of the major initiatives, Meltzer & Martin recommended an independent study commissioned by Sprint to identify the "50 Most Productive Cities in America."

Objectives and Strategy

The announcement of the research results would occur on-site in the city designated as the "Most Productive City in America," centered around an event billed as "the world's fastest press conference." The press conference would feature John Moschitta, "the world's fastest talker," known for his appearances in FedEx television ads, who would describe the attributes that contributed to the city's "most productive" designation and would name some of the small business and categories that helped earn the city this recognition.

In conjunction with the event, the agency worked with an outside vendor to produce a video news release (VNR) announcing the results of the study. The primary objective of the VNR was to further build Sprint's positioning as a telecommunications company that understands small businesses and their need for productivity tools. The agency set a goal of securing four placements in the top markets of the VNR, which closely reflected the key markets on which Sprint placed a special focus during the year.

Execution

The announcement of the 50 most productive cities in America was held in the top city on the list: San Jose, California. Meltzer & Martin PR then enlisted the participation of the San Jose Metropolitan Chamber of Commerce. Because the goal would be to distribute the VNR over the satellite as soon after the event as possible, the agency arranged to shoot and edit certain footage in advance of the actual announcement, including comments from the Chamber of Commerce, comments from Sprint representative, background footage of San Jose, and the narrative voiceover. Final filming occurred at the actual press conference to announce the results of the study, and all footage was reviewed at a postproduction facility near San Jose. The VNR was finalized that afternoon and first distributed over the satellite at 4 p.m. A media alert had been distributed a week earlier to secure initial interest from the media.

Because of an unanticipated media event, a stunning decline in the U.S. stock market that virtually eliminated the opportunity for broadcast feature coverage, the agency and outside vendor agreed to rebroadcast the VNR once again the next week when news media would again be receptive to feature material.

Evaluation

Sprint's announcement of the "50 Most Productive Cities in America" was successful by all measures.

- In total, the VNR generated 39 placements—almost 10 times the original goal—and reached nearly 4.7 million viewers.

- Sixty-eight percent of the VNR placements appeared in the top 50 designated market areas (DMAs), including eight placements in Pittsburgh, four in San Francisco, one in Houston, and one in Cleveland.
- Ninety-nine percent of the placements in the top 50 markets ran during a prime-time news program.
- One hundred percent of the placements conveyed Sprint's productivity message.

And the success of the program was not only external. At the conclusion of the project, Sprint's senior director of small business marketing deemed the study "the best, most strategically strong effort of its type to date."

WHAT CLOUT IS ALL ABOUT

As in any other business or profession, the ability to reach influential people pays off. In advertising, it is often contacts rather than creativity that win new accounts. So it is in PR.

Media relations people at the largest PR counsel firms have clout by virtue of the standing of their clients. It is certainly an accepted practice for an editor to agree to do a piece on Client A in exchange for an exclusive interview with the controversial CEO of Client B.

A media relations person who is established as a source of information about a subject, or even as a source of sources, also exercises clout. This cooperation makes an editor's or reporter's job easier, and ultimately benefits the PR person.

One well-known New York PR professional, known in the business as an "image fixer," is often asked to repair damaged images. He is successful at it because of many years spent accumulating important friends in the media. It also helps that he has been on the other side of the desk, both in the business world and in government.

This PR practitioner has unparalleled access to the power of the press, particularly important when he represents unpopular clients or causes. In one case, he served as PR counsel for the editors of an arch-conservative college newspaper who were suspended from school for harassing a black professor whose teaching style and political views they found objectionable. Here, this PR counsel functioned as a criminal attorney. He tried to convince the public that the editors' punishment amounted to a violation of their right of free speech.

In another case, he was called on to represent three cigarette companies who were jointly defending themselves against a lawsuit brought by a man whose wife had died of lung cancer. Their defense was that there is still no proof that heavy smoking is lethal and that, regardless of the warning on the pack itself, the man's wife chose to smoke of her own free will.

He is able to justify his high hourly fee because he delivers. He can immediately reach top columnists, the managing editor of *The New York Times*, ABC's Peter Jennings, CBS's Dan Rather, CNN's Larry King, and NBC's Tom Brokaw. This access doesn't guarantee that his clients will always win, but it certainly assures that they'll get a fair hearing.

TIPS OF THE MEDIA RELATIONS TRADE

We discuss the operations of Infocom Group, publishers of *MEDIA RELATIONS INSIDER*, *Lifestyle Media Relations Reporter*, *PR AGENCY INSIDER*, and *BULLDOG REPORTER*, in chapter 21. The information in these excellent publications is designed for the skilled PR practitioner and offers the insight necessary to penetrate the minds of editors, reporters, and broadcast news directors.

We list here some tips culled from various issues of these publications. They clearly indicate the high degree of specialization in the craft of media relations:

- Make yourself an expert—know more about the industry than the journalist you're pitching to.
- Show your face—visit a local TV station's or newspaper's newsroom to introduce yourself to the journalists face to face and to see firsthand how they operate.
- Send releases in common language, not industry-speak.
- Train CEOs (in your own or your client's company) to tell their story in three to five messages so that they're comfortable repeating them throughout each media interview much like politicians do during campaigns.
- Research your client's industry by reading more "trades" (industry publications and Web sites) and ask clients for trends.
- Keep abreast of media people moves in daily newspapers, broadcast media, and consumer and business magazines.
- Focus on the language of the market you're trying to reach.

STAGING A SPECIAL EVENT

Special events take many forms, and planning them, of course, requires many different approaches.

The National Air and Space Museum, part of the Smithsonian Institution, creates at least one event a year. On the 20th anniversary of the *Apollo 11* moon landing, an outdoor public ceremony was held at the museum attended by high-ranking government officials, the astronaut crew of *Apollo 11*, and scores of VIPs. A late-night "Lunar landing Party" was staged with actual footage of the Neil Armstrong moon walk shown on closed-circuit monitors around the building.

Planning the event began 18 months in advance, with regularly scheduled meetings with all departments of the museum participating. Early planning also involved negotiations with officials at NASA, whose primary interest was maximum public relations impact.

For the communications staff of the Smithsonian, the hard work paid off. Press coverage was extensive, with a total of 75 camera crews covering the event for local and network TV. In addition to the media exposure, the event enhanced the museum's image. It also produced goodwill and a spirit of community among the local participating groups. The event gave the Smithsonian staff members a feeling of pride and confidence in the institution. For the public, the event provided an educational, family-oriented, festive happening.

ARRANGING A PRESS TOUR

One of the major assignments of media relations people is the press tour. It is used when a movie star does satellite tours to promote a new movie or when a celebrity goes on a tour to promote a new product bearing his or her name.

If you are best-selling author John Grisham you don't go on those wearisome book tours. Add to the elite group of nontourers Robert Ludlum, Tom Clancy, and Danielle Steel. Their new books make the best-seller lists and stay there for months without touring.

Less eminent authors do go through the rigors of book tours. Jay Kordich is "the Juiceman." His publisher, William Morrow, promoted his book, *The Juiceman's Power of Juicing*, with a tour that took in 19 cities in 32 days. In addition to the trip, the author did interviews that resulted in numerous newspaper and magazine stories.

So important was the tour for Kordich's publisher, it employed a publicity and tour-management firm to handle arrangements. Today, e-mail and the Internet have speeded up details for tours such as this one.

The book industry's leading trade publication, *Publishers Weekly*, has gone high-tech in its efforts to publicize and promote books. *Publishers Weekly* has a biweekly e-mail service for agents, scouts, and editors, where it provides up-to-date information on book, movie, TV, and licensing deals.

A Creative Media Opportunity

In the early 1970s, when I was publishing *National Lampoon*, we were a hot item. Everything we did was news, whether we contrived it or not. We also received a large volume of "fan" mail, from an assortment of crazies, racists, and even ordinary citizens who hated the magazine.

One day a package about 6 × 9 inches arrived in the mail. Our mailperson didn't think that was so unusual; we received many packages. But this one was different—it was ticking.

Seizing the moment, one of our editors immediately called the bomb squad of the New York City Police Department, the three networks, wire services, *The New York Times*, and *The Daily News*. To the press he said in a panicked voice, "This is the *National Lampoon*, and we've just received a bomb. Come quickly."

Within minutes they all arrived—the police with their specially padded bomb wagon, the media with their cameras. It didn't take the police long to detect that the ticking "bomb" was actually an alarm clock. That night on the 11 o'clock news all three local news shows carried the episode, including an interview with a *Lampoon* editor. No, the event had not been planned. But it made for a short, humorous news feature, with even some doubt over its legitimacy.

THE NEW REALITY FOR SERVING PUBLIC RELATIONS CLIENTS

Marketing expert Peter Pitts complains that too many public relations counselors focus on the wrong things in serving clients—media, messages, and tactics.

"Not correct," says Pitts. "Effective communications must begin and end with a clear focus on getting through to the target audience, having them believe in the communications delivered, and ensuring that they remember what they have been told. In today's world of message mayhem, the smart communicator understands that it's not what you say, it's what they remember."

How one pulls off that considerable communications task is the subject of an article he wrote for the winter 2001 issue of PRSA's publication, *THE STRATEGIST*.

> The word "communication" comes from the Latin word "communico," which means to share. Those of us in the communications trade are in the business of helping our clients share a message.
>
> Sounds simple.
>
> In practice, however, it's an intellectual, emotional, and often a physical challenge. But the rewards are worth the effort. Too bad so many people don't know what they're doing.

Choosing the Right Agency

How to choose a communications firm is almost as tough as when to hire one. Most CEOs understand that they can't produce their own television commercials. It's technical. They understand what an advertising agency does. But when those same corporate executives are faced with a communications crisis, they're not sure where to turn.

It doesn't help that the "name" public relations firms all present programs that, while complete, are at times useless and always expensive.

That's not to say the majority of experts aren't skilled at their craft—they are. The problem is that very few in the fields of marketing and public relations really understand that successful communication isn't driven by what you say.

It hinges on what your target audience remembers. And, it ain't the same thing.

Examining the Memory Model

By investigating the dynamics that drive the memory of a targeted listener, a model emerges that explains why a person or audience hears certain things—what makes that person or group believe what's being said and, most importantly, why some things are remembered, while others forgotten and still others are entirely misunderstood.

Most public relations firms talk tactics because that's what most clients expect—a schedule of press releases, weighty information packets and media tours. They load the weapon before identifying the target. Success is measured in newspaper clippings, television interviews and Web site click-throughs.

But do media mentions equate to message retention?

It's not what you say—or what is written about what you say—it's what your target audience remembers.

"Words," wrote Rudyard Kipling, "are the most powerful drug used by mankind." And the best doctors diagnose first before prescribing medication. Otherwise it's only intuition—and malpractice.

Define Before Jumping

It's wiser to clearly define the situation before jumping to tactical solutions.

- Who is the intended audience? Customers? Stockholders: Employees? Community activists? Government regulators?
- How best to communicate the right message to the right target?
- And how to insure that the strategically developed message is the one that's remembered?

And, not only remembered, but passed on. People get their information from a multitude of sources, but most public relations firms focus only on what has been dubbed the "formal network of communication," press releases, brochures, annual reports, company newsletters, Internet sites, and advertising, all of which are controlled information networks.

As important and useful as these are, it is not where real credibility resides. Such communications are considered, if not entirely compromised, at best suspect. "The company says" are not the three most trusted words in the English language. Perhaps the three most important words in public relations are identified by what one person in your target audience says to another, "I heard that ..."

Most "established" communications pros concur that it doesn't matter what the media says as long as they talk about you. This may be true for some (and even that's plenty arguable), but it is certainly not so for a corporate client anticipating or in the middle of a crisis. Surely executives at hospitals and nursing homes nationwide are not thrilled about being on the front pages of the newspaper when the stories are about Medicare fraud and FBI investigations.

Hearing, Believing, Remembering

The only thing of consequence is ensuring that your target audience listens, believes, and remembers the message you want to get out.

Merrie Spaeth, Dallas-based communications consultant and former head of White House media relations for President Reagan, has pioneered the inverted communication pyramid. Rather than following the traditional model which calls for a PR strategy built on a foundation of background detail, supported with proof and a bit of sell at the top, Spaeth has it flipped over on its head.

Effective communications, according to Spaeth, must begin with a strong, punchy, pithy headline, followed up with proof, such as facts, statistics, examples, anecdotes and quotes (from any expert or individual meaningful to a target audience.) The detail comes dead last. Sound familiar? It's exactly the way a good news story is presented. Effective communications is not about education; it's about your message. It's the job of the communications professional to take the truth—the message—and make it more interesting than fiction—to make it memorable. It's a formidable challenge.

Author Eli Djeddah wrote, "We constantly think that other people will be persuaded by the intelligent presentation of facts or the force of our convictions—when, in reality, these glance off them like raindrops off a car roof. We have totally ignored the need to prepare the ground for the emotional climate, which will make people listen to us, trust us and be persuaded by us."

Corporations cannot afford (in either time or treasure) to retain a consulting firm that doesn't do anything until a crisis point. But that's precisely what many do—to their own strategic disadvantage.

As *NEW YORKER* writer Kurt Andersen has observed, "Truth is supposed to be stranger than fiction, but it's interesting how often truth is exactly like fiction—contrived, implausible and stupid."

It's the job of the communications professional to take the truth—the message—and make it more interesting than fiction—to make it memorable.

Communications warrior, Peter J. Pitts, is Managing Partner of Wired World, an Indianapolis-based marketing firm and a senior fellow at the Institute for Strategic Communications. He is the author of the book, Become Strategic or Die.

MEDIA RELATIONS AT THE AMERICAN MEDICAL ASSOCIATION

Many professional and trade groups pursue active public relations programs. To understand the workings of PR in this field, let's focus on one such group, the American Medical Association (AMA). The AMA represents almost 300,000 medical practitioners in the United States. Its communication activities are varied, part of an overall strategic plan aimed at strengthening public and professional confidence in the organization and its members.

Here's how the AMA implements this program:

1. The Media Relations Department handles well over 500 telephone calls each month from the news media and the public seeking clinical, socioeconomic, and health policy information.
2. AMA officers and executives visit dozens of cities each year speaking to groups and conducting media interviews promoting the AMA and issues important to America's patients and physicians.
3. Relevant AMA policies on medical ethics, public health, healthcare costs, and health policy are discussed in the media.
4. Officers and trustees deliver speeches before civic and business groups. Three full-time speechwriters produce approximately 200 speeches each year for top AMA leaders.
5. The AMA conducts science conferences in cosponsorship with universities, highlighting for reporters advances in medicine and health care. The AMA also partners with other organizations and corporate entities to sponsor media briefings on important issues affecting health.
6. The AMA publishes the highly respected *Journal of the American Medical Association (JAMA)*, which enjoys the largest circulation of any medical journal in the world. Its U.S.-based edition reaches 360,000 readers in 148 countries weekly, while its 18 international editions, published in 13 different languages, reach another 390,000 readers globally.
7. A packet of news releases from *JAMA* is distributed to almost 1,500 journalists weekly.
8. As a function of its formidable advocacy and lobbying efforts, the AMA is continually in touch with Congress, executive departments, and other federal agencies regarding healthcare issues and the interests of its members.

Many more communication and PR activities are carried out by the AMA. For our purposes, just think of the kinds of jobs available in such an organization. Science writers, editors, speechwriters, and media relations people are just a few that come to mind.

An Interview With a Senior PR Executive at the American Medical Association

Mike Lynch is currently the director of media relations at the American Medical Association. He has worked with reporters on a wide variety of issues affecting health care and medical practice during his 5 years on the job. Recently, Mr. Lynch played an integral role in the AMA's 2000 "National House Call" campaign, which followed Presidential candidates on the campaign trail, calling media attention to the candidates' views on healthcare. In 1999, he effectively managed media attention surrounding the AMA's decision to create a labor organization for employed physicians. The AMA vote became the top domestic news story for 48 hours, airing on all network newscasts and grabbing front-page headlines in *USA TODAY, The New York Times, The Wall Street Journal, The Chicago Tribune*, and other leading newspapers across the country.

Prior to joining the AMA, Mr. Lynch served as chief speechwriter and communications coordinator for the American Academy of Pediatrics. Before joining organized medicine, he worked as a reporter for *The Daily Herald* newspaper in suburban Chicago.

AMA officers and trustees are quoted frequently in the media. What role does your office play in this process and how do you work with your spokespeople to ensure their success?

Our Media Relations office is involved every step of the way. AMA trustees, who serve as our official spokespeople, learn from their very first day on the job that all media inquiries must be routed through our Media Relations office. There are several reasons for this, but mainly it helps ensure that the AMA is speaking with a unified voice and a consistent message. That cannot occur if our spokespeople operate independently.

Most of our spokespeople recognize that routing media calls through our office is in their best interest. Doing so offers our Media Relations staff an opportunity to find out exactly what reporters are looking for and to provide them with background information that can better focus interviews. Most of our spokespeople are practicing physicians so their time is limited. The more we can do to inform reporters before they speak to spokespeople, the better the exchange is for all parties. We make every effort to be sure our spokespeople are well briefed and know what to expect going into an interview. The cardinal sin in media relations is sending your spokesperson into an interview situation ill-prepared.

We do a lot of proactive media outreach as well. It's not enough to simply respond to reporters' inquiries, you need to pitch story ideas and spokespeople to reporters whenever possible. Most reporters are willing to consider good story ideas, but to be successful in gaining their attention, you need to know the kind of stories they write. Not taking the time to learn a reporter's beat shows a lack of respect for the reporter and your pitch is doomed to fail.

Our staff does intensive media training with all new AMA trustees, as well as offer ongoing feedback to those already doing interviews. Even the most expert spokesperson can benefit from staff input. Rarely is a message delivered perfectly. There are almost always ways to improve it. Our staff is constantly looking for examples, stories, statistics, or metaphors that will resonate with a reporter or audience. The real challenge is developing a message that is compelling, yet can be delivered concisely. For better or worse, the media loves "sound bites" and if you can't communicate your message in fifteen seconds or less, chances are you're not going to be heard.

Who does the speechwriting, and do these writers perform other functions as well?

The AMA speaks to several hundred audiences a year from all fields and in all corners of the country. Three full-time speechwriters produce approximately 200 speeches each year for top AMA leaders. Speechwriting for a medical organization is challenging, but not lacking for topics, anecdotes, and apt metaphors. In addition, the speechwriters often help in the preparation of op-ed pieces for newspapers and other appropriate publications.

What are your department's core responsibilities in terms of media relations?

Our staff of 12 professionals receives some 500 to 600 inquiries from the media each month on every topic imaginable. Some of these calls can be handled simply by presenting the reporter with background information. Others require coordinating an interview with an AMA spokesperson. Some inquiries are best handled by referring the reporter to a source outside the AMA. As much as possible, our goal is not to have reporters go away empty-handed. Even if the AMA cannot furnish the necessary information, we try to offer an organization or individual that can. I think reporters appreciate our efforts and are more likely to return to us when they are working on stories to which the AMA can offer meaningful input.

In 2000, the AMA issued over 100 press releases and statements. We're responsible for disseminating these, posting them to our Web site, and making sure they get into the hands of reporters—and ultimately in front of the public. Our staff also writes letters to the editors that comment on timely issues affecting the AMA. During the past year, the letters from the AMA have appeared in *USA TODAY, The New York Times, The Wall Street Journal, Chicago Tribune, Los Angeles Times, Dallas Morning News, Detroit Free-Press, Denver Post*, and other leading newspapers across the country. Letters to the editor are a good vehicle to respond to news reports we feel are unfair or inaccurate, or to offer support for views on which we agree.

The other major responsibility our media relations staff performs is coordinating media events such as press conferences, media briefings, and editorial board visits. While these events are time-consuming and demand thoughtful planning and execution, the payoff can be great. We use these events judiciously, however. When we conduct one of these events, we make every effort to ensure that reporters come away with more than they would get from a simple press release. During a typical year, the AMA conducts approximately 10 to 12 press conferences, 6 to 8 media briefings, and makes 5 to 6 editorial board visits.

Does the AMA engage outside PR counsel firms in addition to the in-house staff? What do they do?

On occasion, the AMA has worked with outside PR counsel. It can be helpful to have other communications professionals look at what our staff is doing and get their input. However, regardless of how good an outside agency may be, there is just no substitute for hiring your own talented, creative people who can learn the "ins and outs" of an organization and use that knowledge to get the job done professionally and expediently. Media relations is a fast-paced, deadline-driven profession. You simply do not have time to get an outside agency "up to speed" so that an issue can be addressed appropriately. My preference is to hire good communications people who can do the job internally. In fact, our staff likens itself to an in-house PR agency—and we view the various departments within the AMA as our clients.

How does the Internet and your Web site fit in with the activities of media relations at the AMA?

The Internet and our AMA Web site have become essential tools for doing our daily work. We use the Internet every morning to track media reports about the AMA and relevant issues impacting its agenda. By 8:30 each morning we distribute electronic news clips of the day's top stories to every AMA employee and our physician trustees. Doing so allows everyone associated with the AMA to know what the outside world is saying about our organization and the issues affecting it. During the day, we use the Internet to stay on top of breaking news affecting the AMA. While medical advances do not occur suddenly, how they're reported certainly does. In addition, the AMA is very involved in many legislative activities in Washington. By monitoring news reports we can work to correct inaccuracies, offer needed clarifications, or provide AMA comment when appropriate. This effort is particularly important in regard to wire service reports like those from the Associated Press, where reporters are updating their stories as information becomes available.

Finally, our Web site is an invaluable tool in helping our staff disseminate relevant information to reporters. We have developed our own "For the Media" Web page that includes AMA news releases, statements, recent letters to the editor, and information about past and upcoming AMA briefings. Our Web page offers reporters a good starting point any time they are reporting on the AMA.

CHAPTER 9

Internal and Employee Communications, Employee Relations, and Employee Publications

In the year 2000, among all the mergers and consolidations of big business, one stands out: the joining of Internet giant AOL and Time Warner, a power in publishing and entertainment and owner of the CNN network. An article in the December 4, 2000, *New York Times* was headed, "A 'Tank' Rolls Through CNN Before Merger." The tank referred to was Steven J. Heyer, president of Turner Broadcasting System, CNN's parent company.

The article pointed out that months before the actual merger was finalized in 2001, hundreds of jobs were eliminated. The situation assumes almost biblical proportion over who shall live and who shall die.

In the new management team's actions, how will they assure the employees who remain with the company that there won't be further mass layoffs to produce maximum revenues in the merged company? Mergers are a dominant issue in today's practice of employee relations, and occur with frequency whenever two powers come together or when globalization or lower profits cause plant shutdowns and divestitures, situations that are reported on daily in the pages of *The Wall Street Journal*.

Yet, in a benevolent gesture, AOL and Time Warner agreed to give stock options to all 85,000 employees of the combined firm after the merger was completed in 2001.

THE ISSUES, APPROACHES, AND TOOLS OF EMPLOYEE COMMUNICATIONS

Whether it's a global corporation, an association, or a government agency, the area of employee communications and employee relations plays a significant role. In most organizations, the corporate communications department reporting to top management is responsible for employee communications. Often, the organization will bring in its PR firm or other specialists to implement this program.

In February 2000, PRSA's publication *TACTICS* had a series of articles that put the spotlight on issues in employee communications.

Carolyn Bobo, assistant vice president for public relations at Cook Children's Health Care System in Fort Worth, Texas, called for a strategic emphasis on employee communications. When competition is fierce and globalization real, communication is more important than ever to an organization.

According to Bobo, senior management must realize that communication is a strategic function. Management must know what employees want and how to implement such a program. She recommended that the organization communicate issues in at least three ways—face to face, memo, e-mail, video, closed circuit TV, and even by letter.

Julie Khan, a manager of organizational communications for GE Capital's Financial Assurance Partnership Marketing Group, stressed that management should not only deliver the messages to its employees, but also evaluate how well they understand the messages.

"In understanding the audience for these messages," said Khan, "management should realize that employees are people first, then audiences, and that they have heads, hearts, hopes, fears, and families . . . to advance the (organization's) business, we need to connect to employees emotionally. But we can't do that without really listening first."

Alison Davis is president of Davis & Company, a consulting firm that helps companies reach, engage and motivate employees. She advocated a program for communicating change (mergers, firings, etc.) in a brave new way. Among her concepts are these;

- Create a change strategy that directly addresses the organization's climate and culture.
- Translate and articulate "management speak" into plain language and tangible contents.
- Relentlessly measure progress (about change) and fine-tune the process.

CORPORATE IDENTITIES

McGraw-Hill Introduces New Corporate Identity

There once was a McGraw and a Hill. In the late 19th century, they were competitors until they joined forces in 1917. We also know McGraw-Hill from our textbook days. But perhaps we don't know that at this writing the company has more than 15,000 employees worldwide and produces 101 publications in four divisions: corporate, financial services, educational and professional publishing, and information media services.

In 1996, an internal survey determined that a majority of employees were "uncertain" and "unaware" of how many divisions, publications, and services existed as part of the McGraw-Hill Companies. McGraw-Hill then decided to launch a new identity campaign to enhance employee understanding of the scope of the company's resources and talents. The vehicle chosen to accomplish the first step of the new corporate identity program was a fast-paced, 14-minute video starring McGraw-Hill employees from around the world, called "We Are One."

To counsel the company in this effort, McGraw-Hill brought in Boxenbaum Grates, Inc., a strategic communications counseling firm, a unit of the high-ranking PR counsel firm, GCI Consulting North America.

The video was built around the five core values reflective of the organization's new culture: principled, brand-rich, global, dynamic, and technologically sophisticated. McGraw-Hill's CEO and president appeared on camera and addressed these issues.

Employees were used in the video instead of actors to convey an authentic sense of the company's diversity and uniqueness, and they were filmed in their own workplaces, not on a set.

The "We Are One" concept became a regular campaign that was extended to the organization's monthly employee newsletter, employee breakfasts, and management forums.

The Marriage of Boeing and McDonnell Douglas

In chapter 3, we referred to the downsizing at Boeing and its subsequent merger with McDonnell Douglas. A Cipra 1998 award details the strategy and creativity used in the employee communications phase of the merger.

The transition period from the time of the announcement to the final approval of the deal took 8 months. In the interim, many decisions had to be made, not least of which was the fate of both companies' employees and their families. Let's look at some of the creative steps the two leaders took on the road to an intense, creative program of employee communications:

On December 12, 1996, the two CEOs called a "communicators only" meeting with their 10 top communication pros, including employee communications executives. Then, on December 15, the process of gaining official approval from government agencies and shareholders began.

But even with these approvals, the communicators agreed that the employee public was crucial to the long-range success of the merged organization. Here are the actions top management and their communicators pursued in the area of employee communications:

- A preliminary communications plan with employee emphasis was immediately written.
- Research findings were used to complete the internal plan. Execution followed, with all internal activity keyed to the research-based plan. Research with 21 employee focus groups was conducted after the announcement to determine levels of understanding and to provide a base for ongoing communications. Two prevailing messages came out of these meetings: communicate, communicate, communicate; and treat the merger as a celebration, not as a funeral.

Day one/week one challenges and planning continued at a high pitch, with the employees kept up-to-date at all stages. The big day, August 4, when the merger was final, heralded a week-long series of events at all the two companies' locations:

- An information plan including videos, brochures, and a new logo pin was mailed to employee homes.
- At 52 work locations, 176,000 employees gathered to view a live Day One telecast, the press conference, special events, and air shows at plant locations.
- Advertising in international and national media announced the merger.

Then, in a stab at show biz, CEOs Phil Condit and Harry Stoneci-
pher launched "Phil and Harry's Excellent Adventure," a road show
that had them walking production lines, shaking hands, flipping
"merger burgers" at outdoor employee lunches, signing autographs,
answering questions, and sharing the moment with employees. At one
plant in Huntington Beach, California, their arrival was greeted with
sustained employee applause for 7 minutes.

For the two former rivals and their companies, the merger went
well, especially to those employees who weren't excessed.

How a Bank Gave Away $20 Million

An article in *Public Relations Journal* tells how the Bank of America
got a warm response from its 50,000 employees: It gave them stock
worth $20 million.[1]

From 1985 to 1987, Bank of America lost $1.8 billion. It dropped
its stock dividend and even sold its headquarters building. It reduced
its staff and fought off a hostile takeover attempt.

The loss was cyclical, and by February 1989, the stock dividend
was reinstated. But there was another problem. A survey determined
that only about half the bank's employees were satisfied with the
recognition they received.

To remedy this situation, the bank awarded each employee 10
shares of stock and an extra day off. The gift was mailed simultaneously to all employees, and the package included a letter of praise
from the bank's CEO.

Employees were totally surprised and gratified with the gift, and
thousands sent the CEO expressions of appreciation. They even called
local newspapers to publicize the bank's generosity.

There may be no correlation, but 1989 was a great year for the
Bank of America. Its profits soared to $1.1 billion, until that date the
most in its 85-year history.

EMPLOYEE COMMUNICATIONS IN PRINT,
VIDEO, SATELLITE, AND ONLINE

The preparation of employee communications in every form is an important component of an organization's total PR program. The concept of employee communications and publications has been around

for more than 70 years and today has reached a high degree of specialization.

The primary role of employee communications is to boost morale. But in a larger sense, it does more. It tells employees:

- How well the company is doing in the marketplace.
- Where the company is headed and how it is going to get there.
- How employees fit in with these plans.
- What technological developments have occurred within the company and industry.

Typically, company publications emanate from the corporate employee communications department. Often, in a large organization a permanent staff of editors, writers, and designers is responsible for these publications and films. Many companies publish multiple employee publications targeted to specific audiences within the organization. At one point, AT&T even published a daily newsletter available on 75 electronic mail networks within the company. Recipients posted paper copies for coworkers who didn't have computers.

The Tools of Employee Communications

Here we look at some individual components of employee communications.

Annual Reports. These are produced primarily for stockholders and the investment community, but some organizations distribute them to some individual employees. At times, a corporation will publish an abbreviated employee annual report. We cover annual reports in the chapter on investor relations.

Bulletin Boards. The old-fashioned bulletin board with its safety information and social notices is still with us. It hasn't gone high-tech, but today it's more graphic.

Internal Video. Video is used internally to announce corporate policy, and even for assembly line workers for training purposes. Some videos even show the company's TV commercials and sponsored programming.

Management and Employee Publications. Large corporations publish employee publications for various reasons. One giant auto manufacturing organization conducted management research that uncovered a lack of trust between management and labor, poor communications throughout the division, decision making limited to a handful, minimal employee involvement, and unpredictable leadership. Top management was determined to improve the division's negative image among employees.

A number of programs were instituted, including face-to-face discussions between supervisors and employees and a complete overhaul of the division's employee publications. The program was a success. Management and labor interaction vastly improved employee relations, and a comprehensive network of employee publications geared to specific audiences was launched.

A single-page daily newsletter was distributed to 20,000 employees consisting of news about the division, the entire industry, and the parent company.

A six-page monthly tabloid was mailed to every employee's and retiree's home.

A bimonthly newsletter, *Report to Supervisors*, was distributed to 3,000 managers and supervisors. The corporation also published a quarterly newsletter, *Joint Activities*, written and funded by the division and its union.

What we see here is a progressive approach to the improvement of employee relations—the use of company publications to reach employees with specialized information.

Some Unique Employee Publications

In 1999, PRCENTRAL's Cipra awards honored a number of outstanding employee publications. We discuss a few of them here.

The e-IBMer. Here's a unique employee publication. Until July 1998, IBM was publishing a paper newsletter for its Chinese-speaking employees in mainland China. The company decided to convert it to a quarterly intranet webzine and engaged Ogilvy PR Worldwide to oversee the development and production of the project.

Ogilvy was involved in conceptualizing and designing the layout template of the webzine, as well as in the copywriting, translation, graphic design, and technical work required to put the project together.

The *e-IBMer*, as the webzine was named, became a Chinese-language publication available to IBM employees around the world through the company's intranet system. It was available in both simplified and traditional Chinese characters and had stories, photographs, and images in each edition.

Ogilvy supervises the production of the e-zine, including copy, design, and layout, while another vendor handles web design and programming. Plans call for the *e-IBMer* to become a Web site with regular updates and a wide variety of Chinese-language content.

IBM reports strong positive feedback for the e-zine, and employees appreciate having a Chinese-language resource. Not only is this e-zine more effective than a print magazine, it's also cheaper and faster to produce.

Newsletters. Various kinds of organizations issue employee newsletters. Some are printed in color and showcase new company developments. These newsletters often include folksy employee profiles with questions on "all-time favorite movie" and "most unique item on my desk." New appointments and company awards are another staple of these publications.

Online Communications. E-mail messages are very popular. Intranets are also used to exchange information. Some companies communicate with employees via an internal wire service carrying company news online every day. Many of these are also used to communicate serious issues such as profits, possible pay cuts, and firings.

Satellite TV. Large organizations use satellite TV as part of a multimedia system for communications with their employees and management groups.

Federal Express Corporation beams original informational programs via a satellite TV system to its 85,000 employees in more than 1,100 locations in north America, Great Britain, and other parts of Europe.

Ford Motor Company uses satellite TV as part of a multimedia system for communications with its 360,000 employees and management groups.

Using Video as an Employee Communications Tool. When the Boeing Company wanted to convey to its employees its new policy on drugs and alcohol, it created a 16-minute video narrated by a

Boeing employee who described herself as a "recovering alcoholic" in an emotional plea to her fellow workers.

Videos are also being used to turn out sales promotion motivational films. They are used in stockholder meetings and as a means to tell the company's financial story to security analysts.

How does the development of video and VNR as a PR tool fit into the plans of future PR people? It creates a demand for visually literate specialists—producers, writers, directors, and editors.

Wal-Mart uses founder Sam Walton's store visits as simultaneous video meetings with thousands of stores by hooking them up with very-small-aperture terminals (VSATs).

Southwest Airlines produced an internal rap video with its CEO, Herb Kelleher, as a veejay, and employees from maintenance crew to pilots extolling the virtues of the carrier.

EDELMAN PUBLIC RELATIONS WORLDWIDE WINS SILVER ANVIL AWARD FOR SELF-ASSESSMENT OF ITS INTERNAL COMMUNICATIONS

In 1999, Edelman Worldwide's Employee Satisfaction Survey determined that the firm was moving so fast it was not communicating its mission to its own employees.

Edelman set up an international task force to implement a comprehensive program it called VMV (Vision, Mission, and Values). The effort was so well executed that the firm submitted it to PRSA's Silver Anvil Awards competition 2000, where it won the prize in the Internal Communications category. We present the text of this award here as an outstanding example in this practice area:

Creating a Shared Focused Future
Edelman Public Relations Worldwide with Edelman Public
Relations Worldwide
Silver Anvil Awards '00 Category 12A Internal Communications
(6BW-0012A07)

Overview

The more than 1800 employees of Edelman Worldwide are working at a firm that has been going through a period of enormous growth and change. In the last four years, the company has increased its staff globally by 73%, expanded its network into such diverse geographical areas as South America and Asia, and extended the number of offices handling more global accounts by 25%. All this has been exciting, productive and positive. But the more the firm changed, and the bigger and more diverse it became, it emerged that Edelman needed to crystallize a center. It was imperative to identify a core set of principles and beliefs that the staff could share and that would help them every day in making decisions, in defining who they are, and in guiding where they are going.

Research

A 1998 Employee Satisfaction Survey taken by Thomas L. Harris/ Impulse Research and prepared for Edelman Worldwide found that the firm's employees: felt the company was moving in the right direction (76%); wanted the firm to develop a way to universally communicate the company's values and commitment to its employees as only 38% felt they were well-informed about the company's goals.

During the 1998 International Managers' Meeting, 80 senior executives:

1. Reviewed the firm's current Mission Statement and felt it represented the company as an international firm, not a global one. It also didn't communicate specific values nor use language that was culturally connected with all offices.
2. Endorsed a process to evolve the firm's VMV.
3. Stipulated ground rates for the process and suggested potential roadblocks.

Secondary research indicated there is a need for an organizational culture, whose strategies, processes, and people are managed by a common vision, purpose, and set of values.

Planning

Evolving the firm's Vision, Mission, and Values was developed in concert with the Ken Blanchard Companies, but executed by the employees of Edelman Worldwide working with the firm's Human Resources Department. The two-phase plan incorporated findings from the research, and the firm's business and personal employee objectives.

Objectives.

- Evolve Edelman Vision, Mission and Values to represent the company's business and its employees.
- Launch VMV into the Edelman global culture.

Strategies

- Involve all levels of employees in the firm's VMV process.
- Leverage each office's culture and people to launch VMV.
- Demonstrate corporate commitment to insuring VMV implementation.

Target audience: Employees.

Materials and resources used: Focus groups, online questionnaires and global online chats, newsletters, e-mail alerts, screensavers, plaques, adaptable presentations, and a video demonstrating senior management's commitment to the VMV process and the need for employees to give feedback.

Execution

Phase 1

A series of meetings brought employees together for input on the firm's VMV:

- The VMV recommendations from the 9/98 International Managers' Meeting were reviewed and adapted by the Executive Committee that includes Richard Edelman.
- An International Task Force of 13 employees met (1/99) in New York to refine the Executive Committee draft so it represented a multicultural voice. They then scheduled a series of focus groups (March–April) in each of the firm's 38 offices, or asked employees to give input on-line to the firm's Knowledge Channel Intranet site.
- Feedback from nearly 800 employees was coded, assessed, and delivered (May–June) with recommendations to the Task Force, who through a series of online global chats redefined the 1/99 draft to reflect employee input.
- The Task Force presented the VMV statements at the International Managers Meeting (7/99) and recommended launch activities to communicate the VMV. The statements were applauded by all in attendance. In one year, the process had come full circle.

Phase II

To respect each office's culture, every office was given the opportunity to launch VMV in its own way. Collateral materials were sent with the window of launch (9/99–11/99).

- Local VMV "directors" (employees) worked with regional task force members. Launch included an adaptable presentation, discussion topics, role plays, and collateral materials.

- Corporate Edelman demonstrated its commitment to VMV by incorporating the Values as criteria in the performance Management Process and the Employee Incentive Plan.

Evaluation

Objective 1: Evolve Vision, Mission, and Values to represent the company's business and its employees.

- More than 69% of those who participated viewed the initiative as positive, and more than 62% valued the feedback opportunity.
- There is strong employee consensus that the VMV process had been true to the original goals, and the final statements reflect staff input. As the Frankfurt office wrote: "the down to earth tonality of the statements proves that these values were developed by those who should live them and not by executives in some top-floor office".
- Employees feel the VMV encourages staff to be accountable to each other, their clients and the industry. The Singapore office said: "they are, a comprehensive overview of what we need to make Edelman a strong company".

Objective 2: Launch VMV into the Edelman global culture.

- An estimated 95% of employees attended the VMV introductions in the firm's 38 offices. Reports indicate global acceptance and support for the VMV in actions, and in the daily use of the paperweights, screensavers, and plaques as reminders to live the Edelman values.
- Each office created special implementation programs to take VMV beyond the launch: VMV Employee Awards, designated "Living the Values" months, VMV training seminars and workshops, Values "buddy office" systems, community volunteer programs, and so on.
- The VMV Champions continue to be an active network with Edelman HR to develop new internal VMV programs, and are now beginning to take VMV to clients and the industry.
- Employees are using the Employee Appraisals that incorporate the Values system, and management is using VMV as criteria in the Employee Incentive Program.
- Although Edelman did not publicize the VMV process externally, *InsidePR* in its "1999 Agency Report Card" wrote: "There's an increased emphasis [at Edelman] on values—quality, integrity, respect, entrepreneurial spirit, mutual benefits."

Face-to-Face Communication at Navistar

A letter from John R. Horne, CEO of Navistar International, a large manufacturing organization, to the Cipra 2000 judges won an award in the practice area of employee communications.

Navistar manufactures trucks, school buses, and engines. It employs 19,000 people at 14 major locations.

Horne forgoes the traditional newsletters and videos in favor of face-to-face meetings with all his employees throughout the year. At some plants he spends 12 straight hours in the plant so he can meet with employees from all three shifts, but eschews handshakes in favor of meetings with small groups at break areas next to the assembly lines or in nearby conference rooms. He has informal lunches with front-line supervisors, local diversity councils, wellness committees, and plant staffs.

Members of Horne's communications team work with the sites in advance to draw up a flow for the visits. Then, during the visits, they take notes and keep track of items to be followed up.

Other company executives visit work sites during the year, then have periodic meetings with Horne at headquarters once a month to review the program's progress.

The visits also give Horne and his staff opportunities to meet with union presidents, bargaining chairmen, and stewards. He credits one such meeting at a plant in Canada as the reason the company got a very competitive union contract.

Horne's communications team is made up of his own corporate communications staff, consultants from PR firms, and subject experts from different areas. Horne says that the face-to-face program has given him an opportunity to meet employees. In one situation, he met a front supervisor who routinely found a way to cover the work of a woman who had to leave periodically to care for her brain-damaged child.

Employee communications and employee relations make up a sophisticated public relations component. At many large corporations, employee relations is a province of the public relations and public affairs department. Also, large public relations counsel firms have specializations in this area.

CHAPTER 10

Speechwriting, Speechmaking, and Executive Presentations

W rite dynamite speeches. Get to hang out with the CEO. Make $100,000 a year, and move up the corporate ladder. That's the fantasy of many young PR people. The reality is that few climb to the upper rungs of this specialization, and many corporate speechwriters are called on to write speeches for less-than-dynamic speakers about unglamorous subjects.

Yet speechwriting remains an attractive pursuit even when it means writing for a corporate head facing a group of skeptical stock analysts or a big-city mayor addressing a belligerent city council.

How wide is the market for speechwriters? It is estimated that about one-third of Fortune 500 companies have a "chief executive speechwriter" whose main responsibility is writing speeches for CEOs. And yes, these are power jobs. At least half of the top speechwriters earn at least $100,000 per year with an average of about $85,000.

Salary is not the only factor in these jobs. The clout and prestige come from being close to the top strata of management. In a sense, speechwriters also act as advisers to their bosses.

But before you rush off to take speechwriting 101, let us remind you that not all speechwriters write for CEOs. Some are considered midlevel employees and write speeches for lesser folk for less money.

How long does it take to write a speech? Chief executive speech-writers spend an average of 50 hours on a major address, of which 20 hours are spent on research and 15 on the first draft, and they prepare an average of 30 speeches per year. What do speechwriters do with the rest of their time? Often, they ghostwrite bylined articles for executives for the trade and consumer press and the investment community. And they do lots of reading and spend time reading other's speeches.

FOUR SKILLS OF SPEECHWRITING

1. Speechwriting is a creative craft. Some CEOs and executives choose to speak from an outline rather than from a prepared script. Doing so frees the executive from having to read every word and instead allows the speaker to concentrate on motivating the audience. The speechwriter's preparation is no less intense.

2. The speechwriter must be able to write the way one speaks, not the way one writes to be read. And, although the speechwriter cannot instill dynamism in a speaker with a dull voice and presentation, he or she can sprinkle a speech with enough humor and spice to make it listenable.

3. It is important to stress "openings" in attracting the audience's interest and attention. Use humor, but don't blow it with a bad joke, and realize that your speaker is not a skilled stand-up comic. Surely, many of us have seen stand-ups fall on their faces in comedy clubs.

   A basic rule for using humor in a speech comes from Helen K. Copley of the Copley Press: "Make sure the joke is inoffensive, self-directed, short and clear, requires no explanation, and has a snappy punch line comprising single-syllable words."

4. Wittiness and conciseness are key attributes of good speeches. Here's an excerpt from "The Executive Speaker":

   > Presenters (speechmakers) would do well to remember when adapting their goals to their group what the Reverend William Sloane Coffin said about the length of an effective sermon: "No souls are saved after twenty minutes."

The Executive Speaker (www.executive-speaker.com) is a clearing-house for speechwriters and speakers, offering information about books, seminars and workshops, video and audio cassettes, and an archive of more than 6,000 speeches.

It also conducts a full spectrum of business communications seminars. Readers can download a free copy of Tom Kirby's "117 Ideas for Better Business Presentation" from its Web site.

Here are a few highlights on the subject of speechmaking:

- Control nervousness by knowing your subject cold. Be overprepared, and know exactly what your opening line is going to be.
- Keep your audience's attention by speaking so the person in the last row can hear you, using "first person" stories when possible, and be sure to pause occasionally.
- Concentrate on your opening remarks. The well-known comic George Jessel said this about speeches: "If you haven't struck oil in three minutes, stop boring!"
- In handling Q&A and trying to get people to ask questions, break the ice by asking easy "conversational" questions yourself.
- Don't deliver a speech verbatim. It's a painfully boring process.

Kirby includes in his "117 Ideas" a few dozen absolute no-exception don'ts, specifics on financial and technical talks, and on-camera techniques.

Another source for group and individual programs on writing and delivering speeches is "The Professional Voice." Log onto its Web site: www.professionalvoice.com.

In his book *The Practice of Public Relations* (7th edition), Fraser P. Seitel divides the speechwriting process into four essential phases: preparing, interviewing (the speaker), researching, and organizing and writing. He also stresses the need for the speechwriter to know the topic clearly and have it well defined before the research is begun.

One veteran speechwriter, Ed Stanulis, adds some additional tips to speechwriters:[1]

> I imagine myself as my chairman speaking to stock analysts at the Harvard Club in New York as he's about to promote his company's stock to these analysts in a speech. I become a character actor for him and try to imitate him when I write.

To get to know the executives he writes for, Stanulis reads the magazines they read, watches the TV programs they watch, learns about their outside interests, and knows their historical background.

He never knows when some tidbit from these activities or background can be used in a speech.

Stanulis writes the middle of the speech first, then writes the introduction and conclusion last. His output at the time of the article was about 40 or 50 speeches a year.

RESEARCHING THE SPEAKING EVENT

The speechwriter must research the event thoroughly. One speechwriting professional has a checklist of 25 pieces of information he needs to know before he writes a speech. These include:

- Will the speaker stay behind the lectern or will he or she wander among the audience members?
- What is the male-to-female and minority composition of the audience?
- What is the audience's attitude toward the corporation or group?
- What is the physical setup of the room in which the speech will take place?

Timothy J. Koranda, a veteran speechwriter, sums it up: "Speechwriting is a personal service like psychiatry. And like a psychiatrist, the speechwriter needs to know what's on the chairman's mind. Ideally, the speechwriter should report directly to the chairperson and be his or her alter ego."[2]

CAREER TIP: HOW TO BECOME A SPEECHWRITER

1. Listen to the great speaker/motivators: Jesse Jackson, Robert Schuller, and Deepak Chopra.
2. Access speeches on the Internet. Evaluate their subject matter.
3. Attend speechwriting forums. They're held in dozens of cities, including Boston, Detroit, Minneapolis, Houston, Chicago, and Washington, D.C. The local club of PR professionals will know the dates of these forums.
4. Volunteer to write a speech for a local political group or charitable organization.
5. Network with the chief speechwriter in your organization. Go through the steps he or she takes when writing a speech.

6. Invent a topic and write a speech about it—say, a speech your CEO will make to a group of Japanese businessmen interested in investing in your industry.

7. Read all you can about speechwriting and speechmaking. Two good books are Peggy Noonan's *What I Saw at the Revolution* and Richard Goodwin's *Remembering America*. Noonan wrote speeches for President Ronald Reagan and the senior George Bush. Goodwin wrote speeches for four presidents.

While researching this chapter I came upon one of the best speeches I've ever read. And what was it about? Making and writing speeches. It was written by Charles Francis and delivered to the New York chapter of the International Association of Business Communicators (IABC). The speech deals with the bête noir of all speech professionals—the "b" word, boredom. His message is for those who make and write speeches, and even for those who have to listen to them.

Francis worked as a journalist with United Press International (UPI), and then spent several years working in public relations for the University of California at Los Angeles and Santa Barbara. Later, he held senior corporate communications posts with IBM.

Today, Charles Francis runs IdeaBank, an Internet research service designed specifically for professional communications people. A free trial to this service is available by logging onto his Web site at www.idea-bank.com.

Here is a transcript of Charles Francis's IABC speech.

How to Stop Boring Your Audience to Death

By Charles Francis
Charles Francis is president of IdeaBank, Inc. His remarks were delivered to the New York Chapter of the International Association of Business Communicators in New York City on January 16, 1996.

As professionals who earn your living communicating with people, and helping others to do the same, I know you all grapple daily with that implacable force—audience boredom.

It's a challenge, no matter what medium you are using—print, video, or human speech. It isn't that people aren't interested. It's just that, from the time we open our eyes in the morning to when we go to bed at night, all of us are assailed by messages of every kind and description. They emanate from the radio, newspaper, television, magazines, the daily mail, billboards—even the screens of our personal computers. I read recently that no less than 70% of what one hears is forgotten an hour after hearing it. There is a catchy acronym for this lack of memorability. It's called MYGLO for "My Eyes Glaze Over," a physical phenomenon that takes over the minute you lose the audience's attention.

The famous advertising man David Ogilvy perhaps said it best, "No one ever sold anybody anything by boring them to death."

There are three magic talismans that can greatly increase your ability to hold people's attention. They are known to every professional writer and speaker but even professionals don't call on their occult powers as often as they could. These three powerful Genies are, simply: quotations, anecdotes, and humor. Let's examine each of them in turn.

For reasons I have never been able to understand, some speakers shy away from using quotations, thinking perhaps that their use will make their remarks sound stilted. [Former] President George Bush was on record as telling his speechwriter that "I don't want any more quotations from that guy Thucydides." True, the name of that ancient Greek historian is a mouthful for anyone, but if the thought is important enough to express, why not just say "A famous historian once said," etcetera?

No one made better use of quotations than that unrivaled communicator Winston Churchill. By his own admission, quotation collections were a filling station to fuel his eloquence. "Quotations," he said, "when engraved upon the memory give you good thoughts."

As someone who has on his library shelves more than 1,000 quotation books of all descriptions, I can assure you that Churchill was right. Browsing through them can be stimulating and thought-provoking even if you end up not using a single quotation. That is because there is not a thought in our heads that has not been worn shiny by someone else's brains. Mark Twain used to maintain that Adam was the only man who could say something with the assurance that he was the first man on earth to say it.

Presidents Jack Kennedy and Ronald Reagan—two of the most gifted speakers of the 20th century—both were fond of quotations and used them with great effectiveness. As a young man running for Congress in his native Boston, Kennedy carried around a loose-leaf notebook containing his favorite quotations. Reagan, who before entering politics was a professional speaker for the General Electric Company, learned to use quotations, anecdotes, and humor with a skill that later on in his presidency earned him the title, "The Great Communicator."

Both Churchill and President Franklin D. Roosevelt occasionally used poetry to strengthen their communications. During the early days of World War II, when Britain stood alone against Hitler, and before America entered the war, Churchill sent Roosevelt an urgent appeal for supplies and arms to aid Britain in its desperate plight. As he struggled with the political difficulties of doing this, Roosevelt sent Churchill a personal message in his own handwriting containing the following verse from a poem by Longfellow, adding that this "applies to your people as it does to us."

> Sail on O Ship of State!
> Sail on, O Union, strong and great!
> Humanity with all its fears,
> With all the hopes of future years,
> Is hanging breathless on thy fate!

On receiving the American President's message, Churchill renewed his plea for aid in a radio broadcast from a subterranean command center. He read aloud the Longfellow verse Roosevelt had sent him, concluding with these words: "Give us the tools and we will finish the job." He got the aid he requested and it sustained his embattled nation until help arrived.

Since I am owner of an online research service used by many professional speechwriters, I am sometimes asked how many quotations one can put in a speech. Certainly, too much of anything is never a good idea. However, I once had occasion to analyze an eloquent speech by the noted educator and public servant John Gardner. He was addressing a prestigious group of management consultants on the importance of personal and corporate renewal.

Gardner, who possesses one of the most original minds I know, used or alluded to 17 different quotations during a 20-minute talk. Yet the entire presentation was totally seamless. Blended into his text were quotations by such diverse personalities as S. N. Behrman, Yogi Berra, Norman Douglas, Joe Louis, Logan Pearsall Smith, Robert Louis Stevenson, and Pope John XXIII. It was a cornucopia of interesting and provocative thought on an important subject. When he was finished, Gardner received a standing ovation.

A kissing cousin of good quotations are proverbs. They are the distilled wisdom of all nations. Many are humorous and all are memorable. The Afghanistan proverb, "If you deal in camels, make the doors high," says as much about how to achieve customer satisfaction as any article in the *Harvard Business Review*.

Each of you probably would define what an anecdote is in a different way. My own definition is simply that an anecdote is a story that has a point or moral. Anecdotes are probably among the most powerful communications tools ever discovered by man. Jesus used them for his teaching and we know them as parables. Abraham Lincoln used them and filled them with a wry humor that came from his boyhood on the American frontier.

Once, when Lincoln was telling one of his stories at a Cabinet meeting during the darkest days of the Civil War, he was criticized by a Cabinet member for telling humorous stories in such terrible times. Lincoln replied, "If I didn't tell stories at times like these, I think I should die." Then he asked the cabinet to read the draft of a document he had been preparing for months. It was the Emancipation Proclamation.

Lincoln used anecdotal stories with telling effectiveness all his life. As a young lawyer in Illinois, he was pleading a case before a jury when he became convinced that he was losing, even though right was on his side. So he told the jury this story.

"A farmer back home was sitting on his front porch," Lincoln said, "when suddenly his six-year old son came running from the barn saying, 'Father, father, the hired man is in the hayloft with Big Sister. The hired man is pulling down his pants and Big Sister is lifting up her skirts, and I fear they are going to pee on the hay.' 'Now, now, Son,' said the farmer calmly, 'you have all the facts right but you have reached the wrong conclusion.'"

The jury roared with laughter and Lincoln won his case handily.

While we are on the subject of anecdotes, let me say that no anecdote is more effective than one which comes directly from your own experience, something you saw with your own eyes, something you heard with your own ears. Audiences remember these long after the rest of your talk is forgotten. But if the anecdote you tell makes the point you are trying to make, that is what you are after anyway.

Pete Peterson, the Wall Street financier, is in demand as a speaker all over the world. He has said he frequently meets up with someone who has heard him speak months or years before and they will compliment him on the fine speech he gave. "But," he says, "they never play back to me the serious remarks I made, they always remember some bit of humor I used to dramatize a serious point." For this reason, he has developed what he calls the Peterson Principle. "If you want anything to stick to the bone, use some humor that is relevant to your message."

When one talks about using humor in speeches, many people think you mean putting a joke at the beginning to warm up the audience. It doesn't matter to them whether it has a relevant point or not, just to do it is funny. Nothing could be worse or more counterproductive to gaining favor with the audience. Real humor reaches out to members of the audience and includes them in the fun. Real humor shows them you are someone they would like to know better. Real humor is always in good taste and should always be appropriate to the message you wish to get across.

John Cleese, a British comedian who has made a fortune in the field of business humor [videotapes, etc.], says that "If I can get you to laugh with me, you like me better, which makes you more open to my ideas. And if I can persuade you to laugh at the particular point I make, by laughing at it, you acknowledge its truth."

Unless you are a gifted raconteur, telling a joke is one of the world's most dangerous activities. *New York Times* columnist Russell Baker likens it to walking among a nest of rattlesnakes. If the audience doesn't laugh, you are standing there with egg on your face. It is much safer to use a few humorous quotations at appropriate places in your speech. If the audience doesn't laugh, you haven't lost anything. If you get a few chuckles, that's a bonus, and if you get some loud laughter, that's wonderful!

Sam Ervin, Jr., was a U.S. Senator from North Carolina who earned fame for leading the investigation of the Watergate scandal. A gentleman of the old school, with a Southern accent that dripped with charm, Ervin wrote the following definition of humor when he was 85. I have never seen better.

"Humor," he said, "is one of God's most marvelous gifts. Humor gives us smiles, laughter, and gaiety. Humor reveals the roses and hides the thorns. Humor makes our heavy burdens light and smooths the rough spots in our pathways. Humor endows us with the capacity to clarify the obscure, to simplify the complex, to deflate the pompous, to chastise the arrogant, to point a moral, and to adorn a tale."

If I have convinced you that quotations, anecdotes, and humor can be powerful preventatives to a sudden outbreak of MYGLO in your audience, where do you find the really good material? The answer, of course, is *everywhere*.

Read your daily newspaper with an eye for items that catch your fancy and that can be used to spice up a talk or article you are planning. Television is filled with good material. Everything can be grist for your mill—even a funny remark made by one of your children at the dinner table. A little girl's comment that "Socrates was a wise man who went around giving people advice, but they poisoned him," could make a wonderful self-effacing opening for a talk at your local service club on how to solve some local problems.

Then, of course, there are computer-driven sources such as CD-ROM collections of material, online sources such as America Online, Compuserve, Prodigy, and even the Internet. These give you access to all kinds of information and it just takes some practice to use them efficiently.

Once your head is bulging with useful material, there remains admittedly the painful process of boiling it down into an interesting and memorable presentation. For most of us, the task unfortunately is very much like novelist Gene Fowler's description of writing. "Writing," he said, "is easy. All you do is stare at a blank sheet of paper until drops of blood form on your forehead." But do persevere. And never forget the cardinal rule in any communications. You must convince the audience that what you are saying will make a difference in their lives. "You" is the most important word in the English language.

After writing your speech comes practice giving it and everyone agrees this is of utmost importance, time-consuming as it may be. Famous athletic coaches all agree that preparation is the key to winning championships and the same is true of giving a successful speech. You will find the confidence practice gives you is a wonderful panacea for the nervousness you may experience when you mount to the podium.

Backed up by your research, the magnetic power of your three magical servants—quotations, anecdotes, and humor—and several successful run-throughs, you are a candidate for, if not a standing ovation, a really satisfying audience response to your message. You won't end up feeling frustrated like the famous Mexican revolutionary Pancho Villa, who is reported to have said on his deathbed, "Don't let it end like this. Tell them I said something."

CHAPTER 11

Public Affairs, Lobbying, and Issues Management

When George W. Bush won the election in December 2000, did all those defeated members of Congress and White House officials make the mean trek in the snow to the unemployment insurance offices, or did they instead have their drivers chauffeur them to their new lucrative jobs on K Street in downtown Washington? K Street, for the uninitiated, is the home of hundreds of lobbying and public affairs organizations eager to employ these legislators and officials for their influence and relationship with former colleagues and inside knowledge of the legislative process.

To deal with the Washington power structure, PR firms and corporations pay as much as seven-figure salaries to defeated brand-name senators and $200,000 to $400,000 to lower profile names. And it doesn't matter which party they're from; the business community wants the best lobbyists on issues such as tax cuts, social security, mergers, and Medicare.

Some public affairs pros maintain that political campaigning and lobbying is an ancient art. They claim that the first recorded political consultant was Quintus Cicero, author of a handbook on electioneering. He wrote it to help his brother win the consulship of Rome in 63 B.C.

In developing the important component of public affairs, let's first begin with some basic definitions from Richard Weiner's book *Webster's New World Dictionary of Media and Communications*:

> *Public affairs*—the aspect of public relations that involves working with governments and groups with regard to societal (public) policies, action, and legislation; the relationship between an organization and a government, community or society in general; public affairs sometimes is used as a synonym for public relations, but more often the term refers to activities that are thought to be in the public interest. In a corporation, a public affairs officer or public affairs director is involved with external publics and not with employees or shareholders.
>
> *Lobbying*—originally [the lobby was] the area adjacent to the assembly hall of a legislature; it was open to nonlegislators, including individuals who congregated there to meet and influence the lawmakers. Lobbyists, in their modern context, act on behalf of special-interest groups (sometimes called *lobbies*); that is, formal or informal organizations seeking to influence public policy by urging the legislator to vote for or against bills or other matters. The same process of *lobbying* may also be used in an effort to influence government agencies and other bodies.
>
> *Issues management*—the process of identifying problems and subjects relevant to an organization and then developing and executing a program to resolve the problems. This systematic identification and action generally involves public policy matters.

LOBBYING TODAY

To understand the interlocking network of lobbying, government, and business today, it becomes necessary to go back more than 50 years. Lobbyists then would buttonhole legislators on behalf of local issues, and later maybe buy them a drink and dinner.

In Washington, D.C., up until the 1980s, a small number of lobbyists cultivated the committee heads of the Senate and the House of Representatives on legislation relevant to the interests of their client corporations or association groups. But with the dramatic growth of multinational corporations, and the developments in information and technology in the 1990s, lobbying took a global turn. Multinational corporations now needed representation not only in

Washington, D.C., but also in Brussels, Beijing, and other world capitals.

These developments hastened the need for talented people in tune with the needs and demands of today's business environment. Here's one example of today's top-level lobbying in action.[1]

In 1992, the Cassidy Companies, run by veteran Washington lobbyist Gerald S. J. Cassidy, represented the Electric Boat Division of General Dynamics, manufacturer of the Seawolf class of nuclear attack submarines. Before he left office, former President George Bush canceled the project. It was Cassidy's job to keep it alive with the incoming Clinton administration.

First, Cassidy brought all the Seawolf suppliers to Washington for a meeting. Then the firm sought support from unions and oversaw letter-writing campaigns, paid retired admirals to speak in local districts, and arranged meetings with as many editorial boards of newspapers as were willing to listen.

Cassidy's big break came when President Clinton came out in favor of the Seawolf. Eight years later, the project was still alive, in spite of periodic raids by Congressional budget cutters who maintained that the attack submarine was superfluous.

In 1999, Cassidy's company received a total of more than $20 million from their lobbying efforts. But they needed to expand to effectively run a global operation. Their umbrella at that time covered lobbying operations (two companies), a public relations firm, a research company that offered opinion and polling services, and a group that specialized in law-related public relations.

But the story hardly ends there. In November 1999, Shandwick USA, one of the 10 largest PR firms we covered in chapter 4, purchased Cassidy and its associate firms for about $75 million.

And no one doubts that in the George W. Bush administration the influence of lobbying and public affairs in government will continue to rise as it has in the previous decade.

Andrew Card, President George W. Bush's White House Chief of Staff, came from the ranks of Washington lobbyists. According to the Web site www.tompaine.com, Card helped the Big Three automakers, Ford, General Motors, and Daimler Chrysler, spend nearly $25 million on their lobbying efforts in the 5-year period preceding President Bush's inauguration.

By the year 2001, there were about 40,000 lobbyists in the United States, and the cost of lobbying efforts reached $100 million a year. And with the increasing sophistication of lobbying and public affairs, a number of huge firms are being formed offering many services including public relations, lobbying, research, polling, direct-mail canvassing, and specialists who work on drumming up "grass-roots" support for issues.

Who are the clients of lobbyists or groups who employ lobbyists? We have already mentioned multinational corporations, but we add to the list foundations, industry and trade associations, labor unions, philanthropic organizations, and advocacy groups.

One such group is the National Rifle Association, headquartered in Washington, D.C., with the single-issue orientation of opposing legislation that would restrict the use of guns. To achieve this objective, the NRA engages in a sophisticated campaign directed at legislators and their staffs, as well as at the general public.

Politically, lobbyists work across the spectrum from liberal groups such as Americans for Democratic Action, the American Civil Liberties Union, and Planned Parenthood, to the Conservative Caucus and the National Right to Life Committee.

A LOOK AT LOBBYING IN A PRESIDENTIAL ELECTION YEAR

Readers of my book *The Newspaper: Everything You Need to Know to Make It in the Newspaper Business* know that you don't have to read more than your newspaper's headlines and subheads on the front page to gain a sense of what you may or may not want to read about.

In the 2000 election year, I scanned the headlines of the *Los Angeles Times* for stories that offered an insight into the oft-maligned profession of lobbying. Here are a few selections:

> Convention 2000/The Democratic Convention, August 17, 2000: "Receptions Here are Warm—and Fuzzy." Exclusive parties give lobbyists and executives prized access to public officials without the scrutiny or disclosure that lobbying usually requires.
>
> Convention 2000/The Democratic Convention, August 13, 2000: "Cash Making Its Presence Known at the Conventions." The events bring together private interests that need friendly treatment from government with officials who need money for an attention-getting political gala.
>
> "Internet Firms Gain Foothold in Washington," March 12, 2000. Policy: Debates over privacy and taxation force many

high-tech firms to set up lobbying branches. Move to influence legislation is a sea change from prior attitudes toward dealing with government.

Campaign 2000, February 20, 2000: "5 Lobbyists, as Friends, Help Gore's Rise." Campaign: Very nature of inner circle raises questions. All insist they do everything to avoid appearance of conflict.

For our own comment, we plead the Fifth.

LOBBYING OFF THE BELTWAY

Clearly, Washington is the home base of hundreds of lobbyists, but lobbying and advocacy are no less important elsewhere. The issues and the conflicts may be in Europe, Asia, or even Africa. The solution still requires educating and activating the constituencies.

Let's look at some examples of lobbying that illustrate its use in various situations and places:

- In a Western state, a firm that placed TV in classrooms paid lobbyists $640,000 to fight legislation that would ban television commercials in school programs.
- A heated battle over Canadian forests became a PR war about the environment. A Greenpeace pioneer lobbied for British Columbia's timber industry with a message targeted at the United States.
- Waste firms courted politicians with lobbyists at City Hall in Los Angeles in their attempt to get lucrative contracts for landfills and waste bins. They spent almost $1 million in 3 years for high-powered lobbying campaigns.

GRASS-ROOTS ACTIVITIES MEAN PUSHING DIFFERENT BUTTONS

Lobbying and advocacy for public affairs professionals most often mean selling their positions on issues to elected officials and bureaucrats. Yet today these practitioners are vastly stepping up grass-roots activities to reach their objectives, particularly at the state and local level.

What form does grass-roots activity take? A basic approach is meeting with citizen boards and community activists, as well as newspaper editors, labor and education leaders, local business people, and, of course, the general public.

Grass-roots activities often call upon mobilizing the public to write, phone, fax, and e-mail state and federal legislators about issues. Newsletters are another tool, as are op-ed columns in local newspapers.

Common Cause and Public Citizen are watchdogs in grass-roots efforts to expose sham groups posing as consumer organizations.

POLITICAL ACTION COMMITTEES

Political action committees (PACs), a political development of the last 30 years, are a sensitive issue. PACs are defined as a group of people in business, labor, the professions, or other areas organized by special interests to raise funds to be contributed to candidates, political parties, and others involved in government and public affairs. They are controversial because of their role in funding and influencing elections. By the end of 1999, PACs were contributing more than $200 million a year to Congressional candidates alone.

Lobbying and PACs are components of the broad subject of public affairs.

THE PUBLIC AFFAIRS COUNCIL AND THE FOUNDATION FOR PUBLIC AFFAIRS

The Public Affairs Council is a Washington-based membership group of more than 600 companies and noncorporate organizations that seeks to advance the practice of public affairs.

The Foundation for Public Affairs is the research and information clearinghouse affiliate of the Public Affairs Council.

Home Depot, AT&T, Hallmark Cards, the National Association of Broadcasters, Pfizer, Inc., the Bank of America, the Association of American Medical Colleges, and all the major PR counsel firms, corporations, organizations, and associations are members of the Public Affairs Council.

Headquartered in Washington, D.C., this dynamic group offers advice, counsel, and research on topics of vital interest to any corporate or association public affairs practice.

When we define public affairs today, these are some of the issues we address:

Politics: campaign finance, PACs, political education, voter registration/get-out-the-vote efforts, good citizenship programs.

Public affairs management: performance measurement and evaluation, benchmarking, strategic planning, organization and staffing, technology utilization, staff training and development, Professional ethics, communication tools, maximizing external resources, public affairs competencies.

Government relations: local, state, federal, international.

Advocacy: coalition building, grass-roots programs.

Corporate community involvement: community relations, corporate contributions, volunteerism.

Corporate issues: emerging issues, issues management.

From this list we can readily understand the complexity and diversity of the broad area of public affairs. Issues management, for example, takes place in a number of arenas: federal and state issues, social trends, economic analyses, and international events. And a large corporation is involved with its community, which may be international and may involve issues of contributions and volunteerism.

The Dynamics of the New, New Public Affairs

Douglas G. Pinkham, president of the Public Affairs Council, used the title "The Dynamics of the New, New Public Affairs" for an article in the 2000 Annual Report of the council. In it, he reviews the mercurial growth of Internet access in the United States—70% by the end of 2000—more than the combined circulation of *The New York Times*, *Washington Post*, and *Los Angeles Times*, *The Wall Street Journal*, *USA Today*, *Time*, and *Newsweek*. And the number of Web sites went from only 26,000 in 1993 to more than 5 million in 1999.

What are some of the ways this technological development has manifested itself in the field of public affairs?

- Activists have launched watchdog Web sites to challenge a corporation's policies.
- In the 2000 presidential election all major party presidential candidates maintained Web sites. The White House has been online since 1993.

FIGURE 11.1 The Foundation for Public Affairs report, "Creating a Digital Democracy," covers the widespread impact of the Internet on public affairs. (Courtesy the Foundation for Public Affairs)

- In 1998, Jesse Ventura used e-mail and the Internet to mount his successful third-party run for governor of Minnesota.
- Leading companies are posting key issues on their intranets and then asking staff to provide information updates and share ideas on how different business units can address the same issue.

One would think that Congressional staffers would find time for reading all the media. An Opinion Leader Study conducted by the Holm Group in October 1998 offers some interesting statistics on the use of information by the staffers.[2] Eighty percent read the *Washington Post* and access the Internet almost daily, while only about 30% read *The Wall Street Journal* and *The New York Times*. About 50% watch the network news daily, but only 30% watch public television news, even though the "Jim Lehrer Show" is a breath of fresh air in the miasma of most network television news.

What are the major uses of the Internet for public affairs work?

- Monitor/research legislative/regulatory issues at the federal level.
- Monitor/research legislative/regulatory issues at the state level.
- Monitor media reports.
- Monitor/research public interest groups.
- Monitor news groups.

These are listed in the 1999–2000 *State of Corporate Public Affairs Survey.*

In addition to the responsibilities shown here, a number of large PR firms offer expertise in other areas of public affairs. An example is *ally development*. Firms like Ogilvy PR form alliances by uniting independent entities that share in the outcome of an issue.

Another service of PR firms in the public affairs area is *litigation support*. This role is accomplished by managing the communications environment surrounding litigation, which then creates opportunities to shape balanced and fair perceptions and attitudes.

CASE STUDIES IN PUBLIC AFFAIRS

The Largest Merger in the History of Telecommunications

In May 1998, the giant SBC Communications planned a merger with another titan, Ameritech. SBC's purchase price was a whopping $56 billion. It would be the largest such transaction in the history of

ANNO 2001

Public Affairs Review

JOURNAL OF THE PUBLIC AFFAIRS COUNCIL

FOCUSED CHANGE

What's Wrong With the Political System, and How Can It Be Fixed?
Alan Rosenthal
Page 2

Meet the Chief Privacy Officer. You'll Be Working Together Soon
Tom Price
Page 8

How'd *We* Get to Be the Bad Guys?
Managing the Public Affairs Function Under Fire
Douglas G. Pinkham
Page 14

Teaching Management How Government Impacts Business Strategy
Michael Watkins
Page 18

With the Annual Reports of the Public Affairs Council and the Foundation for Public Affairs

FIGURE 11.2 The 2001 edition of the Public Affairs Council's journal, *Public Affairs Review*, covers the salient issues, "Managing the Public Affairs Function Under Fire," and "What's Wrong With the Political System, and How Can It Be Fixed." (Courtesy of Public Affairs Council)

telecommunications. But mergers like this one set up powerful challenges from competitors, from employees fearing lost jobs, and from the media, using expressions like "phonopoly."

SBC faced its most daunting task in gaining state and federal regulatory approval, particularly from the Federal Communications Commission. Consider the size alone of this merged colossus: $46 billion in annual revenues, more than 203,000 employees, and investments in 22 countries.

To overcome objections to the merger, SBC and its PR counsel firm, Fleishman-Hillard, structured its case on the premise that the merger would increase competition, offer greater consumer choice, and offer the ability to serve global customers worldwide.

The SBC team conducted a telephone survey of 1,200 residential and business customers in three Midwestern states. The results determined that customers were most interested in improved telecom technology and job growth.

SBC buttressed the research with the successful results of its 1997 merger with Pacific Telesis, which created 4,500 new jobs in California, improved customer service, and resulted in the launch of a $50 million program to support technologically underserved schools and communities.

SBC's first objective was regulatory approval. Then its strategy was to shift the debate from contentions of monopoly and lost jobs to the positive findings of its research efforts.

The company also documented its excellent relationships with labor unions and announced plans to offer service in 30 major markets as part of its national expansion strategy.

Once the merger was announced, SBC began publicity efforts in many of the new markets it planned to compete in after approval of the merger. The publicity campaign would be national as well as local. First, SBC provided full documentation of the results of the previous SBC–Pacific Telesis merger. Then a "truth squad" was formed, which gave the media and employees ammunition to counter misinformation from those opposed to the merger.

Many media relations tools were used to spread the word, including talking points, letters, intranet updates, and fact sheets.

Media briefings were held outside the doors of hearing rooms. Editorial board sessions featuring key representatives from both companies were conducted with major regional and national publications.

Commitments were made in the Ameritech region to keep employment levels and school and community support at or above premerger levels. Progress on some promises was made even before the merger approval.

The merger was approved by all regulatory bodies and received the support of the Communications Workers of America, the largest telecommunications union. More than 200 elected officials, business, and consumer groups endorsed the merger, as did almost all the daily newspapers in the new Ameritech region.

SBC continued to issue key messages affirming that the merger would maintain prices and improve customer service.

On the day after the merger was completed, SBC announced it would proceed with local competition outside its traditional territory. It unveiled the name of its new brand, SBC Telecom, and announced it would serve new markets in Boston, Miami, and Seattle in October 2000.

For their efforts in this campaign, SBC and Fleishman-Hillard received the coveted 2000 Silver Anvil Award in the category of public affairs: business/services, given by the Public Relations Society of America.

How the Drug Industry Lobbies Washington

An article in *The New York Times* for November 4, 2001, is headed "A Muscular Lobby Rolls Up Its Sleeves." Its essence: the drug makers gain enormous access in Washington by spending more money than any other industry to push its legislative agenda. According to the advocacy group Public Citizen, the total for the year 2000 was about $92 million, spent on such issues as Medicare, prescription benefits, drug pricing, foreign drug imports, patients' bill of rights, and patents.

Consider the issue of patent extension. Drug companies receive patent protection for their drugs for a fixed number of years. Economically, this policy is necessary in order to compensate for the huge research costs needed to bring a prescription drug to FDA approval and to market. Once the drug reaches this stage, the pharmaceutical company will spend many millions of dollars to convince the medical community and the general public that its drug is superior to that of its competitor. Example: GlaxoSmithKline makes Paxil, while Eli Lilly produces Prozac, American Home Products makes Effexor, and Pfizer, Zoloft, all of which are drugs used in the treatment of depression.

Lobbying, a component of public affairs and public relations, enters the equation when a drug's patent protection period is over and cheaper generic drugs reach the market. In one situation quoted in *The New York Times* article, Bristol-Myers Squibb, the maker of the diabetes drug Glucophage, sought a three-year extension to its exclusivity so that the drug's effectiveness on children could receive further study. Analysts estimated that the company would yield an additional $1 billion in sales for every six months the patent was extended.

The patent issue went high profile during 2001's anthrax crisis. The Bayer company's Cipro was considered to be the primary drug for treatment of this potentially deadly disease. Cipro's sales in 2000 were $1.6 billion out of Bayer's total pharmaceutical sales of $5.8 billion. Although Bayer toughed out a price reduction, it finally agreed to lower its price substantially rather than risk loss of the patent.

The Players in the Lobbying Scenario

Obviously, with the high stakes in the prescription drug game, drug makers need maximum access in Washington to promote their interests before the halls of government. How do they do it? One key resource is the employment of defeated or retired congresspeople and former government officials. As we noted earlier, these influentials amble their way to Washington's K Street, there to gain employment as high-priced lobbyists, in many cases for the pharmaceutical industry. And, Democrat or Republican, they clearly do not need a road map to press the issues to the right bodies on Capitol Hill and government agencies.

Bristol-Myers has hired fifteen lobbying firms with fifty-seven lobbyists, including Haley Barbour, a former chairman of the Republican National Committee, and Thomas H. Boggs, Jr., a prominent Democratic political figure.

The Drug Industry's Powerful Advocate

The Pharmaceutical Research and Manufacturers of America (PhRMA) is the major lobby group for the U.S. drug companies in Washington, DC. It serves as an important adjunct to the activities of the industry's lobbyists and the drug companies' own public affairs departments. Here are some of the federal government issues PhRMA dealt with at the time of this writing:

- The Medicare Preservation and Improvement Act, the right direction for seniors and Medicare reform.
- Direct-to-Consumer Advertising.
- The Canadian Health Care System, no model for America.
- How Government and the Rx Industry Cooperate for Benefit.
- Defending the Risk and Cost of the Drug Industry's Research and Development Activities.

Log onto www.phrma.org for an understanding of how this important group functions in the public affairs arena.

WHO SPENDS THE BIG BUCKS ON ELECTIONS

The year 2000 Presidential elections broke records for campaign spending. Leading the charge was the nation's drug makers. They spent more than $80 million to defeat Democrats in Congress, who they feared would pass the kind of Medicare prescription drug benefit they oppose.

But on other issues such as abortion rights, groups such as the National Abortion and Reproductive Rights Action League and the Planned Parenthood Action Fund kicked in a total of $20 million to defeat candidates opposed to their issues.

Once the elections were over, the opposing groups' lobbyists took over their respective causes.

Presidential elections are by no means the only time special interests spend heavily on causes and issues they favor. One group, the Pharmaceutical Research and Manufacturers of America (PhRMA), representing about 100 companies in its $100 billion industry, has a huge budget to advance its agenda, using lobbying, image advertising, research, and education. The money is allocated to civic and government groups, public policy institutes, biomedical research, and disease advocacy groups.

THE MEDIA INDUSTRY AND LOBBYING

The Center for Public Integrity monitors the lobbying activity of media companies, defined as companies that derive half or more of their revenues from broadcasting, cable operations, publishing, online media and their content providers, and their trade associations. Congressional legislators from both parties share in the lobbying largesse dealt out by the media.

It's significant to learn what the media want from the legislators. The Center for Public Integrity has compiled a list of the top 10 lobbyist issues pursued by the media from 1996 through 2000:

- Intellectual property.
- Violent programming restrictions.
- Satellite systems.
- Tax issues.
- Telecommunications.
- Political ads/campaign finance.

- Cable issues.
- Tobacco/alcohol advertising.
- Antitrust/ownership issues.
- Broadband/spectrum issues.

For further information on jobs in public affairs, log onto the Public Affairs Council's Web site: www.pac.org. We also recommend the *Public Affairs Handbook*, edited by Joseph S. Nagelschmidt, published by AMACOM, a division of American Management Association.

CHAPTER 12

Public Interest, Public Service

C ommunity relations, corporate social responsibility, corporate philanthropy, corporate image, cause-related and social marketing, image building, support for the arts, education, and the environment, grass-roots volunteer campaigns, development/fund raising, multicultural affairs, special events, disaster relief, association nonprofits: All these categories are the ribs of the public interest and public service umbrella. They're considered components of public relations and are carried out by foundations, trusts, schools, Fortune 500 corporations, and individuals, and often involve the spending of large sums of money and commitments of time. They also employ large numbers of people.

To illustrate their function, we give practical examples of each category.

COMMUNITY RELATIONS

Corporations and other business organizations engage in public interest, public service, and community relations programs for a variety of reasons. They find that it is good business to put their best foot forward to bring an image of quality, social consciousness, and responsibility to the attention of their various publics: stockholders, competitors, employees, and customers.

AT&T, through its AT&T Foundation, spends hundreds of millions of dollars on educational and philanthropic programs. But does the homeowner choose AT&T Long Distance instead of another service because of the company's good works? Does an investor buy AT&T's stock because of the company's exemplary public service? The answer is an obvious no. Most consumers and investors don't even know about the AT&T Foundation. Yet the company chooses to be one of our foremost public citizens.

IBM is one of our largest corporations. Its program in this area is called "A Commitment to Corporate Citizenship" and counts education as the top priority in its philanthropic efforts. IBM's program paves the way for systematic reform in school systems nationwide through partnerships with whole school districts and entire states. Here are three of their specific programs.

IBM launched a TryScience Web site in collaboration with the New York Hall of Science and the Association of Science-Technology Centers, the first worldwide science and technology center.

In 1999, IBM hosted the National Education Summit, where governors, CEOs and education leaders made a series of key commitments to continue progress in standards-based reform.

IBM and the Singapore Ministry of Education formed a major partnership to leverage technology and enhance teaching and learning in the country's classrooms.

In New York, New Jersey, and Connecticut, McDonald's conducts an "Arching Into Education Scholarship Program," which awards $175,000 to tristate students through three scholarship opportunities.

And here's a commendable community relations initiative undertaken by ViaHealth Rochester General Hospital. Alarmed at seeing so many head injuries in children as a result of bicycle accidents, a group of concerned physicians at the hospital began distributing bike helmets to a few of their patients during routine office visits. These physicians and the hospital's medical staff felt strongly about becoming more heavily involved in preventing these head injuries and in educating children and their parents about safe bicycling. The hospital's public relations team created what became an annual event, "Bicycle Helmet Safety Day." The hospital handed out over 2,000 bicycle helmets to local children, and each helmet was custom fitted to each child.

A dozen local organizations supported the campaign, along with the leadership effort of the public relations team, physicians, volunteers, marketing staff, educational professionals, and community organizations. The evaluation: The number of children with head injuries due to bike accidents entering the emergency department of the hospital declined steadily from 93 in 1996 to 18 in 1999.

PHILIP MORRIS AND CORPORATE IMAGE

The Philip Morris Companies make Kraft Foods, Miller Beer, and Philip Morris cigarettes. They've been sued for billions by survivors of cigarette smokers.

In the 1998 tobacco settlement, cigarette manufacturers agreed to stop marketing to minors, but ads still run in magazines with significant youth readership. Finally, cigarette manufacturers, including Philip Morris, suspended some of their advertising—but not all.

Philip Morris has chosen to burnish its corporate image with support for the arts and corporate advertising that highlights these efforts. An ad in *The New Yorker*, for example, promoted "The Next Wave Festival," a 2-month performance series in dance, music, and theater at the Brooklyn Academy of Music. At the bottom of the ad, the line read, "Supported by the Philip Morris family of companies," and the companies listed were Kraft Foods, Miller Brewing, and Philip Morris U.S.A.

Another Philip Morris ad in *The New York Times Magazine* and the October 2000 issue of *Brill's Content* featured an exhibition at the Brooklyn Museum of Art of the work of Lee Krasner, Jackson Pollock's wife.

Still another Philip Morris magazine ad in these publications was on behalf of the National Network to End Domestic Violence Fund and Doors of Hope, the domestic violence shelter sponsored by the company. At the bottom of this ad, before the Philip Morris list of companies, was the line "Working to make a difference."

We make no moral or value judgments here, but only give examples of how one corporation uses corporate advertising.

CAUSE-RELATED AND SOCIAL MARKETING

Webster's New World Dictionary of Media and Communications defines cause-related marketing as "a promotional technique in which a company is linked with a nonprofit organization, a public service, or another cause."

Avon is in the cosmetics business. It refers to itself as "the company of women." This translates not only to marketing products to women, but also to engaging in an active involvement in women's health issues. In 1993, the company introduced the Avon Breast Cancer Crusade, which supports nonprofit early detection programs for women, particularly those who are medically underserved.

Avon's major fundraising effort is the Avon Breast Cancer 3-day event in which about 2,000 men and women walk nearly 60 miles over 3 days. The commitment not only entails physical stress, but also requires that each participant raise a minimum of $1,700.

In 1999, the event was held in five major cities and generated net proceeds of $20 million for Avon's Breast Cancer Crusade.

Media coverage promoted by Avon and its PR counsel, Bragman Nyman Cafarelli, was substantial in both print and broadcast. In addition, the PR firm implemented a grass-roots PR strategy and became the virtual "personal publicists" for the participants. Questionnaires were distributed to walkers on registration to learn their motivation for participating. The most compelling stories were selected and featured in the press materials.

In terms of results, the message of early detection received widespread coverage, and large sums of money were committed to breast cancer education and early detection programs.

In 1999's campaign, more than 500 TV stories were aired, including network programming like "The Rosie O'Donnell show," "Good Morning America," CNN, "Dateline," and MSNBC. Hundreds of print media also covered the event.

Results are carefully measured in evaluating a special event of this nature beyond the goodwill factor. Avon and its PR counsel, BNC, reported that for the 1999 event, 330 million print and electronic impressions were garnered through preevent and postevent media coverage.

TARGET'S "TAKE CHARGE OF EDUCATION" CAMPAIGN

Target (some call it "Tar-zhay") has built a retailing empire on cheap chic. It's known as an "upscale discounter." The chain advertises in *Vogue*. You can even buy animal-skin cowboy hats at Target for $14.99 that are very similar to the ones sold at Nordstrom's for $28. At this writing, there are 978 Target Stores in 46 states. So successful is the Target brand, the parent company changed its name from Dayton Hudson Corporation to Target Corporation.

Target does many things well. The secret to its success in marketing is the chain's ability to renew its brand constantly with innovative and unique marketing initiatives that echo the brand's experience. One such campaign is Take Charge of Education (TCOE), created and implemented with Minneapolis-based Martin/Williams, an advertising, public relations, response marketing, and retail image management agency.

Background

America is awash in credit cards. In the past 10 years, the number of cards in use has expanded by 50% and card debt has doubled. Target needed to promote guest card acquisition and usage in an environment cluttered with competitors offering more and more card enhancements.

Target and Martin/Williams differentiated Target's guest card by effectively tying it into Target's ongoing commitment to education. The program fit their "family" guest profile perfectly, and addressed one of this audience's most pressing concerns, the support and health of their local schools.

Strategy

When customers use their Target TCOE credit cards for purchases, 1% of their total goes to the specific school of their choice. The ability to "target" support to an individual school is an important key to success and really anchors this program locally to the community.

To communicate this message, Target and Martin/Williams created a fully integrated campaign including broadcast, print, in-store signage and merchandising, direct mail and promotion, web support, and a comprehensive in-school program.

Results

In the first 9 months, the program exceeded its annual goal by 36%. After 3 years, there were over 3 million TCOE cards in use, roughly

25% of Target's total charge cards. Additionally, TCOE cardholders visit twice as often as other Target guests and their average purchase is three times greater. Finally, out of approximately 110,000 schools in the country, 93,000 are enrolled in the TCOE sponsorship program, a tremendous local anchor for the Target brand.

The campaign has been awarded a gold Effie, a gold AME (Advertising/Marketing Effectiveness), and the Heinemann Award at the Retail Advertising Conference.

Take Charge of Education is a consummate example of cause-related marketing with a big payoff.

SOCIAL MARKETING

In chapter 4, we discussed Porter Novelli and its innovative social marketing program. This agency has successfully harnessed the many disciplines of marketing to promote social change on behalf of the world's largest and most highly regarded NGOs (nongovernmental organizations), corporations, professional bodies, and government agencies.

Porter Novelli bases its social marketing program on four key elements:

- Audience research.
- Strategic planning.
- Powerful integrated marketing communication programs.
- Continuous audience feedback, which is then used to refine programs.

With the compounding of the world's social problems, we can expect the discipline of social marketing to increase enormously in the early part of the 21st century.

THE RELATIONSHIP OF PUBLIC RELATIONS AND FUND RAISING

First, here are some definitions from Kathleen S. Kelly's academic text *Effective Fund-Raising Management.*

Fund raisers are paid specialists and volunteers who assist in the process of obtaining gifts. They are skilled communicators, trained to manage relationships with strategic publics and add compensated value to the organizations they serve.

Kelly defines fund raising as a subfunction of nonprofit public relations, similar to investor relations in the business sector. She calls public relations "an academic home for fund raising." Others believe that fund raising is a specialization of public relations.

In a 1988 study, the Public Relations Society of America (PRSA) incorporated the subhead "Fund Raising" as the seventh element and function of the public relations practice, along with media, employee, community, government, consumer, and investor relations. Says Kelly, "The public relations function has developed many specializations to manage organizational relationships with important stakeholders."

How big is philanthropy in America? Almost $200 billion is contributed to charity each year, and giving is no longer dominated by the society matron writing checks to a well-heeled foundation. Today's new philanthropist is as likely to be a thirty-something Internet millionaire setting up his or her own foundation or retiring early to help build schools in Chile.

In 1997, software magnate Paul Brainerd set up a foundation that is a model of "venture philanthropy" and offers a new businesslike approach to giving. Each of the foundation's 193 partners pledges at least $5,000 a year and is expected to volunteer with one of the donor organizations receiving the grants.

Where People Work in the Nonprofit Sector and How Much They Make

A special insert on the subject "Giving" in *The New York Times* for November 20, 2000, discussed the wide range of nonprofits and the jobs within that periphery. First, here are some general numbers. In 1996, there were 1.14 million nonprofit organizations in the United States, big and small, and more than 100,000 professional fund raisers. Colleges, cultural, and other organizations use the word "development" or "resources development" euphemistically for fund raising.

For example, the University of Michigan's web site, www.umich. edu, offers an insight into the development niche. The school was the first public university to raise more than $1 billion in a campaign (1992–1997: $1.4 billion). The job offering sought development people to work on a forthcoming fund-raising campaign that was to be the largest in its history.

One job for Development Officer I (entry level) had these duties and responsibilities:

- Assist in developing solicitation methods and marketing development programs.
- Assist with gift solicitation and program planning.
- Assist in organizing and training volunteers.
- Provide consultation to university units, alumni, and student groups regarding fund-raising activities.

For this lowest level development officer job, the candidate needed a bachelor's degree and some experience in marketing, public relations, communications, or a related field.

The job offer for the top-rung spot of Development Officer III listed duties and responsibilities that are more managerial, and included recruiting and training volunteers, preparing reports on fund-raising activities, and developing solication methods.

The qualifications for this higher level job included experience in marketing, advertising, public relations, communications, or a related field, and some experience in public speaking and promotional writing was necessary.

If you work for a publicly traded company, there is no question that you'll make more money than at a nonprofit company. A public relations executive at a nonprofit makes about $41,000 a year, while the same job at a public company pays $118,000.

And the director of government relations at a nonprofit makes about $70,000 a year, but his or her comparable person at a public company earns about $137,000.

Why work for less? Many have made the move because of the challenge and the fulfillment of the nonprofit world. One top executive, Lawrence M. Small, was making a multi-million-dollar salary at Fannie Mae, the home lending organization. At 59, well before retirement age, he moved to the Smithsonian Institution in Washington, D.C., as Executive Secretary for only $330,000.

Multicultural Affairs

Billionaire Bill Gates of Microsoft has spent millions in battling federal antitrust charges. In January 2001, Microsoft faced new challenges on the management policies of the company toward seven African American employees. These employees filed race discrimination suits, charging that they were not evaluated fairly, promoted, or as highly paid as White employees. Therefore, they claimed that Microsoft is in violation of federal civil rights law.

Microsoft's spokeswoman made the requisite public relations response when she announced that the company had welcomed more African Americans in recent years and has donated more than $100 million to fostering interest in technology among young women and minorities. The Bill and Melinda Gates Foundation has assets exceeding $17 billion, making it the nation's largest foundation.

But not everyone can do it like Bill Gates. At the age of 41, Tony Paquin sold his $10-million computer consulting company and didn't buy a 60-foot sailboat to explore the South Pacific. Instead, he spent more than $100,000 of his own money and 16 months to run for Congress in Idaho. He lost the election, but found a new outlet for his energies. Paquin and his brother Gary started Netivation.com, an Internet-based company serving political campaigns. With the money he makes, Tony Paquin plans to start a foundation for children.

What conclusions can we draw from the examples of the public-interest and public-service programs we have discussed? Certainly these companies and hundreds of others participate in them because they regard doing so as good business. Perhaps they even regard this positive image building as a balance against criticism about a corporation's environmental policy or some future negative occurrence such as a strike or an accident. And of course many of these public-interest and public-service programs are tax deductible.

As a career source, public service and public interest are among the most rewarding areas in the whole field of public relations. They may be less stressful than media relations and crisis management. They may pay less, but they pose a challenging career choice that can be pursued at many levels—corporate, not-for-profit, or governmental.

The Good News About Working for the Nonprofits

In an article in the August issue of PRSA's *TACTICS*, a commentary by Kathleen S. Kelly, "The Top Five Myths Regarding Nonprofits," explodes many of the conceptions about this sector:

Myth 1—Nonprofits Cannot Make a Profit. Yes, nonprofits can make a profit, but they can't distribute them to those who control the organization. Most nonprofits have huge endowments. A study estimated that about 22,000 nonprofits have $600 billion in retained earnings.

Myth 2—Nonprofits Are Small in Number and Size. Half of the 1.4 million nonprofits are charitable. From 20,000 to 30,000 new nonprofits are started each year. Nonprofits employ about 11 million people, or 7% of the U.S. workforce.

Myth 3—Nonprofits Deal With Charity. The National Football League and the PGA (in golf) are neither government, business, nor charity, yet they fall into the nonprofit sector because they don't distribute their profits.

Myth 4—Gifts Account for Most Nonprofit Revenue. Gifts are not the primary source of income for nonprofits in general. Dues and fees make up most of the group's revenues.

Myth 5—Most Gifts Come From Corporations and Foundations. Wrong again. Of the roughly $190 billion contributed to charitable organizations in 1999, individuals gave 84%.

Kelly concluded: The nonprofit sector represents a rich and unexplored territory for most practitioners. Its scope and diversity deserve attention—and accurate understanding.

Note that Kathleen Kelly, PhD, APR, Fellow PRSA, is professor of communication and PR at the University of Louisiana. She is also the author of the nonprofit field's first text, *Effective Fund-Raising Management*, mentioned earlier in this chapter.

CHAPTER 13

Strategic and Integrated Public Relations and Brand Marketing

In the broad areas of public relations and marketing covered in this chapter, let's deal first with the subject of strategic public relations as it is practiced by a corporate or other organization.

Applying strategic management to public relations involves six steps, according to Paul Forbes, a veteran counselor to senior corporate management.[1]

- Scanning the future.
- Building scenarios for this contingency planning.
- Reviewing the mission of the organization on an ongoing basis.
- Setting objectives, strategies, and policies as to where the organization wants to go and how to get there.
- Implementing this strategy.
- Evaluating and updating the plan annually.

Forbes sums up strategic planning as "what you do now to bring about a future result."

To be strategic, public relations must pass one basic test: At a minimum, everything done must be aligned with the corporation or other organization's vision or mission—its reason for being—and must contribute to achieving its strategic objectives.

Strategic marketing refers to the practice of selling a service, a product, or a group of products to a specific market or audience. Integrated marketing combines advertising, public relations, and other activities in a coordinated strategy using messages and media. Often they are coordinated through a single planning system.

We offer here a few Silver Anvil and Cipra award-winning campaigns in the practice area of strategic and integrated public relations and marketing.

SURVIVING THE STORM: A CRISIS IN CREDIBILITY

Publishers Clearing House with Rogers & Cowan (New York)

I spent about 35 years as a magazine publisher. Because most of my magazines depended on subscriptions as well as newsstand sales, I had numerous dealings with Publishers Clearing House (PCH), the world's largest multimagazine subscription service. PCH awards prizes to recipients of its mailings in order to solicit subscriptions.

All went well until the mid 1990s, when PCH was caught in a web of bad publicity due to a competing subscription service defaulting on its promise of prizes. This was purely a case of guilt by association, because PCH legitimately awarded the prizes it promised. In a June 14, 1999, article in *The New York Times*, media reporter Alex Kuczynski wrote, "Indeed, magazines are scrambling to flee American Family Publishers and Publishers Clearing House faster than Ed McMahon can say, 'You're a winner.'"

With magazine subscriptions from this source down dramatically due to the negative publicity, and PCH's sales in a free-fall, the company called in a highly respected PR agency, Rogers & Cowan. The resulting campaign, "Surviving the Storm: A Crisis in Credibility," won a Silver Anvil Award 2000 in the category of marketing consumer sources. Here are details of the Rogers & Cowan campaign.

Research and Planning. National opinion polling revealed the ongoing portrayal that all sweepstakes were "frauds" and never awarded the prizes they promised. To persuade consumers to reenter the contests, the customers would have to see firsthand that someone in their town had won a prize. This was accomplished by the rewarding of many surprise awards delivered by PCH's Prize Patrol. The theme of the new plan was that PCH's contests were "open and honest."

The media plan also called for focusing on developing a highly visual, TV-friendly, and emotional platform favorable to PCH. The target audience/target media was defined as women 25–54 and heavier than average viewers of TV news. The influential target outlets were isolated as local TV news and national entertainment media. Rogers & Cowan concluded that these groups would respond best to immediate news about PCH, not dwelling on the past negative news. The budget for the campaign was set at $500,000, inclusive of all program costs.

Objective. First, arrest the response in free-fall, halt the customer loss, impact the company's critically important June mailing, and finally convey the message that PCH awards its prizes.

Strategy. (1) Address "consumer despair" by dispelling misconceptions identified by research. (2) Gain third-party endorsement for the fact that people really do win. (3) Utilize emotion to gain media coverage when people learned they had won a cash windfall delivered by PCH's Prize Patrol.

Concept. PCH would give the media complete access to the giving of a happy surprise to winners by the Prize Patrol. In total, 100 prize deliveries in the top 100 media markets would occur in just the 3 days before the strategic mailing arrived.

Preparation and Execution. To accomplish this Promethean task, 66 PCH employees were trained to perform as the Prize Patrol and as media spokespeople. The "Prize Patrol Boot Camp" resulted in a major segment on "Entertainment Tonight." Susan Lucci, the soap star who had just won a Emmy after losing for 19 consecutive years, was enlisted to deliver the first surprise award. The segment broke on "Access Hollywood" and "Extra." Additionally, an ABC satellite feed was carried by local newscasts in 34 top markets. The Prize Patrol segment also broke on "Inside Edition" and CBS's "Late Show With David Letterman."

Evaluation. Despite breath-taking logistics and just 40 days to prepare, the program met its challenging objectives:

- It arrested the response in free-fall.
- It had a positive impact on the June PCH mailing nearly three times greater than its competition.
- With six waves of coverage from the national media in less than 2 weeks, the program successfully conveyed to a large audience that people really do win. Many media outlets endorsed the PCH sweepstakes, saying that it pays to send back entries.

GET ON BOARD: STEERING A NEW COURSE FOR THE BEEF INDUSTRY

The National Cattlemen's Beef Association (NCBA) with Ketchum Public Relations

Since 1980, the beef industry has been down. Falling demand, falling volume, falling prices. In 1998, the NCBA began noticing a significant and alarming shift toward chicken usage in restaurants. Beef was flat at 7.1 billion servings while chicken was up 6% to nearly 4.7 billion servings. The dominant player, the beef industry, needed to counter the increase in chicken servings with an increase of its own or continue to lose market share.

Research. Ketchum and the NCBA learned that although beef was the more frequently ordered item, chicken represented an almost equal share of the menu because, on average, it is used as an ingredient in an entrée five times, where beef is used only four.

In 1999, Ketchum and the NCBA developed an entirely new strategic direction for beef, based on new, value-added "easy beef" products to change foodservice perceptions. The campaign earned Ketchum and the NCBA a Silver Anvil 2000 Award in the category of Integrated Communications.

Planning. The program objective was to generate awareness, build demand for beef in the food-service channel, and stimulate trial for value-added (e.g., precooked, preseasoned) beef products.

Strategy.

- Create excitement for beef via major "events" to premiere the "new" beef industry.
- Demonstrate beef's versatility and convenience.

- Leverage "hot" comfort food trends like pot roast, sandwiches, and ethnic flavors to remind operators of the popularity of beef.

Target Audience. The campaign was directed to the top 200 chain restaurants, high-volume independent restaurants, and the top 25 institutional management companies, such as schools and employee cafeterias.

Budget. The budget broke down as $1,280,000 ($615,000 agency fees, $290,000 out-of-pocket, $375,000 trade media advertising).

Execution. Here's Ketchum Public Relations/San Francisco's campaign for the beef industry's new strategic direction.

Multiple-page ads were placed in *Nation's Restaurant News* featuring restaurant industry leaders promoting new "easy beef" products to the food-service industry. Other ads featured "hot" menu concepts like "precooked beef strips" and "preseasoned, precooked prime rib."

Advertorials in food-service publications stressed the convenience aspect and reported compelling research on labor issues and consumer demand for these new beef products.

Restaurant operators were given more than 75 innovative convenient beef recipes for the menu trend, and recipe cards were produced to fulfill requests generated by the ad campaign and trade show promotion.

Thirty-two executive research and development chefs from the top chain restaurants met for a 2-day culinary program sponsored by the NCBA.

Evaluation. One year after the program began, beef had increased by 100 million servings, and items like steak sandwiches rose 17%. Some chains agreed to test fully cooked beef entrees.

Seminars were held for chefs from national and regional restaurant chains. Follow-up surveys indicated that 75% had a greater understanding of value-added beef products and would consider them for future use in their operations.

LAUNCHING AN E-BANK

WingspanBank.com with Ogilvy Public Relations Worldwide

In 1991, Ogilvy Public Relations Worldwide was given a challenging assignment in the area of Brand Development: marketing an online bank for a primarily female audience, and doing it with a limited budget of $150,000.

Situation Analysis. WingspanBank.com received a generous amount of media attention when it was launched in 1999. Ogilvy's job was to build up appeal to women while not excluding men and to show consumers the benefits of banking online.

Objectives.

- Increase awareness of women as the household financial officer.
- Position Wingspan as a bank that understands women.
- Differentiate Wingspan from the competition.
- Drive traffic to the Web site.
- Improve the flow of information to media via a dedicated press Web site.
- Develop initiatives to include original research, third-party endorsements, and a media event.

Audience. Target the audience for the campaign as women and their role in managing and controlling family finances.

Research. Use Wingspan's own findings. For example, 70% of women pay the family's monthly bills and their use of financial service Web sites is growing.

Planning. With only a 3-week turnaround time, the dedicated press Web site had to be structured, a job that included creating links, catchy splash pages, and essential visuals.

For consumer media relations, the team researched an appropriate third-party spokesperson, developed the WingspanBank Financial Index, organized a press event to announce the findings, created an "e-teaser" to build excitement for the Female Finance Factor, and wrote numerous press releases.

Strategy.

- Stress the woman as family financial manager.
- Sell Wingspan as a bank that knows women.
- Position Wingspan as the leader in personal financial management.

Execution/Tactics. Ogilvy conducted qualitative research to bolster the premise of women as financial controller in the home. The findings were branded as the WingspanBank Financial Index, and the trend was called the Female Finance Factor.

Ogilvy engaged financial expert and author Dr. Judith Briles as the voice of Wingspan.

Reporters were invited to a Consumer Breakfast Event at the St. Regis Hotel in New York, where computer terminals were set up enabling journalists to check out the Wingspan Web site, as well as the press site.

Dr. Briles was featured on an audio news release that promoted the WingspanBank Financial Index.

Measurement of Success.

- The campaign met many objectives, primarily that of increasing awareness of women in control of household finances.
- The media coverage was extensive with 544 placements, 3.4 million broadcast impressions, and 20.2 million print impressions. A broadcast impression is based on the total audience of the radio and TV shows that carried the Wingspan coverage. A print impression is the total readership of print publications covering WingspanBank.com. For the first time, Wingspan was covered in such high-profile women's and parenting publications as *Reader's Digest, Family Circle, Woman's Day,* and *USA TODAY.*
- Wingspan.com was very clearly aligned with female consumers.
- The Wingspan Web site had a daily increase from the campaign beginning of 33%.
- The flow of information to the media via the dedicated press Web site was improved.

EDDIE BAUER MAKES THE E-COMMERCE TREK

Eddie Bauer with Edelman Public Relations Worldwide

Eddie Bauer is a respected name in upscale apparel with a special appeal to outdoor sports people. In 1999, Edelman Public Relations Worldwide was given the assignment to position Eddie Bauer as the leading e-commerce retail site. Here's how the agency handled this strategic marketing assignment.

Challenges.

- Broaden excitement and relevance around the Eddie Bauer brand; focus on brand interest and relevance for male consumers.
- Support and build on Eddie Bauer travel-related marketing initiatives.
- Position Eddie Bauer as the leading e-commerce retail site.
- Reclaim Eddie Bauer's Northwest American Heritage.

Strategies.

- Virtual Editor Showroom: Establish Eddie Bauer as the industry forerunner by implementing an online showroom. Fall 2000 viewing is easy with "click and pick" showroom.
- Editor Edventure Press Trip: Invite six to eight key editors to experience "A Day in the Life of Eddie Bauer," such as hiking, kayaking, whale watching, and tour of the Eddie Bauer campus archives.
- Holiday: North by Northwest Fashion Preview: Promote Holiday 2000 collection to key media. Position collection in a venue that inspires the transient feeling of "Heading Home For The Holidays."
- *National Geographic*/Eddie Bauer Lewis & Clark Journey: Promote EB/NG partnership by recreating a modern-day Lewis & Clark cross-country journey.
- Eddie Bauer–Riverkeeper Challenge: Eddie Bauer teams with Riverkeeper, an environmental group, to promote appreciation for the sport of kayaking and preservation of America's waterways. Also, leverage Eddie Bauer's sponsorship with US Canoe and Kayak to create media buzz and consumer awareness.
- Ongoing News Bureau Placements: Use New York contacts and in-house product closet to ensure ongoing, yearround consumer and trade placement.

Results. The objective in this marketing assignment was to take advantage of the brand name and its Pacific Northwest orientation. The Edventure Press Trip puts editors in the Eddie Bauer environment so they are better able to write about it.

Tying in *National Geographic*, Eddie Bauer, and the Lewis & Clark journey is great marketing by association.

WHEN MARKETING BACKFIRES

Burger King is big, McDonald's is bigger, and although the number 2 chain wins the taste tests for its burgers, the Golden Arches make the top fries.

In 1998, Burger King embarked on a campaign to topple McDonald's from its perch by formulating a new fry. It would be a potato stick coated with a layer of starch designed to help retain heat and add crunch.

An article in *The Wall Street Journal* in January 2001 told how Burger King spent $70 million and 3 years to win the french fry war—and lost.

When Burger King first launched its new, improved product, children's meal toys in the likeness of Mr. Potato Head, who would be the fry's official "spokespud," were ordered. January 2, 1998, was designated "Free Fryday" with 15 million servings handed out nationwide.

At first, Burger King franchisees were elated over the new fry's prospects, particularly since the product's profit margin was as high as 80 cents on the dollar. Statistically, Americans consumption of fries per capita is 26 pounds a year, or a half pound a week.

But soon after the new fry was introduced, a super-glitch developed. One franchisee said the taste was terrible and the fry snapped like a potato chip. People actually began avoiding the chain's stores because of its french fries.

Says Jennifer Ordonez, who wrote *The Wall Street Journal* article, "In the annals of consumer product flops, this one has quietly amounted to a whopper."

Back at Burger King headquarters, the flopped fry fiasco extended to the potato suppliers, who had been sent a 19-page set of specs on how the fry should be prepared.

At the root of the problem was taste. Said company spokesman Rob Doughty, "They were soggy, they would get cold easily, they were lumpy, they weren't competitive," while market research simply showed that people only wanted a fry that was crispy and would remain hot.

Now comes an element in this saga that would have made a great piece in the *National Lampoon* had I still been publishing the magazine. To guarantee the adequate crunch factor, Burger King's 19-page tome on the new fry's specifications required that for each mouthful of french fry, the degree of crispiness was to be "determined by an audible crunch that should be present for seven or more chews . . . loud enough to be apparent to the evaluator." Would it be taken off the market if the customer had false teeth that didn't result in the required number of chews?

In an example of how big-time marketing works, Burger King assembled a team of 100 marketing executives, food scientists, franchisees, and others to look into a coated fry that, when dipped in a batter of potato starch, retains heat longer and will be warm and crunchy even when eaten at home.

Extensive testing followed until the company was finally satisfied with the taste and texture of its fries. Burger King even booked expensive TV commercials during the 1998 Super Bowl and launched other big-budget promotions.

But by summer 2000, Burger King still had lost the quality contest to McDonald's. Sales of the fries dropped, and complaints by Burger King franchisees mounted. So it was back to the product development people for a new improved fry that would be in restaurants by spring 2001.

OTHER EXAMPLES OF STRATEGIC MARKETING CAMPAIGNS

We have seen how strategic marketing and communications can be practiced in three different situations. Here are capsules of other campaigns that further illustrate the practice:

For client Hallmark, Fleishman-Hillard initiated a marketing campaign for a new line of 99-cent greeting cards called "Warm Wishes."

Ketchum Public Relations and its client Mine Safety Appliances (MSA) introduced MSA Safety Works, a consumer product line featuring protective eyewear, dust masks and respirators, hearing protection, and hard hats.

In an advertising and public relations campaign, J. Walter Thompson positioned diamonds as the ultimate symbol and gift for the millenium.

BSMG Worldwide Services reached the hot teenage market with its Milk Mustache, Cat Boots, and Youth Smoking Prevention programs.

Positioning yo-yo use as a real sport, HPK Marketing and Medialink promoted the Bandai 1999 World Yo-Yo Championships.

Cone, Inc., created ConAgra's "Feeding Children Better," a national initiative dedicated to ending childhood hunger, for its client, ConAgra, the world's largest food manufacturer.

Polaroid contemporized its brand with the Porter Novelli strategic marketing plan for the Polaroid I-Zone Instant Pocket Camera, a cell-phone-sized camera that takes instant miniature photo stickers.

To combat the overwhelming intrusions of cell phones, manufacturer Nokia and the city of San Diego called on Ketchum to create Cell Phone Courtesy Week, raising the consciousness of the problem, as well as the image of the sponsors.

In these examples we see the wide variety of situations in the practice of strategic marketing and communications. The procedure in these programs is typically an identification or overview of the issue or problem, a situation analysis and objective, research, planning, execution, and evaluation of the result.

CORPORATE PUBLIC RELATIONS, CORPORATE REPUTATION, CORPORATE ADVERTISING, AND BRANDING

Marken on Corporate Image

An article in the spring 1990 issue of *Public Relations Quarterly* by industry veteran G. A. "Andy" Marken was headed "Corporate Image—We All Have One, But Few Work to Protect and Project It." Marken quoted an Opinion Research Corporation (ORC) study that finds that people do business with a given firm or buy its products for more than the quality of the goods or services. The collected knowledge of customers, stockholders, bankers, brokerage houses, dealers, distributors, and the media regarding a company can affect its sales, earnings, valuation, ability to obtain loans, and ability to attract quality employees.

Influences on Image

Advertising and publicity are only two aspects of a firm's image. Everything a company is, says, and does, according to Marken, is a component of its image. What are these elements?

- Product: Consistent high quality from companies like Hewlett-Packard, Compaq, IBM and others has positioned these companies above their competition.
- Service: IBM may not always have the most advanced products, but no one questions the level of service it provides.

- Finance: Even well-known, reputable companies have periodic setbacks in sales, but their overall financial strength can override long-term fears about their future health.
- Employees: Happy, productive employees are a powerful market influence. The attitudes of a firm's employees often influence the way it is perceived by clients, trade partners, and competitors.

Launching an Image

Marken suggested these steps in launching a corporate image communications program.

1. Evaluate the strengths and weaknesses of the company's current image.
2. Define the image that the firm wants to project.
3. Determine a course of action that appeals to the largest possible number of your target audience.
4. Coordinate every channel of communications to build the desired image.

Launching an effective image development and/or reinforcement campaign means defining your target publics. Who are they? We listed them in an earlier chapter, but add a few here: employees, communities, suppliers, and, of course, the media.

Marken summed up:

> A sound corporate image is no substitute for fair dealings and quality products. However, first impressions have a lasting effect. A company's ability to communicate a favorable and progressive image to its many publics places it ahead of its competition and, subsequently, has a profound effect on the bottom line.

Corporate Advertising

IBM is a long-time advertiser in *The Wall Street Journal*, but never has it committed more dollars than for its 1-day, 32-page insertion on December 13, 1999. *Editor & Publisher* called it possibly the biggest newspaper ad ever.

The thrust of the ad section was to e-business owners and executives. IBM was stressing its capability as "The Biggest Dot.Com of Them All."

One typical full-page ad in the spread was headed "e-chiaroscuro." It bore a full-page photograph of a room in Russia's Hermitage Museum showing a woman and a child examining a classic work of Renaissance art. The copy went on to say that Russia's historic museum uses IBM Digital Library software, high-resolution imaging, and IBM UNIX servers to put 2,000 pieces of art online.

Editor & Publisher estimated the price of the insertion as nearly $2.8 million and noted that each copy of that day's *WSJ* weighed 1.84 pounds.

Now, why did IBM feel it necessary to spend all that money to reach 2 or 3 million movers and shakers? Surely it wasn't to generate a flurry of orders for its UNIX servers to museums. The ad had more intrinsic purposes. It reinforced IBM's brand and image as a world business machine powerhouse, a province of corporate branding and reputation.

In today's marketplace the corporate brand name, be it IBM or Philip Morris, is accepted as a valuable asset. Maintaining the primacy of a corporate brand takes research, segmentation, analysis, identity development, strategic planning, brand expression (targeting, messaging, program execution), and measurement/program refinement.

We've given one example of how the giant IBM spent a huge sum of money on a single multiple-page ad insertion that would equal the yearly budget of many advertisers. Few organizations have the reputation of Big Blue. Others need to build a brand from scratch or repair a tarnished one.

At Ogilvy Public Relations Worldwide's corporate practice, brand and corporate reputation issues are addressed according to a plan:

- *Brand Strategy* strategically repositions a company to regain competitive advantage.
- *Workplace Performance* analyzes employee's behavior so that it aligns with the strategic direction of a company.
- *Media Works* favorably positions a company and its management in the national business media.
- *Financial Relations* deals with a fair evaluation of a company's stock.
- *Brand Shield* helps a company to properly manage a crisis that can severely harm its reputation.

- *Cause-related Marketing* monitors a company's philanthropic activities to develop a better return on investment. The total check-up is called "Brand Works."

Corporate Advertising That Delivers Reputation Results

An ad for United Airlines in *The Wall Street Journal* shows a 9 × 10-inch photo of an airport's baggage carousel, but instead of luggage, the chute is delivering musical instruments. The headline reads, "Proud Sponsor of the Los Angeles Philharmonic," the text says, "United Airlines is happy to help the L.A. Philharmonic and Hollywood Bowl continue enriching the Los Angeles community. After all, it's not just flying we want to make more enjoyable It's life UNITED AIRLINES."

The ad is so effective as a corporate image, it will at least compensate for the next two times you wait for three-quarters of an hour for your luggage at a United terminal.

DuPont has a series of corporate image ads called "To Do List for the Planet." A recent color ad in the November/December 2000 issue of the *Columbia Journalism Review* was headed "Develop Medicines That Fight HIV." The bottom of the ad bears the DuPont logo and the tag line, "The miracles of science," with an 800 number to call for information and with a Web address. This ad is perfect as a combination of good corporate public service and corporate reputation.

I noted a 6 × 9-inch ad in the November 12, 2000, *New York Times* for Target. But instead of selling its wares, the ad had a color background of "Snoopy," the dog in the "Peanuts" comic strip, and the copy superimposed, "The Children's Museum of Manhattan will be temporarily relaxing its No Dogs Allowed policy."

The bottom of the ad read, "Target is proud to sponsor free admission every Friday in November to *Good Grief!*, an exhibition at the Children's Museum of Manhattan that helps kids resolve conflicts."

All three ads bolster reputation by associating the corporation with culture and good works. Typically, the ads appear in influential and "think" publications to reach the desired audience.

Fortune produces the "Fortune Most Admired Companies" and Fortune/Roper Corporate Reputation Index databases, which track more than 400 of the Fortune 500 companies on eight attributes driving reputation. These databases provide a look at how business influentials, financial analysts, the general public, and individual investors regard America's most admired corporations. Firms like Burson-Marsteller, which conducts an active Corporate Reputation practice, own these indices. This firm's comments on creating a sense of mission are: "With companies in a constant state of flux, managing change is a necessity. One key is communicating clearly on corporate mission and values, and making sure that communications has measurable goals."

CHAPTER 14

Financial Public Relations and Investor Relations

W hat happens when, at the last minute, General Electric, the nation's largest conglomerate, upsets United Technologies, another giant corporation, in United's bid to buy the not-so-small Honeywell International? How is the press informed of the details amid the secrecy of the intense rounds of deal making that culminates in G.E.'s acquisition of Honeywell? Here's part of the play-by-play.

Honeywell, a company with 120,000 employees and annual sales of $24 billion, was in the final stages of merger talks with United Technologies in October 2000 when G.E. topped United's bid and agreed to acquire Honeywell for $45 billion. G.E. has 340,000 employees and annual sales exceeding $110 billion.

The merger was finalized on Sunday, October 22, and therefore presented great deadline pressures for G.E.'s investor relations team, as well as for the media. The page one headline of *The New York Times* on Sunday, October 23, read:

General Electric Buying Honeywell In $45 Billion Deal

Then on page 22 of the same issue, *The New York Times* goofed when its headline read:

G.E. Is Acquiring Honeywell for $45 Million in Stock

The implications of a merger like this one are enormous. How would the merger affect the stock of both companies? How many of Honeywell's 120,000 employees would lose their jobs? Would Honeywell's CEO continue to run the newly merged division of G.E.? Would the deal affect G.E. Chairman Jack Welch's decision to retire in early 2001? What about G.E.'s 340,000 employees?

Once the deal was signed by the boards of G.E. and Honeywell on Sunday afternoon, October 22, G.E.'s and Honeywell's investor relations and financial communications people took over. They were charged with the responsibility of announcing the deal to the print and broadcast press and to the companies' financial publics, which included:

- The financial press.
- Present G.E. and Honeywell stockholders.
- Stock exchange member firms, customers' brokers, branch office managers.
- Mutual fund owners.
- Investment counselors and advisory services.
- The investing public.
- Security analysts.
- Investment bankers.
- Commercial bankers.
- Trustees of estates.

Although G.E. and Honeywell could not reach all these publics directly, they could reach the most important ones. For example, their hundreds of thousands of present stockholders were informed of the deal in the next quarterly report.

A merger like this one is important financial news. It doesn't mean that the stockholder will immediately decide to buy more stock, but it does show that the company is growing on a sound basis—that is, paying a fair price for increased future profits.

Perhaps the most important publics in a merger are the security analysts for brokerage firms, banks, and mutual funds that hold stock in these companies for their clients and make investment decisions based on the profit potential of the merged companies.

When one speaks of the financial press as a public these days, the reference is no longer only *The Wall Street Journal*, *Barron's*, and a handful of other print and broadcast sources. Financial information today travels at an instant rate of speed. When the *Bloomberg Financial Markets, Internet Wire*, or TheStreet.com sends out the G.E.–Honeywell story on the Internet, online users worldwide receive the information when it happens.

The daunting task of communicating with the press and the other publics on financial situations like the G.E./Honeywell merger is the responsibility of investor relations (IR) personnel at the companies, with support from their PR counsel firms.

All this merger activity was for naught. The deal was killed in summer 2001 by the European Union charging that the merger would cause unfair competition to other aircraft and aerospace manufacturers.

THE CHANGING RELATIONSHIP BETWEEN INVESTOR RELATIONS AND PUBLIC RELATIONS

According to an article in the September 1998 issue of *Inside PR*, until the late 1980s many major companies didn't have an IR function. If there was an individual responsible for financial communications, he or she was typically a midlevel manager within the public relations department.

IR is a spring trap that can ensnare even the wiliest corporate participants. We give as examples the Lucent and Mattel debacles of the year 2000, with the concomitant severe drop in their stock prices and the negative publicity that ensued. The issue of "getting the ink" in the investor relations area is particularly vital because it often affects the rise and fall of a company's fortunes.

At this writing, almost every company has not only an IR director, but an IR department. And often the IR department reports not to the senior public relations executive, but to the company's chief financial officer (CFO).

In terms of compensation, the senior IR person is better paid than his or her counterpart in PR and has better access to the CEO and other members of the management team.

According to the *Inside PR* article, most public relations executives make the case that IR should be one of their responsibilities because it falls within their role as managing the relationship between the company and all its publics.

The National Investor Relations Institute (NIRI) has 3,800 members who represent 2,200 companies. Forty-one percent of its members have corporate communications or public relations backgrounds, and 45% come out of a financial background.

At times, says *Inside PR*, professionals move from PR to IR. Larry Bishop began his career in PR, moved into IR, and became responsible for both functions at the Boeing Company. He feels that his ascent from the senior IR position to his new role may be illustrative of a new trend. When CEO's are looking for someone to whom they can trust a centralized communication function, they are increasingly choosing IR people over their PR counterparts.

An ideal background in today's corporate climate would be someone who studies public relations in college, earns an MBA, and develops writing skills.

Requisites for a Career in Investor Relations

In his book *Experts in Action: Inside Public Relations*, Bill Cantor detailed the duties of the financial public relations executive.[1] We offer some of them here:

- A clear understanding of the guidelines for publicity in the Securities and Exchange Acts of 1933 and 1934, as well as the disclosure requirements of the national stock exchanges and court cases relating to these laws.
- The ability to analyze and evaluate financial statements.
- Very detailed knowledge of the business activities of a company or client.

The scope of responsibilities and functions of financial public relations includes the following.

Liaison With Executive Management.

- Board of directors, primarily through the board chairman.
- Executive and finance committee.

- Key officials and department heads.
- Directors of public relations, industrial relations, and employee relations.

Financial Publicity.

- Uncovering and developing news of interest to stockholders.
- Contacting and cultivating friendships with financial editors at media sources.
- Directing the preparation of financial press releases, annual and interim reports, financing, and mergers.
- Interviewing media financial reporters to determine their needs.
- Supplying requested information to investment services, brokerage houses, investment banking firms, and others.

Stockholder Correspondence. Handling inquiries, complaints, explaining financing, form letters covering exchanges, and so on.

Conducting Stockholder Surveys. Preparation of corporation annual report and quarterly earnings statements.

Preparation of Other Stockholder Publications.

- Quarterly earnings statements.
- Folders interpreting company policies.
- Dividend stuffers and inserts.
- Reprints of speeches and articles by company officials.
- Preparing biographical digests of executive officers and members of board of directors.

Financial and Educational Advertising.

- Cooperating with a corporation's financial executives, advertising manager, and outside PR firm handling IR assignments.
- Supervising and writing financial publicity, financial advertising, and announcements of mergers and acquisitions opening of new plants.
- Preparing institutional advertising, including annual reports and quarterly advertisements, announcements of acquisitions, opening and closing of plants, and more.

Planning the Annual Meeting of Stockholders.

- Organizing program, selecting place of meeting.
- Preparations for answers to questions and criticisms.
- Entertaining press representatives.
- Arranging closed-circuit TV and other communication to reach stockholders in other parts of the country.

Regional Meetings of Stockholders.

- Assisting stockholders in sale of large blocks of shares.
- Offering gift packages of company products.

Working With Security Analysts.

- Questioning analysts to determine the extent of their knowledge of the company and their attitudes toward the company.
- Arranging analyst meetings with company's executives and tours of plants and research facilities.
- Preparing and distributing informational materials to analysts.

As we can see here, IR and financial communications make up a very specialized and demanding area of public relations. Its practitioners are well paid and are on a fast track to high executive positions.

HOW IR IS PRACTICED AT THE TOP PUBLIC RELATIONS FIRMS

Let's say that a multinational corporation is in the process of acquiring another multinational organization, but many roadblocks must be hurdled before the deal can be finalized. Regulatory agencies must approve many aspects of the acquisition. There may be a proxy contest from a group prepared to better the offer. Dissident stockholders voice their fear of a dilution of their interest. The financial press casts doubts about the efficacy of the deal. The solution: Call in the outside specialists. This may mean giving the assignment to a large public relations firm, or even to a specialist financial PR firm. What can a PR firm accomplish that the multinational can't?

FIGURE 14.1 IR specialists cooperate with others in corporate structure to build better financial communications. (Courtesy PRSA)

Here are some examples:

- Conduct a program that will define and clarify the deal by placing stories in the right media.
- Arrange an international public relations campaign to be implemented by the firm's offices abroad.
- Set up road-show presentations for the top brass of both parties in the merger.
- Use the firm's public affairs and lobbying team to smooth the path in Washington.
- Prepare advertising messages to counter the claims of critical stakeholders.
- Reach the investment community with accurate information about the operations of both parties to the deal.
- Promote the merger on the Internet.

Public Relations Firms Define Their Role in Investor Relations

We scanned the IR practice profiles of a number of large PR firms to come up with some highlights of their programs.

The share price of Ogilvy Public Relations' client McKesson HBOC fell by nearly 50% in 1 day—a result of the first of three earnings restatements. Ogilvy provided crisis communications support. Later, the company's actions were viewed as a triumph of the corporate governance process.

BSMG Worldwide Services works with companies to help evaluate the benefits of mergers and acquisition programs, refocus investment positioning, rebuild investor sponsorship, and repel dissident shareholders.

Edelman Public Relations Worldwide practices financial communications in global markets. Some assignments have been helping Visa International raise awareness of its initiatives in electronic commerce; managing BankBoston's media relations; and promoting Charles Schwab's products and services to consumer and institutional investors.

Burson-Marsteller's IR practice emphasizes the perceptions of a company's management—its depth, strategic focus, and vision. Burson-Marsteller's philosophy is that how well a corporation understands and manages these perceptions can influence investor confidence, resulting in a buy or sell decision.

Fleishman-Hillard guided an unknown startup, the Internet Capital Group (ICG), to success in the uncharted area of business-to-business (B2B). ICG could then position itself as a holding company, making investments in the B2B e-commerce area by helping the building of ICG's business and investments in other e-commerce companies. In 5 months of operation, ICG's portfolio grew to 52 companies.

The Elements of a Major Merger
Between Two Corporate Banking Giants

On September 13, 2000, the consumer banking powerhouse Chase Manhattan announced its plans to acquire J. P. Morgan & Company, an investment banking giant. The price: $30.9 billion in stock.

According to *The New York Times*, September 14, 2000, "The combined J. P. Morgan Chase & Company would have the size to claim a spot among the world's financial titans. It would have about $660 billion in assets, more than 90,000 employees around the world and a stock market value of about $95 billion." The newspaper devoted about 8,000 words to the coverage, including a chart that traced Chase's ownership from Aaron Burr and Alexander Hamilton to the Rockefellers and beyond.

Consider the financial communications and public relations elements of such a major merger. The two banks, their in-house corporate communication and IR teams, and their outside PR counsel firms had to prepare concise answers to dozens of key questions and issues the media would certainly ask about. And all this preparation had to be accomplished with utmost secrecy. Among the media's obvious questions were:

- Who will run the combined company?
- How many employees will lose their jobs?
- What effect will the merger have on the earnings of the combined company?
- Did Chase pay too hefty a price above J. P. Morgan's market price?
- Is investment banking already too crowded?

In an example of sound employee communications, e-mail messages about the deal were sent to thousands of employees of both companies early in the morning of the day the merger was announced to the press. Industry analysts estimated that about 10,000 employees could lose their jobs.

The toughest assignment in a merger of this size and impact for the firm's top management is facing the all-knowing stock analysts, who see the deal's immediate and long-term ramifications the moment the merger is announced. In the Chase–Morgan deal, the CEOs of both companies discussed their proposed merger at an analysts' meeting in New York on the day of the announcement.

In early 2001, the new entity, J. P. Morgan Chase, began trading on the New York Stock Exchange. Its share price held up fairly well and the company continued to pay its premerger dividend.

Financial Stories That Make It to *The Wall Street Journal*

The Wall Street Journal is our largest circulation newspaper—about 1.76 million, just ahead of *USA TODAY*. Its influence in the financial community and among investors is unsurpassed by any other newspaper. A favorable story about a company in the *WSJ* can move its share price 5 or 10 points in a day. The paper receives thousands of financial press releases, yet no one can predict which stories the paper will use and how it will play a particular story. We examined our copy of *WSJ* for January 23, 2001, for some answers:

On page A3 (first section), the headline read:

Dell Warns Net Will Fall Short of Expectations

Dell is the second-largest personal computer maker. Its earnings picture may mirror the whole PC business. The story quoted three security analysts and the company's chief financial officer (CFO). It also mentioned that Michael S. Dell, the company's chief executive, had conference calls with investors on the day of the announcement. This is a common practice in investor relations.

But a newspaper like *The Wall Street Journal* is independent and unpredictable. As part of its coverage of this financial news, it ran a chart titled "Dell's Doldrums," along with the company's not-so-promising previous 9 months' sales picture. Dell, incidentally, had a full-page ad in the same issue the article appeared.

A third story in that day's *Journal* was about the chip maker Texas Instruments, which boasted of a fourth-quarter profit and sales increase. The company's CFO was quoted as saying that Texas Instruments was on track "until the very end." The *Journal*, however, surveyed analysts who said the profit was lower than expectations. The stock dropped 5.5% for the day.

A 25-Year-Old Entrepreneur Makes It in the Venture Capital Business

Page 1 of the business section of the 1.1-million circulation *Los Angeles Times* is a coveted spot for investor relations staffers. The size of a company is only one factor in the business editors' selection process. Editors look for a story angle that will attract the interest of a large percentage of the newspaper's readers, rather than a smaller number of hard-core investors.

On December 18, 2000, page 1 of the paper's business section carried a color photo of a smiling, tieless and jacketless young man, Adam Winnick. The headline below the picture read, "Fund Bolsters University Ideas," and the subhead, "ITU Venture Focuses on Entrepreneurship from Grad Schools."

Now why did this story make the grade? First, Winnick is the 25-year-old son of Gary Winnick, one of the richest men in Los Angeles. Gary Winnick at one time had a net worth exceeding $6 billion, thanks to the rise of his telecommunications firm, Global Crossing. Winnick père invested $5 million in son Adam's business. In total, Adam Winnick's firm had raised $29 million in venture capital for his investment firm, ITU Ventures.

ITU's strategy is to use a network of graduate students and faculty members to find promising new tech ideas. The fund then works with professors and students by providing seed investments ranging from $100,000 to $1 million.

In the first year of its operation, ITU developed networking relationships at MIT, Stanford, and 10 other major universities and had made a $100,000 investment in a small optical and wireless firm founded on Caltech's Pasadena campus.

A story like this one is a slam dunk for a financial communications professional. It has all the right elements—a bright young man with a good concept fostering successful companies on university campuses.

Adam Winnick even knew how to give the right quotes to the reporter covering the story, saying that his company is on the way to building a strong brand, admitting that his family name doesn't hurt, and concluding with, "We're building a reputation here."

Summing Up the Role of an Investor Relations Professional

The investor relations officer (IRO) plays a key role in a publicly traded company's relationship with the financial media, security analysts, portfolio managers, and individual investors.

"On any given day," says Cynthia Clark, assistant professor in the College of Communication at Boston University, "an IRO may need to discuss what's happening with the company's management, its stock, its products, or its inventory."

"An increasingly pivotal issue for an IRO," says Clark, "is disclosure of material information, both qualitative and quantitative, according to the requirement of the Securities and Exchange Commission (SEC). One debatable issue, for example, is whether posting information on a Web site satisfies full disclosure by itself."[2]

IROs must realize that the business press sees the same language every day. It is their job to be different, to write with candor and not hype, and to be fully conversant with the issue, news, or situation presented to the media.

An excellent source of information about investor relations is the National Investor Relations Institute (NIRI). This organization offers text and trade books, reprints of articles, audiotapes, and other valuable information to assist IR professionals in expanding their horizons. Download the NIRI listing at www.niri.org.

THE ANNUAL REPORT

I receive about a dozen annual reports. For the most part, I give each report about a half hour of my attention, although the average reader only spends 300 seconds. I pretty much know how well each company has done financially, so I spend most of the time looking at the graphics and reading some of the text.

Recently, I read a report from the Tribune Company. Tribune is a diversified media company with interests in television and radio broadcasting, newspaper and educational publishing, and Internet services. Tribune also has a 25% stake in the WB television network (home of "Buffy the Vampire Slayer") and the Chicago Cubs baseball team.

The 1999 Tribune annual report, handsomely prepared, was an occasion for the company to boast. It was their eighth consecutive year of growth, the stock had split, and the company had aggressively repurchased some of its own stock, always a sign of financial good health.

One gap in Tribune's fortunes seems to be the Chicago Cubs. The annual report had only a brief reference to the team. Obviously, although Tribune adhered to the Securities and Exchange Commission (SEC) regulations about what was required coverage in its annual report, the Cubs probably failed on the diamond and at the ticket office, so why talk about them?

The Annual Report as Corporate Compass

An article in the June 2000 issue of *Reputation Management* by Stephanie Zschunke comments that although an annual report can make a good first impression or foster negative thoughts about a company, it is, nonetheless, important as a corporate compass and as an investor relations tool.

"In today's free-flowing technology, with up-to-the-minute financial information available on the Internet," says Zschunke, "some executives think the annual report is no longer important. Yet others regard it highly as a communicator of a company's vision, a statement of the company's direction, and a dialogue with potential or present shareholders."[3]

Ted Pincus, chairman of the Financial Relations Board, maintains that annual reports influence prospective stockholders' investment decisions. The report is a branding tool, and it is a company's compass. Done well, an annual report can solidify good public opinion of the company.

A Closer Look at Some Individual Annual Reports

In Stephanie Zschunke's *Reputation Management* article, experts examine a number of 1999 annual reports. Among their comments are these:

DuPont. William Dunk of William Dunk Partners commends DuPont's openness, the company's changed outlook such that from an old-line brick-and-mortar company, DuPont is remaking itself through the Internet, knowledge economy, e-commerce, and strategic alliances. Dunk adds, "This is the first time I would ever accuse DuPont of producing a modern report ... it has a few small graphics and is very easy to read ... it is designed to look like a sketch plan for the future complete with hand-drawn diagrams and a hand-written 'To Do List' on the cover."

DuPont uses the report to enthusiastically explain both the why and how of its changes. Dunk believes this report does a good job tying all the elements of a knowledge economy together.

Southwest Airlines wins the straightforwardness award for the cover of its 1990 annual report. In big, bold white letters on a black

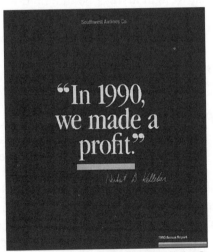

Southwest Airlines Co.

FIGURE 14.2 Designers say the annual report cover is the single most important graphic element. CEOs, they say, should view the cover as seriously as magazine editors do. The cover has to say, "Open me! Read me!" Southwest Airlines' annual report does just that. (Courtesy Southwest Airlines Co.)

background are the words:

> "In 1990, we made a profit"
> [signed] Herbert D. Kelleher
> [Southwest's CEO]

That was the only copy on the report's cover. What stockholder would not open the report and read it!

Southwest Airlines has always projected a funky, informal image in its advertising. Its 1999 annual report is a thin book on heavy stock with graphics in the front around the text, but none to distract from the financial figures. The images and text of the report give the airline a place in history, telling of the significance of the invention of flight alongside the significance of low-cost flight accessible to all, which is what Southwest is all about.

Alongside 500-year-old sketches by Leonardo Da Vinci's feather and inkwell, and then beside compassed sketches by the Wright brothers, to the blueprints of the modern airplane, and, finally to the kitschy collectibles of modern flight (pens, pins, and vacation photographs), the annual report for Southwest Airlines tells the story of the company as a figure in history. The report states, "Wherever the future takes us, we will always be indebted to the dreamers who gave us our first glimpse of the freedom to fly."

"Reading such text," says Hank Moore of the Management Resource Institute in the *Reputation Management* article, "gives a feel-good warmth as if the airline is a staple for our rights. There is a definite sense of company pride and generosity to the public all at once."

There are many people who don't like Nike. They don't like its influence on amateur and professional sports, and many have protested the company's labor practices. Some people don't even like its shoes.

An article in the August 1998 issue of *Inside PR*, titled "Nike Annual Report Shows Company Still Has Sense of Humor," discusses the company's unusual frankness in its 1997 annual report.

The report opens with a simple statement: "Everyone's entitled to an opinion." Then it proceeds to include excerpts from dozens of letters, telephone calls, and e-mails from satisfied and dissatisfied customers.

The letters are set against a backdrop of newspaper headlines: "Hypocrisy Is Nike's Sole Purpose," "Watchdog Group Slams Nike," "Nike to End Ties With Indonesian Companies."

One letter in the report says, "How dare you and your marketing jackals manipulate the world's athletic stage for your own ends." This letter writer has another gripe: "Get on the ball and get the stock price back up to where I paid for it."

These two letters in the report are my favorites:

> "My dad has many of your t-shirts and *colord* shirts. But almost all of his shirts *butins fel* off."

> "I am writing to ask your permission to have a Nike swoosh tattooed on my right butt."

The letter in the report from Nike chairman and CEO Phil Knight to the stockholders contains a single short paragraph defending the company's labor policies, and urges consumers to become better informed rather than just alarmed.

However, while acknowledging that the company has had a tough year, Knight's letter is a forthright piece that begins, "This year produced considerable pain." He then proceeds with a blunt assessment of Nike's problems and a refusal to offer any easy solutions, saying, "We'll have good numbers again. It's just not obvious when."

According to Nike's director of corporate communications, Lee Weinstein, the company's CEO was closely involved in the production of the annual report, which was produced by a team that included a senior writer, the director of investor relations, and a Nike designer.

Annual Reports Come of Age

The Securities and Exchange Commission (SEC) sets the guidelines for annual reports. Certain basic financial information and disclaimers must be included. These guidelines have been mandated for the protection of stockholders. However, companies have increasingly used their annual reports for image-building purposes and to strategically position a company in a particular direction.

What we have also seen in reports is an active effort by corporations to show their responsibility in terms of global and environmental issues. As one designer of annual reports put it, "Companies are now using annual reports to try to answer questions before the questions are asked."[4]

In terms of disclosure, companies are choosing candor instead of cant. In his letter to shareholders, Reynolds Metals Company CEO

William O. Bourke says, "From a business standpoint, 1991 is a year we are glad to have behind us."

Who Does What on an Annual Report

Robert K. Otterbourg is a free-lance annual report writer. In *Public Relations Journal*, in August 1992, he discussed the process of managing a corporation's annual report.[5]

Otterbourg began the process four months before it was to be completed with a meeting between the corporation's president and marketing service vice-president. In what he called a preliminary "no-holds-barred" session, objectives were stated and themes discussed.

At some organizations the corporate communications director will present the finding from focus group sessions with shareholders and financial analysts. Reaction to the effectiveness of the current report helps set the tone for the upcoming one. Later, a detailed and realistic production schedule is set that establishes firm deadlines and delegates responsibility.

The designer of the report is selected early on. Often, an outside graphic design firm is chosen for this assignment.

Perhaps the most important consideration in producing a report is sensitivity to a company's publics and constituencies—shareholders, security analysts, employees, customers, and suppliers.

The public relations manager in charge of the report devotes 6 months to the project. In the first 3 months, he or she works half-time on the project, and in the final 3 months 70%.

Graphics designer Arnold Saks estimates that creativity takes 15% of the effort, and housekeeping and administrative details take up the balance of time required to complete an annual report.

CAREER TIP: INVESTOR RELATIONS—A GROWTH MARKET

IR is an excellent field for MBAs who have writing and PR training. Opportunities exist at both the corporation and PR counsel firms specializing in financial PR. PRSA has an investor relations section for professionals in this specialty. New York University, the University of California at Los Angeles (UCLA), and other colleges offer training programs in investor relations.

CHAPTER 15

Entertainment and Personal Public Relations

Entertainment PR has existed in the United States for as long as there has been entertainment, predating even P. T. Barnum. When Henry Rogers founded his own entertainment PR firm in 1935 with $500 lent to him by his father, there were already three top publicity offices in Hollywood, all run by women.

Those were the days of the powerful Hollywood syndicated columnists Hedda Hopper and Louella Parsons. Breaking into their columns was the ticket to heaven for publicists. Henry Rogers and his partner, Warren Cowan, broke those columns and many others for a roster of clients that included Joan Crawford, Rita Hayworth, Rosalind Russell, and Olivia de Havilland. By 1965, Rogers and Cowan had become one of the preeminent independent publicity agencies in the entertainment industry and, in the process, had given the field a new respectability.

Under the old Hollywood system, the studio was responsible for the publicity of its movies and its contract stars. Once that system was eliminated, the stars engaged their own publicists.

Broadway has always had its publicists who fed the columnists of their day: Walter Winchell, Ed Sullivan, and Earl Wilson. Today, every running Broadway show has a publicist.

For television, the networks typically have staff publicists to plug their shows. The music industry, both east and west, employs publicists tuned to that genre.

Entertainment PR has grown in sophistication since its early days. Publicists of major stars are in power positions. One leading Hollywood publicity agent, Pat Kingsley, and her company, PMK, control access to more than 140 clients, including Tom Hanks, Jennifer Lopez, Courtney Love, Arnold Schwarzenegger, and Nicole Kidman.

PMK has a staff of 40 employees and grosses about $10 million a year. Clients pay firms like PMK estimated fees of $3,500 to $8,000 a month. Studios pay about $10,000 a month to outside PR firms for help with a film's release.

In March 1999, PMK was sold to a giant advertising agency, McCann-Erickson World Group, which is owned by the Interpublic Group of Companies, which, in turn, owns other large public relations firms.

HOW PUBLIC RELATIONS WORKS IN THE MOVIE BUSINESS

Today, movie stars, directors, and even screenwriters have their own publicity counsel. Movie studios also maintain substantial PR staffs, and on a particular picture the production may engage a unit publicist.

Here's what they do:

A personal publicist is hired by an actor, director, screenwriter, producer, or anyone else involved in the entertainment industry to advise on the most effective use of publicity. The client may hire the publicist to oversee just one particular project that he or she wants to draw attention to, or to oversee the client's career on an ongoing basis.

The personal publicist arranges and counsels the client on which interviews to do. Each interview is arranged to serve the client's best interest. When possible, the publicist has a say in who will do the interview, who will take the photograph, and when and how it will be featured in the publication. It is rare to have total control over a situation, but the publicist tries to manipulate the elements to the client's best advantage.

The publicist also advises the client on which personal appearances to make and then makes all the arrangements. This includes award shows, charity benefits, speaking engagements, and public service announcements.

The studio publicist is solely responsible for the studio's roster of films and for publicity that concerns the studio on a corporate level.

The studio publicity department oversees all aspects of a film's publicity and promotion from preproduction, through production, postproduction, and release. This department oversees visits to a movie set by the press, as well as production stories and magazine, newspaper, radio, and television interviews for a film.

The studio publicity department arranges screenings of the film for the press, organizes the film's premiere or other event, and oversees the still photographs used to publicize the film and the electronic press kit. The electronic press kit (EPK) is a video presentation about a film that may include footage of the film in production, interviews with the producer, director, and stars, and any other relevant information that will be useful to the broadcast media. In addition, the studio publicity department is responsible for the production notes on a film, often with information supplied by the unit publicist. These are handed out to the press to give them background on the film and the creative team behind it. Another function of the studio's publicity department is Web-site marketing.

The unit publicist is hired by the production company or the studio to deal with all publicity activities while a film is in production. He or she is likely to be with the film on location on a daily basis. Unit publicists arrange visits to the set by both broadcast and print press. It is their responsibility to see that these visits are not disruptive to production, but still get the job done.

The unit publicist writes the production notes for the film. The notes include information about the evolution of the project, what went on during production with quotes from the creative team, and short biographies of the stars, director, producer, screenwriter, and director of cinematography (and often other behind-the-scenes people). The completed notes are then handed over to the studio.

The unit publicist stays in constant contact with the studio to let it know how things are progressing or if there are any problems that require studio intervention. The unit publicist is also responsible for ensuring that the actors who have photo approval review all the artwork shot by the film's unit photographer in which they are featured, and then make their "kills."

The negative aspects of being an entertainment publicist are similar to those of any other kind of publicist. One deals with a wide variety of personalities, both as clients and as members of the press. Obviously, some are more demanding and difficult than others. Also, the publicist often wishes that he or she had more control over how a story turns out, particularly when it doesn't turn out the way the client hoped it would. Publicists probably average about 50 phone calls a day—some days more.

The entertainment publicity business is based on relationships. A star's appearance as a guest on "The Today Show" is supposed to be worth more than feature stories in *The New York Times* and the *Los Angeles Times* put together. How are such appearances arranged? What are the strategies used?

To arrange any interview, whether print or broadcast, the publicist first begins by calling the contact at the media outlet to sell the story. In television, publicists contact the talent coordinator for a talk show, or the producer for a news or entertainment program. For radio, they contact either the assignment desk for a particular station or radio network or, most often, deal directly with the interviewer. For print interviews, publicists negotiate with the appropriate editor at a newspaper or magazine, or often with a freelance writer who has a relationship with the outlet; then the writer sells the publication on the story.

The publicist needs a good working knowledge of the media: what types of television programs, radio programs, newspaper sections, and magazines are out there. Half the battle is pitching the right person the right angle and evaluating either the individual client or the project and deciding which idea or angle has the best chance of selling.

The Publicists Guild supports the interests and welfare of entertainment publicists. In 1993, the Entertainment Publicists Professional Society (EPPS) was formed. By 2000, EPPS had 220 members.

Satellite Press Tours

A PR office or a studio often contracts this assignment out to a company that specializes in organizing press tours. Then it works with that company to ensure that the kind of interviews it is looking for are secured.

The idea of a satellite press tour is that the client can sit in a television studio in one city and, via satellite, conduct short interviews with television stations across the country. Previously, one would have to travel from city to city. Obviously, a satellite press tour is much more convenient. Most of the interviews publicists look for are on local morning shows ("Good Morning Cleveland") or local news programs, which usually have a short entertainment section.

The Stars and the Media: A Symbiotic Relationship

In recent years we have seen the introduction of dozens of new TV shows like "Entertainment Tonight" and numerous interview shows focusing on entertainment celebrities. There are also magazines with the same orientation, such as *People, Entertainment Weekly*, and *Premiere*.

The surge in entertainment-related television programs and magazines has provided entertainment publicists with a real boon. The competition offers them the opportunity to have more control over a particular interview. If one magazine won't give a publicist the cover, another probably will. Stars become even more in demand because of the number of outlets wanting interviews with them, and publicists can afford to be more particular, thus keeping the client happy.

The increased coverage of entertainment also means that the media are more apt to do stories on lesser-known figures than they were in the past. They are also more interested in doing features on the behind-the-scenes people (directors, producers, screenwriters, etc.) than ever before.

Magazines like *People, Vanity Fair, Premiere, Entertainment Weekly*, and even *Time* and *Newsweek* run pictures of movie stars and other celebrities on their covers. Often, the inside of the magazine has a story about the cover subject. A great deal of money is at stake on the choice. We'll explain why.

Most magazines derive their circulation income from subscriptions and single-copy (newsstand) sales. Advertising rates are based on a magazine's total circulation. And although the number of subscriptions are fixed from year to year, the newsstand numbers vary, depending upon a number of circumstances, often the cover subject.

So, for example, a magazine may distribute 700,000 copies on the newsstand one month with a young actress on the cover, and only sell 250,000 copies. Another month, the publication may run a cover with a trio of hot Hollywood actresses and sell 550,000 copies. Newsstand distribution is carried out on a consignment basis. Because a magazine's advertising rates are set on its total circulation numbers, there are obviously many dollars involved in making the right cover choice.

The movie studios are also in this picture. The right magazine cover of the star of a forthcoming picture may improve the opening weekend box office by many millions of dollars. And stars know that if their picture does well, their asking price for the next picture will go up three or four million dollars.

Publicity agents to the stars are keenly aware of the media's needs and the nation's obsession with celebrity. As a result, they call many of the shots in entertainment journalism.

In an article in *The New York Times*, veteran show biz journalist Bernard Weinraub wrote, "She [Pat Kingsley] shrewdly manipulates and cajoles magazine editors and television executives, and often demands outright that for profiles of her clients, they use preferred interviewers (usually ones who are in awe of stars and will ask softball questions, as well as glossy photographs."[1]

Journalist Catherine Seipp articulated the media/star relationship in an article in *American Journalism Review*: "The dance of mutual dependence between magazines and celebrities has long been a tense tango, with a media culture so carefully choreographed by publicists that celebrities can be shocked [in an interview] when they encounter a rare unpuffy question. It's the equivalent of getting stomped on by a clod trying to lead. But these days the tango seems to be performed by marionettes, manipulated from above by celebrity publicists."[2]

If you're a Hollywood publicity agent, you'll be one of about 3,000 in your profession, and you'll earn a lot less than agents, managers, and attorneys for the stars. Junior associate agents in Hollywood make between $40,000 and $60,000 a year, whereas senior partners in an entertainment publicity firm can earn $100,000 or more.

Other Players in Entertainment Public Relations

Hollywood and Broadway have hundreds of entertainment PR firms, large and small, and some that are one-person operations. Add to this list the in-house publicity staffs of the major studios, the TV networks, and the TV shows themselves.

Baker-Winokur-Ryder, headquartered in Beverly Hills with an office in New York, specializes in motion pictures, television, talent, and technology public relations. The firm is a division of Ogilvy Public Relations Worldwide, which we cover in chapter 4.

Annett Wolf and Lisa Kasteler run a boutique entertainment public relations business with some mighty clients—Meg Ryan, Nicolas Cage, Cate Blanchett, Alec Baldwin, and Samuel L. Jackson.

Most of the top 10 public relations firms covered in chapter 4 engage in the practice of entertainment marketing and communications. For example, Edelman Public Relations represents the IMAX Corporation, Warner Home Video, CBS, Madame Tussaud's Wax Exhibition, and Hard Rock International.

More recently, Edelman's practice took on branding identity programs for top-selling instrumentalist Kenny G, Gloria Estefan's Millenium Concert in Miami, and world champion figure skater Michelle Kwan.

The Rogers & Cowan Story

Earlier in this chapter we referred to the legendary Hollywood public relations firm Rogers & Cowan. This "praisery," as some have called it, goes back to the 1940s. In those early days, they needed stunts to get the ink. In the *Los Angeles Times*, Daniel Akst writes about how Henry Rogers wired one of his first clients, Rita Hayworth, with the news that she had been selected Hollywood's best-dressed offscreen actress by some fashion group he had invented. The stunt landed her on the cover of *Look* magazine before anyone ever wised up.

Cowan reminisces about other memorable "events" in his firm's career. Figuring out that client Julio Iglesias sold more than one million albums in each of six different languages one year, Rogers & Cowan got this snippet of news into the Guinness Book of World Records, and watched in glee as a British paper headlined the story: "Move Over, Beethoven."

In the *Los Angeles Times* article, Akst writes about how, in the early 1960s, Rogers & Cowan created the first celebrity sports tournament for charity, the Frank Borzage Invitational Golf Tournament. Fred Astaire, Mickey Rooney, and Clark Gable played while Marilyn Monroe kept score, and Frank Sinatra landed on the first tee by helicopter to caddy for Bing Crosby.[3]

Today, Rogers & Cowan is owned by one of our top 10 public relations firms, Shandwick International, and has offices in Los Angeles, New York, and London. The firm is divided into nine groups. The personalities group represents film and television personalities, as well as supermodels and fashion designers. In the music group, the client roster includes concert tour promoters, musical artists, and record producers. The other groups include television, motion pictures, fashion/beauty, promotions, product and product placement, special events, and corporate and consumer marketing.

Rogers & Cowan offers career and internship opportunities. For further information, contact Robin Tucker, Human Resources Manager, rtucker@shandwick.com.

PERSONAL PUBLIC RELATIONS

In movieland, it's not only the stars who have publicists. Even Beverly Hills dentists who specialize in smile reconstructions, dog groomers, philanderers and philanthropists, and the chichi landscaper who runs "Affaires of the Garden"—all have spokespersons, or is it spokespeople?

Someone once said, "In Hollywood, even the press agents have press agents—themselves."

The proliferation of publicists is particularly dramatic in Los Angeles, where manufacturing celebrities is an indigenous industry. No one knows exactly how many people work in public relations in the Los Angeles area. There are more than 700 public relations firms listed in the local business directories.

Celebrities and Crises

In her book *Crisis Communications*, Kathleen Fearn-Banks discussed the privacy issues facing celebrities and their public relations representatives. She pointed out that although the Fourth Amendment of the U.S. Constitution grants the right of privacy to all citizens, it excludes "public figures." Thus, the press can divulge information about celebrities as long as it is legitimate news. The determination of "news," however, is a highly debated subject.

A particular problem arises when the celebrity is a spokesperson for a brand or service. Fearn-Banks pointed out three frequent crises that have occurred when a celebrity acts as a spokesperson:

1. Spokespersons inform the public that they do not use or support the product they endorse.
2. Spokespersons are charged with a crime or are publicly associated with illegal or immoral activity.
3. Spokespersons are charged with encouraging crime related to the endorsed product or service.

The author cited as an examples of a celebrity crisis the Beatles' Ringo Starr speaking on behalf of Sun Country wine coolers and subsequently entering an alcohol rehabilitation center.

Pepsi was not upset when its spokesperson, Michael Jackson, the King of Pop, admitted that he didn't drink Pepsi. Instead, he acknowledged that he drank only vitamin-fortified liquids. Pepsi accepted this denial, saying, "It's not important to us whether he drinks it. He has millions of fans who drink it. What's more, Jackson has a Pepsi vending machine at his home that we supply. We presume he serves it to his guests."

A Personal Publicity Master Tells All

In chapter 8, we offered the media relations comments of Howard J. Rubenstein. His firm specializes in keeping celebrities in and out of the press. Here are his answers to three questions I posed to him on personal public relations.

> *Your firm handles many high-voltage personalities such as Donald Trump. Is PR for these clients managed on an issue-by-issue basis, or is it based on a strategic plan? Do their organizations have their own PR departments and, if so, how do you interact with them?*
>
> It is crucial in all accounts, and particularly with so-called "high-voltage" clients, to understand their operations and their objectives. Since these clients are in the public eye, they are inevitably both newsmakers and targets. There must be an overall strategy to ensure that you are moving in the right direction. But every issue must also be evaluated on a day-by-day basis, with continuing input from the client or his designated representative, to meet the internal logic of each situation, to exploit its full potential (or minimize its damage). A number of our clients do have their own PR departments and we work well with them. Basically, we extend their reach.
>
> The important factor is to speak with one voice, theirs or ours, which reflects the best judgments made after appropriate consultation and review.
>
> *How do you work with the trash tabloids that prey on celebrities like Donald Trump?*
>
> We serve as heat shields or buffers, as appropriate, and politely decline any interviews [the clients] may not wish to do. Our clients, in consultation with us, set the ground rules so that we can make informed judgments about how best to serve their interests. Some questions or

allegations don't deserve the dignity of a response. For many, "no comment" will do. For others, it may be important to squelch a rumor or present a position.

As a fast-growing organization, you obviously are increasing staff. Where do you look for new people?

I believe we have a great staff of Tiffany-quality professionals. Many have been with me for many, many years. Among the qualities I value most are the ability to listen well, to understand a client's needs rather than talk a loud, uninformed blue streak; solid business and political judgment; fast and facile writing; adherence to the highest ethical standards, both personal and professional; commitment and a desire to work hard, which is crucial in a service business like ours; and a love of the profession. My top people—and those I continue to seek out—come from government, private-sector companies, other agencies, and the media.

CAREER TIP

Want to make it in entertainment publicity? UCLA Extension in Los Angeles has an outstanding nine-session evening program that covers every phase of this specialization. More than 20 entertainment industry public relations heavyweights serve as guest speakers.

Topics covered include developing a publicity plan for a movie or TV show, the three phases of motion-picture publicity, campaigns for individual actors and other creative talent, music publicity, and new media's importance in the marketing of entertainment products.

This course is a requirement toward the school's entertainment publicity concentration and is an elective credit toward the certificate in public relations.

Contact jrprfr@uclaextension.org.

ACKNOWLEDGMENT

I am grateful for the contribution by the late John West of some of the information in this chapter.

CHAPTER 16

Healthcare Marketing and Communications

Here's a tale of two pills. In December 1998, the pharmaceutical giant Pharmacia received Food and Drug Administration (FDA) approval for the arthritis pain reliever, Celebrex. In May 1999, pharmaceutical giant Merck won FDA approval for another arthritis pain reliever, Vioxx.

The medical benefit of these two new drugs is their capacity to lower the risk of developing ulcers, a problem that exists for arthritis patients taking pain relievers like aspirin and ibuprofen.

The potential here for the makers of Celebrex and Vioxx is enormous. These days it is not uncommon for a successful drug to have annual sales exceeding $1 billion.

An article in *The New York Times*, "Pushing Pills With Piles of Money," by Melody Petersen, told how Pharmacia and Merck spent millions of dollars to gain dominance for their new brands.[1] One promotional technique the two drug companies used was the employment of Bruce Jenner, Dorothy Hamill, and Bart Conner, celebrity athletes who were taking the pain relievers for their sore joints.

TV commercials and print ads aimed at consumers were used extensively, and hundreds of doctors were given fees to speak on behalf of the drugs' benefits in alleviating the pain of arthritis. More than 4,000 representatives of Pharmacia and Merck visited doctors to promote the drugs.

During the first 4 months of 2000, Merck spent $67 million to advertise Vioxx to consumers, more than any company spent to advertise any other drug. The blitz marketing campaign paid off big time. Doctors prescribed the drugs, and patients rushed to their pharmacies to buy them, at a cost of about $86 for a month's supply. By comparison, generic pain relievers on the market cost about $11 for a month's supply.

The sales results for Celebrex and Vioxx far surpassed the previous hot drugs of the late 1990s, Lipitor and Viagra.

When the FDA voiced warnings about the side effects of these new drugs, Pharmacia and Merck launched a massive campaign to educate physicians about the drugs' benefits. Pharmacia, partnered with Monsanto as the maker of Celebrex, enlisted members of the American Gastroenterological Association in a paid effort to encourage people with arthritis to take a quiz to see if they might be at risk for developing serious ulcers from taking Celebrex. Those who were at risk were encouraged to talk to their doctors before taking the new drug.

Free samples of Celebrex and Vioxx were distributed in hospitals, even though claims and counterclaims over both drugs' efficacy were raised. At one point, in late 2000, the FDA told Pharmacia and its marketing partner for the drug, Pfizer, to cut a widely aired TV commercial for Celebrex. It was the third time in 14 months that the FDA had cited Celebrex marketing, addressing improper claims made by the drug's sales representatives. One ad showed arthritic people engaged in such activities as zipping around on scooters. The FDA said that was too much. Nonetheless, the huge promotional and advertising campaigns paid off. The two companies sold about $4 billion worth of the painkillers in 2000.

THE MONEY SPENT ON DRUG ADVERTISING AND MARKETING

An article in *The Wall Street Journal* for January 2, 2001 details the big marketing bucks drug companies spend to promote their products.[2] In 1999, drug companies spent $12 billion on medical journal ads, samples handed to doctors, and other expenses. To reach consumers, the companies spent almost $2 billion on print and television campaigns. TV received by far the largest share of this spending, but newspaper and magazine ads, brochures, and posters got a healthy dose as well.

Balancing the Demands of Diverse Publics

In an article in *Public Relations Journal*,[3] Don Hyman, top PR executive, said that public relations professionals in the pharmaceutical and healthcare business have learned the language of marketing. But there's a lot more to learn, particularly how to deal with consumer advocates, government regulators, and other publics.

Consider the diverse publics involved: multinational corporations, private investors, healthcare professionals, insurance companies, health organizations, government, the managed care industry, patients, and the general public. And in building a positive image for pharmaceutical makers, ways must be found to help consumers become wise patients.

Hyman gave examples of proactive, image-related issues that challenge public relations professionals in the pharmaceutical industry:

- Hazardous waste disposal.
- Animal testing.
- Pricing costly drugs developed for treating AIDS and other politically sensitive diseases.
- Regulating biotechnology research.
- Therapeutic substitution.
- Generic equivalency.
- Product liability.
- Marketing practices abroad.
- National health insurance.

"Finally," said Hyman, "public relations professionals have to develop and implement programs where all sides walk away as winners. They must help guide companies to continue to give back generously and variously to the society they draw profits from. They must engineer situations in which journalists get good stories while physicians and patients get useful, accurate information. They must regulate themselves. If they don't, others will do it for them."

THE LARGEST PUBLIC RELATIONS FIRMS AND THEIR HEALTHCARE PRACTICES

All 10 of the largest public relations firms covered in chapter 4 are active in the health and medical practice area. Some even own specialist firms in this growing field. We offer highlights of these practices.

Ogilvy Public Relations Worldwide

Ogilvy has planned and executed strategic communications programs in virtually all facets of healthcare and for a broad list of clients. Examples include the following.

Cardiology. National Heart, Lung and Blood Institute. Multi-year public education campaigns to help consumers manage risk factors for high blood pressure, cholesterol, heart attacks, obesity, asthma, and sleep disorders.

Oncology. Bristol-Myers Squibb. Prelaunch communications for Orzel, an oral chemotherapy for colorectal cancer.

HIV/AIDS. Glaxo Wellcome. Product marketing for its HIV franchise

Women's health. FDA Office of Women's Health. Social marketing campaign geared to mid-life and older women about using medicines wisely in "Take Time to Care"

Marketing communications. Novartis. To support its CNS (central nervous system) portfolio. Shaped messages and coordinated execution for more than 30 countries for their latest major CNS drug approval.

FKH is a division of Ogilvy that offers specialized communications consulting for the biotechnology industry. The firm also furnishes business development, market research, and strategic consulting services for healthcare clients.

Hill & Knowlton

To be a leader in today's healthcare marketplace, a public relations firm must provide its clients with the kinds of services they do not have in-house. Hill & Knowlton's healthcare and pharmaceutical practice is totally in tune with the fast-paced rhythms of this specialization.

It presents its clients integrated expertise in these key audience sectors:

- *Patient*—HIV/AIDS advocacy groups, women's health organizations, disease education organizations, diversity constituencies.
- *Payer*—managed care organizations, employer coalitions, integrated systems.
- *Pharmaceuticals*—pharmaceuticals, medical devices, biotechnology, animal health companies.
- *Policy*—public health and federal and state legislative contact and regulatory counsel.
- *Provider*—hospitals, health systems, medical groups, physician structures, regional alliances, associations.

In addition to Hill & Knowlton's proficiency in these practice sectors, the firm offers experience in bridging high technology and molecular biology/genomics, and a broad geographical and service-sector reach.

Here are some recent Hill & Knowlton client headlines:

"Study Finds Alzheimer's Indications Early in Life" (*The Wall Street Journal*).
"Online Exchange for HealthCare Companies Could Cut Costs" (*The New York Times*).
"Medical Suppliers Team Up for On-line Exchange for Hospitals" (*Chicago Tribune*).
"Bone Marrow Could Be Endless Source of Nerve Cells (*USA Today*).

Burson-Marsteller

Burson-Marsteller's healthcare practice has a global focus. In practical terms, it means that the firm is positioned to help its clients navigate the new medical, political, social, and economic landscape, creating and managing perceptions that deliver business results. The practice gives clients the ability to translate science into the language and everyday behaviors of people, patients, and politicians.

An example of Burson-Marsteller's healthcare practice is the launch of a drug aimed at the central nervous system, as well as drugs that tackle a variety of virus-related diseases. The firm has also applied its political expertise to ally development and grass-roots mobilization in the healthcare field.

Porter Novelli International

Porter Novelli's strategy is the focusing of close attention on healthcare marketing issues in order to function as a problem solver by utilizing diverse communications strategies to change public perceptions, raise awareness, and increase product sales.

Some of its assignments have been helping smokers around the globe give up the habit, teaching physicians and financial analysts about the life-saving potential new therapies, educating parents about treatments for childhood diseases, and helping ensure fair prices for therapies.

GCI Healthcare

The professionals at GCI Healthcare break down their practice into nine specialized and dedicated services:

Strategic planning and research   Interactive
Advocacy   Corporate
Clinical trial recruitment   Consumer
Media relations   Consensus
Client service

Specifically, GCI's therapeutic category expertise extends to the areas of biotechnology, cardiovascular, consumer health, central nervous system, dermatology, dental, diagnostic, eye care, geriatrics, infectious disease, managed care, nutrition, oncology, and women's health.

Fleishman-Hillard

Fleishman-Hillard's healthcare practice is best exemplified by a Cipra 2000 winning entry, "The Obesity Research Challenge," for clients Knoll Pharmaceutical and the North America Association for the Study of Obesity (NAASO).

Data show that 55% of Americans are overweight or obese, yet media attention is focussed on fad diets and "miracle cures" that often have no legitimate grounding. NAASO attempts to communicate with the public and health professionals about obesity.

Fleishman-Hillard worked with NAASO on the media relations coverage of its annual meeting to communicate the best science about the disease of obesity. Knoll Pharmaceutical Company provided an educational grant to NAASO for support of the annual meeting. This effort increased awareness of the organization and its research. Spokespeople for NAASO were trained to handle on-site and telephone interviews. Five hundred scientific abstracts were presented to health professionals and the public about obesity issues.

Highlights of the NAASO meeting's coverage included seven articles in *USA TODAY*, appearing each day of the meeting, four Associated Press articles, three live appearances on MSNBC "Newsfront," and more than 300 broadcast placements aired about science presented at the meeting.

Edelman Public Relations

Edelman's healthcare practice uses the diverse talents of more than 200 specialists and the global capabilities of numerous complementary practices.

At the earliest stages of a brand's life cycle, the clinical trial, Edelman spearheads the recruitment of candidates for clients like Hoffmann-LaRoche's "flu pill."

Later it disseminates clinical trial data (Eli Lilly), and create groundbreaking professional education programs (CIBA Vision). Finally, when a brand reaches the approval launch and global rollout period, Edelman's healthcare team helps maximize impact.

Edelman's healthcare and reputation management professionals interpret complex scientific issues and benefits and help build a company's most important "brand," its corporate image, for clients such as Pfizer, Cephalon, Merck, and Schering-Plough.

Shandwick International

For many healthcare brands, global product rollouts are a necessity. Shandwick, headquartered in London with offices in 60 other countries, is ideally situated to offer these services. Its reach extends to new healthcare categories like nutraceuticals and biotech products. Shandwick is also expert in exploring new ways of using the Internet to bring information to target audiences, whether they are media or consumers.

Nancy Turett
President, Global Director,
Health

Irene Haas Ph.D.
Managing Director,
Health Communications,
Germany

Mark Deitch
General Manager,
BioScience Communications
Worldwide

FIGURE 16.1 The sophisticated practice of global healthcare requires many so-lutions. Here is a range of Edelman's client activities. Left to right: Introducing the Roche Glucotrend blood sugar monitor in the U.K.; working with Bristol-Myers Squibb on behalf of children with AIDS in Mexico; recruiting patients for flu treatment clinical trials on behalf of Roche Pharmaceuticals; launching Ribena Toothkind in Dublin; reporting on a medical research meeting in Brussels; climbing mountains on behalf of multiple sclerosis and Berlex Laboratories in Argentina. (Courtesy Edelman Public Relations Worldwide)

Ketchum

Ketchum is the seventh-largest agency in the world. It has offices from Chicago to Shanghai and more than 1,200 employees. Its performance in healthcare mirrors the quality of the whole firm.

The pharmaceutical giant AstraZeneca competed against five virtually identical high blood pressure medications with its Atacand products. The assignment called for Ketchum to increase sales force effectiveness, forge relationships with physicians, and establish Atacand as a powerful new choice for managing hypertension.

Ketchum accomplished its client's objectives with "Have a Heart," a grass-roots educational program that enlisted more than 1,800 physicians in 54 cities. Ketchum conducted several programs: "Media Outreach," "Have a Heart Physician Forums," a "Have a Heart Educational Kit," and even a "Hypertension Scorecard" in partnership with regional blood banks.

In a sure sign of success, Atacand's sales for 1999 reached $51 million, exceeding projections by 20%.

BSMG Worldwide

BSMG's medical and health practice serves as marketing communications counsel to companies like Bristol-Myers Squibb, Johnson &Johnson, Pfizer, SmithKline Beecham, and the Pharmaceutical Researchers and Manufacturers of America (PhRMA). The firm's work often begins in the early stages of product development, then moves on to clinical trial recruitment programs, product launches, brand equity development, consumer and professional education, FDA/regulatory support, constituency building, and media relations.

One notable BSMG effort is the milk mustache campaign, which is credited with transforming the national perceptions of milk toward "hip" and "healthy."

Manning, Selvage & Lee Joins with the Upjohn Company in a Campaign Against Diabetes

Manning, Selvage & Lee is one of the world's largest PR firms. It has a formidable healthcare practice. Some years ago, with client Upjohn, the firm launched "Unidos Contra la Diabetes" (United Against Diabetes). Its purpose was to disseminate information to Hispanic Americans about the disease and bring to their attention Upjohn's oral antidiabetes therapy.

Diabetes is the third leading cause of death by disease in the United States.

First, an extensive research effort was undertaken. Some of its findings were:

- Previous campaigns by the American Diabetes Association (ADA) were analyzed.

- The Roman Catholic Church was considered a key ally by virtue of its strength among Hispanics.
- Most family healthcare decisions in the Hispanic community are made by the oldest woman in the family.
- Heavy use of media directed at Hispanics was essential to the program's success.

Planning.

- Two cities with large Hispanic populations, East Los Angeles, California, and San Antonio, Texas, were designated as the target areas of the campaign.
- Local community organizations were recruited, as were doctors and other members of the health professional community in these cities.
- Channels of communication included news media publicity, radio promotion, direct mail, free-standing newspaper inserts, church newsletters, and special community events.

Objectives.

- Motivate 1,000 Hispanic Americans at risk for diabetes to see a health professional for a diabetes evaluation.
- Media coverage was needed to discuss the symptoms, risk factors, and treatments for diabetes.
- Upjohn was to be hailed for its commitment to diabetes education and patient service.
- The total budget for the campaign in both cities was set at $100,000.

Execution. Working with the Los Angeles affiliate of the American Diabetes Association, the Upjohn/Manning team organized the previously mentioned "Unidos Contra la Diabetes," a 6-hour health fair that included patient screening, question and answer sessions with a physician, a nutritionist, and even an exercise expert.

Pre-event publicity included TV and radio interviews with Spanish-speaking physicians and others discussing the warning signs of diabetes. Singer Vicki Carr, a local celebrity, recorded public service announcements in English and Spanish. And an insert promoting "Unidos Contra la Diabetes" was published in eight separate Spanish-language daily and weekly newspapers.

San Antonio's "Strike Out Diabetes Night" was coordinated by the local affiliate of the American Diabetes Association and had the participation of the local San Antonio Missions baseball team, Catholic church leader Archbishop Patricio Flores, radio stations, and a preevent media tour by baseball Hall of Fame pitcher Jim "Catfish" Hunter, a diabetic himself.

Evaluation. In Los Angeles, nearly 1,000 Hispanic Americans attended the "Unidos Contra la Diabetes" event, 563 people were evaluated for diabetes, and 85% were found by ADA staff to be at risk for diabetes and referred to Spanish-speaking physicians for further testing and evaluation at no charge. In addition, media relations efforts about diabetes education yielded 4.4 million impressions in local TV, radio, and newspapers.

In San Antonio, 3,000 attended the "Strike Out Diabetes Night." More than 1,500 people were evaluated, of which 12% tested positive and were referred for treatment. Nationwide, the program received coverage on the Univision Hispanic network and in *Hispanic* magazine.

On the strength of its success in these two cities, the following year the program was extended to Miami.

For its "Unidos Contra la Diabetes" campaign, the Upjohn Company and Manning, Selvage & Lee were awarded a 1989 Silver Anvil Award in the category of special public relations programs.

When a PR Push Goes Too Far

Here's how a company's scare tactics raised public concerns but rubbed some doctors the wrong way.

The thought of having to undergo any surgery is fearsome. But what about waking up on the operating table, conscious but unable to move or speak as the surgeons keep cutting?

An article in *The Wall Street Journal* tells about what anesthesiologists call "intraoperative awareness," a real phenomenon in which an anesthetic wears off, leaving patients awake but still under the influence of paralytic drugs, perhaps even in pain.[4]

In 1998, Aspect Medical Systems brought out its Bi-spectral Index Monitor (BIS), a device that can reduce such occurrences by measuring the brain's electroencephalograph (EEG) signals and the effects of anesthesia.

In the 2 years after the FDA approved the device, more than 800 hospitals, 15% of the U.S. total, purchased it and Aspect's stock zoomed. A single BIS unit costs $8,900, plus as much as $15 per use for the disposable sensors.

As soon as Aspect's BIS began being ordered, the company escalated its promotional and marketing efforts, with a PR campaign to inform the public about intraoperative awareness. But many doctors said that Aspect's claims misled hospitals and patients into believing that the monitor "prevented" intraoperative awareness. Further, to sell the BIS monitor aggressively, Aspect's sales staff even warned doctors that they might face malpractice suits if they didn't adopt the device.

Finally, Aspect backtracked on some of its claims and even informed the American Society of Anesthesiologists that it would shift the focus of its media coverage. But the company continued to market the product by distributing fact sheets to hospitals and the press describing the device as a "solution" to the problem of intraoperative awareness.

Inevitably, once the public perceived the possibility of being awake during surgery, a flurry of lawsuits was brought against hospitals for failure to use the BIS monitor.

To add to the controversy, the chairman of the anesthesiology department at the University of California at San Diego said that use of the BIS monitor might actually increase intraoperative awareness by encouraging doctors to use minimal anesthesia.

Breathe Easy About Benadryl and Sudafed

In a September 12, 2000, issue of *The New York Times*, a full-page ad for Sudafed and Benadryl proclaimed: "Concerned about the recent FDA statement about certain cold medicines?"[5]

Below the graphic of the products was the line: "Every Sudafed and Benadryl product is PPA-free."

Because PPA (phenylpropanolamine) has received a great deal of negative publicity about increasing risk of strokes, it was necessary for Pfizer, manufacturer of Sudafed and Benadryl, to take a positive stand in promoting its cold and allergy medicines. The ad's copy stated that these two products never have and never will contain PPA.

When Healthcare Advertising Meets Healthcare Editorial

An *advertorial* that runs periodically in *The New York Times Magazine* is titled "From Cause to cure." One recent edition had a cover photo of a smiling senior citizen and cover lines that read, "Heart Disease and Hypertension, Cholesterol Levels: What the Numbers Mean, Can Diet Curtail Hypertension, and Congestive Heart Failure: Innovative Treatments Bring Hope."

The inside of the 20-page insert included ads from a number of hospitals with renowned heart centers; the American Heart Association; and PhRMA, the umbrella organization for many of America's pharmaceutical companies.

But here's where a person trained in medical esthetics or a media critic may fault the premise of the insert. The Merck Company, makers of the cholesterol-lowering drug Zocor, ran a three-page ad in the insert. This raises a number of questions. Do the hospitals who advertised in the insert recommend Zocor as the most effective medicine in the treatment of heart disease? What about all the other drugs that treat this disease? And, finally, does the designation "Advertisement" in tiny type at the top of each advertorial page clarify to the reader that the information was written by participating advertisers, not the editorial staff of *The New York Times*?

A Noteworthy Healthcare Public Relations Campaign

We searched the Web site of PRCENTRAL for outstanding public service campaigns by pharmaceutical companies and other organizations. Here are highlights of one outstanding campaign.

America's Awakening With Eli Lilly. One percent of Americans, more than 2.7 million people, suffer from schizophrenia, and until recently there was no hope for a cure or a reduction in the number of people developing the disease.

It took a partnership of the Chamberlain Communications Group (CCG), "Dateline NBC," the National Mental Health Association (NMHA), the National Alliance for the Mentally Ill (NAMI), Fountain House, and Eli Lilly and Company to build a schizophrenia educational program with these objectives:

- Destigmatize schizophrenia in the minds of Americans.
- Build support for the use of newer medicines to treat schizophrenia.

- Awaken America to the hopes, aspirations, and successful return to society of those living with severe mental illness.

The vehicle chosen to tell the schizophrenia story to a large audience was the "Dateline NBC" documentary "Awakening." It told the story of Luca Moylan, a 25-year-old with schizophrenia.

With the help of new medications, a loving mother, and the tender care of his physician, Dr. Ralph Aquila, Luca was successfully reintegrated into society and was able to take classes at a community college.

Chamberlain Communications Group's promotional team decided to use "Awakening" to localize Luca's story across America. The team selected Friday, August 20, 1999, as "America's Awakening."

Segment producers at NBC affiliate stations across the country were contacted about carrying the show on this special date. CCG staff traveled the country conducting media training sessions to prepare physicians and patients to appear on local broadcasts tied in with the showing of "America's Awakening" on the special date. CCG also teamed with local independent public relations firms to manage the event nationwide. Nearly 30 physician/patient teams were interviewed on NBC affiliate stations on August 20, the day of the telecast.

NBC introduced CCG to local market producers, health reporters, and assignment-desk editors, encouraging them to develop local companion feature stories. CCG was to be the resource to coordinate interviews with local physicians and patients.

One benefit that NBC News offers its viewing audiences is a compendium of background information on segments that air on its programs. "Dateline NBC" posted this information on MSNBC's Web site about schizophrenia around the time of the airing of "America's Awakening."

To assure print media coverage of the show, CCG conducted comprehensive media outreach to leading newspaper across the country. The efforts paid off. Favorable reviews were carried in *The New York Times*, the *New York Post*, the *Los Angeles Times*, the *Arizona Republic*, and *The Newark Star-Ledger* on the day the "Dateline" segment aired.

The measured audio for the show was 15.6 million people. "Dateline NBC" won its time slot on August 20, and a total of 27 NBC stations ran local stories, featuring successfully reintegrated patients.

The powerful message conveyed in the show for those living with schizophrenia, those caring for them, and the millions of Americans watching "America's Awakening" was that with newer medications and the right kind of support from family and physicians, a return to normal life is possible.

CHAPTER 17

Crisis Communications and Management

In Chapter 4, we wrote that when disaster strikes, the job of PR is to assess the situation and the damage quickly, to assemble all the facts and background information, and to offer them to the news media, along with the "public's" response. This practice becomes increasingly complex when a large population is involved and when a hostile group is suspected of criminal activity.

On September 11, 2001, New York's World Trade Center towers and a section of the Pentagon were demolished by suicide air attacks carried out, it is believed, by the terrorist followers of the exiled Saudi militant, Osama bin Laden. Thousands were killed.

In early October 2001, in a development possibly related to the World Trade Center disaster, the tabloid publisher, American Media, Boca Raton, Florida, received an anthrax-spiked letter. Seven of its employees were exposed. One died, and another was hospitalized with an anthrax infection.

Later, similar incidents occurred at the New York offices of NBC's Tom Brokaw, CBS's Dan Rather, and the ABC network, fortunately with no deaths.

Soon, panicked New Yorkers were taking antibiotics before being tested for anthrax exposure, and purchasing gas masks, protective full-body suits, and germicidal wipes to protect against this biological scourge.

Since the World Trade Center attack and the anthrax detections occurred on his beat, New York's mayor, Rudolph W. Giuliani, took the reins of his city's PR response to the biological crisis. He conducted daily press conferences where he answered dozens of questions and implored New Yorkers not to panic. According to *The New York Times*, the mayor "sought to balance the appetite for information against the potential for hysteria." To the media, he was carrying out a cautious but sound campaign against fear.

In a crisis of this magnitude, the public relations arms of these government agencies and departments came into play: the Bush White House, the Centers for Disease Control and Prevention, the attorney general, the secretary of health and human services, and the F.B.I. Add to this list from the private sector: Bayer, the maker of the anti-biotic Cipro; and NBC, ABC, and CBS, the three networks where the contaminated letters were sent.

CRISIS AT COLUMBINE

It was a terrifying example of the violence that pervades our society—from the streets to the schoolyard—and it happened in a suburban high school just outside of Denver in April 1999.

Two heavily armed students, clad in dark ski masks and wearing long black coats, went on a killing orgy, setting off homemade bombs outside the school, then gunning down students, and finally using the guns on themselves. The tragedy at Columbine will long be remembered as the worst high school shooting in U.S. history.

In the aftermath of the terror, many questions were asked: Should the two students' odd behavior and Nazi-like clothing have attracted more attention from the school authorities, and why did more than 200 heavily armed SWAT team members and other police officers in body armor stand around discussing strategy while hundreds of children were inside?

Out of the carnage at Columbine, the crisis management efforts of the team at Jefferson County Public Schools' communications services team stands out. For this achievement, the team won the Public

Relations Society of America's Silver Anvil Award 2000 in the category of crisis management.

Rick Kaufman, leader of the Columbine Crisis Communications Response Team, became a familiar presence in national media crisis coverage. One of the first people on the scene at Columbine High School, he coordinated strategic communications about the crisis and its aftermath, plus the 1-year recovery and healing efforts.

Kaufman worked with the various law enforcement and emergency response teams on site, as well as the more than 700 national and international media outlets. He currently serves as district spokesman for all Jefferson County Schools. Previously, he directed the public relations programs for two of the largest school districts in Wisconsin, served as a special consultant with the Wisconsin Department of Public Instruction, and is a past president of the Wisconsin School Public Relations Association.

Accredited by the National School of Public Relations Association (NSPRA), Kaufman is the recipient of NSPRA's Gold Medallion for crisis management, and he was honored by being named the public relations professional of the year. The team at Jefferson County Schools received the Public Relations Society of America's Silver Anvil for crisis communication.

We reprint here the text of Rick Kaufman's winning entry.

THE COLUMBINE TRAGEDY: MANAGING THE UNTHINKABLE—JEFFERSON COUNTY PUBLIC SCHOOLS

Silver Anvil Awards '00—Category 11B Crisis Management

Research

- Assisted, prior to the tragedy, in the development of district crisis management plan, including an emergency response checklist of steps for the first 24- to 48-hour period after a crisis.
- Consulted with school administrative and PR officials from each of the prior school shooting sites, and with the National School Public Relations Association, the National Organization of Victims Assistance, and the Crisis Prevention Institute to identify strategies of crisis response and management.
- Organized briefing with district management team, school board officials, employee association representatives, and community leaders to review responsibilities outlined in the crisis

management plan including the establishment of two command centers—an on-site communications center (near Columbine) and a central operations center.

- Participated in daily briefings with law enforcement, state and federal emergency management agencies, and governmental groups to coordinate the ongoing crisis response and management.
- Created database of media outlets that contacted the district for information and interviews, and used this list to distribute updates on the district's response to the tragedy and its efforts to help the community heal and return to normal. The media list is used today to distribute information on how the school's students and staff and the community are healing and moving forward.
- Analyzed media coverage daily throughout the crisis to evaluate how Jeffco Public Schools' messages were received and to assess changes in media attitude and public perception.

Planning

The Jefferson County Public Schools' Communications Services team developed a crisis communication structure that established key duties and protocols in a crisis. This plan was adapted as a result of the nature and magnitude of the Columbine High School tragedy and continues to be revised to reflect lessons learned from this tragedy and its aftermath.

Communications Objective. The overall public relations objective throughout the crisis was to quickly adjust the school district and community's position from one of response and reaction to one of proactive control, enabling the team to aid in school and community healing. To attain this objective the Jeffco Public Schools' Communication Team:

- Provided on-site guidance and leadership to students and staff.
- Developed key communication vehicles to reassure parents and the community.
- Strengthened proven strategies to propel those affected beyond the crisis to learn and grow stronger.
- Communicated the school and district's point view with professional grace and insight.
- Reinforced the healing process while aiding in return-to-education objectives.
- Cultivated a sense of triumph in the face of tragedy.

While juggling demands from the news media at an unimaginable rate, the driving force behind every decision and event remained the need to help students and staff heal and return to the learning process as quickly as possible.

Another objective was to demonstrate and emphasize the school district's commitment to the emotional and physical needs of affected staff, students, and the families of the murdered and injured students and teacher.

Strategies.

- Implemented a crisis communications command structure. The structure designated primary functions for managing the crisis, including strategic communication counsel, internal and external communication, media management, research and media monitoring, event management, and coordinating volunteers.
- Created several methods for communicating with parents, students, employees, business and community leaders, political and governmental officials, and the public and continually updated those methods for efficacy.
- Responded promptly and honestly to questions for information and interviews from the media, and anticipated changes in news cycles and demands.
- Apprised daily all staff throughout the 89,000-student district of the status of the investigation and recovery milestones.
- Spoke with "one clear voice" and "stayed on message" as determined by the district's management team and developed by the district's communications team.

Target Audiences. Parents, students, faculty and staff, media, state and federal legislators, the Jefferson County community, and the residents of Colorado.

Budget. No organization can adequately budget for a crisis of this magnitude; however, the estimated cost to the Communications Services office is $150,000 in strategic planning counsel and assistance; development of materials; research; telephone, computer, and fax lines; cellular phone use expenses; duplication of materials; and postage.

Execution

The Jeffco Public Schools' Team consisted of six professional and support staff when the tragedy struck, but received volunteer assistance from members of the Colorado and National School Public Relations

Associations. We responded to more than 1,000 inquiries a day from local, national, and international media outlets, for the first 4 weeks after the crisis, and continue to maintain contacts to update media about recovery efforts. We coordinated the media efforts for the special first day back to school event in August 1999, and are currently planning to mark the anniversary on April 20, 2000, We also:

- Managed all communications, including twice-daily press conferences and daily fact sheets and news releases, distributed throughout the state and nation. Drafted daily talking points for district spokespeople.
- Established one-on-one opportunities with local reporters to interview key district personnel involved in the recovery efforts, and to strengthen the relationships with local journalists who would be here long after the national and international media left.
- Created weekly talking points for administrative staff at 143 other district schools to share with staff and parents.
- Met daily with legal and administrative management teams to formulate key messages and address emerging issues.
- Created a community hotline designed to accept offers of monetary contributions and donations of materials and services from around the world. In the first 3 weeks after the crisis, we received over 1,000 phone calls a day.
- Assisted in the development of the Columbine Tribute Web Page, and created a videotape showing the positive images of recovery to replace the negative images that were repeatedly aired on local and national media.
- Coordinated special events, including two large memorial services, separate visits by President Bill Clinton and Vice-President Al Gore, tours of the reconstructed school, and the "Take Back Our School" first day school assembly.
- Developed a presentation—"The Columbine Crisis: Managing the Unthinkable"—for school district officials, emergency responders, and law enforcement officers.

Evaluation

The school district's communications management team personnel did their solemn, professional best in a difficult situation and emotional environment. In the ongoing efforts, we continue to focus on our mission to help students, staff, and the community heal and recover, and share the story of our efforts with all key audiences. Further examples of how we continue to achieve our objectives are:

- We always kept the feelings of the victim's families in the forefront. Today many of our district leaders have personal relationships with families of the murdered and injured students and teachers based on our work with them.
- Target audiences read or saw Jeffco Public Schools' messages in more than 1,550 print stories (primarily local and large national publications) and 450 broadcast stories. A database of all the media coverage has been created, and currently encompasses 700 pages.
- Public perception both locally and nationally was positive and supportive of the district's crisis response, based on letters from the President of the United States, private organizations, national media, and community sentiment.
- A strong working relationship was developed with the Jefferson County Sheriff's Office, the Jefferson Center for Mental Health, the Jeffco and Federal Emergency Management agencies, and the FBI.
- Hundreds of requests have been received from organizations for crisis management training. Members of the district's communications and management teams have presented over 50 seminars and training sessions since August 1999. Organizations requesting presentation/training include the FBI, Fidelity Investments, Los Angeles County law enforcement agencies and school districts, and the American Association of School Administrators, to name a few.
- A special "Welcome Back-to-School" event and picnic for all staff was developed to celebrate the accomplishments of recovery. Over 2,000 staff attended the event, which included the planting of a tree and placement of a commemorative plaque on a large boulder in memory of Dave Sanders, the only teacher killed in the April tragedy.
- Program refinement based on media analysis and community needs.

VACCINATING AGAINST "MAD CORN DISEASE"

An article in PRSA's TACTICS August 2001 issue details how two public relations professionals handled a crisis situation of ominous proportion.

Crises do not provide you with a timeline. They happen when you are least prepared and most occupied with other matters. Crises do not provide you with a comfort zone or a finite conclusion. What a crisis, properly understood and handled, can provide you with, however, is *opportunity*. The most well-known example of a crisis turned positive is the deft handling of the Tylenol scare by Johnson & Johnson. The most current case study is how Mission Foods dealt with unapproved genetically modified (GM) corn found in its taco shells that led to the largest food recall in U.S. history.

StarLink Ain't Tuna

GM corn was first produced in the early 1990s. For farmers, GM corn helps eliminate the need for widespread spraying of pesticides and also significantly increases crop yield—helping to keep corn prices low and allowing the American farmer to feed the world. Every GM corn variety is registered with the Environmental Protection Agency (EPA) and certified as safe for human consumption.

In 1998, a new kind of GM corn with a new kind of protein was certified by the EPA for use as animal feed and for industrial purposes. The genetically modified protein was called Cry9C, and the new corn hybrid (developed by Aventis, a French company) was named StarLink. The EPA approved StarLink for animals and industrial usage—but not for human consumption. The reason StarLink was not approved for human consumption is that the Cry9C protein acts as an insecticide, and all the required safety data—specifically, whether StarLink might cause an allergic reaction in humans—was not available.

As part of the EPA certification, Aventis and its distributors were required to manage and monitor the StarLink harvest to ensure that it went only to animal feed and industrial customers (i.e., for use as ethanol). With this limited EPA approval, Aventis introduced StarLink into the American market.

The Controversy Erupts

Friends of the Earth, an environmental activist group, held a press conference on September 18, 2000, and revealed that testing (conducted for them by Genetic ID, a well-respected international genetics testing company), had detected the presence of StarLink in a wide variety of products manufactured by Mission Foods, the largest producer of Mexican food products in the United States.

The press conference resulted in one of the largest food product recalls in U.S. history—over 300 yellow corn products ranging from taco chips to tortillas (StarLink is a yellow corn).

The impact of the recall was as traumatic to Mission Foods as it was sweeping. Besides switching over to 100% white corn production and dealing with the many tactical issues involved in a massive retail-level recall, lawsuits were filed, sales began to suffer—and the media began to call. Merrie Spaeth, president of Spaeth Communications, and Peter J. Pitts, managing partner of Wired World (a strategic marketing communications firm with expertise in crisis management) were called in to develop and implement a crisis communications plan.

First, Spaeth and Pitts developed an honest Q&A to detail "what Mission Foods knew and when did they know it." They advised that being as open and honest as possible with the press was the only credible strategy. Second, they wrote a position paper on the issue so that the media would begin reporting on what *should* happen—rather than on what was happening. After all, the media reports what is made available to them and, in the absence of new news, will continue to report on what it already knows.

In the wake of a crisis, Spaeth and Pitts explained, the press is looking for what is going to happen next. Mission Foods, by talking about how to solve the problem, refocused the attention of the press by positioning the company as the expert rather than the perpetrator. Lastly, Spaeth and Pitts positioned the recall of all yellow corn products and the move to 100% white corn as "the only responsible thing to do."

Further, they urged Mission Foods to identify and speak directly to the audiences most important to them: 1) their customers (food retailers); 2) consumers; 3) government regulators; and, most importantly, 4) the thousands of Mission Foods employees nationwide. All messages were crafted to have a positive impact on one or more of these key constituencies.

Spaeth and Pitts developed the position that the recall was driven by prudence. "Since we can't be 100% sure we decided to be 100% safe" was the sound bite developed for Mission Foods and reported widely in the national press.

Statements to the press (reported in news media ranging from *The New York Times* and *The Wall Street Journal*, to "NBC Nightly News" and National Public Radio) that "Mission Foods is becoming a 100% white corn company until the government can guarantee the safety of the national yellow corn supply" helped move Mission Foods to the "White Hat" position, the responsible industry leader—a position that Spaeth and Pitts then moved to reinforce and enhance.

On December 6, 2000, Mission Foods sponsored and participated in "The StarLink Summit," a public policy conference held by the Hudson Institute, a leading national think tank with an international reputation for its work in the field of agricultural innovation. The keynote address was delivered by Mission Foods CEO, Irwin Gordon. Mission Foods was now dealing with its target audiences through the media rather than having the media control the boundaries of the conversation.

Without side-stepping the controversy, Gordon called for an open and honest debate about the broader issues of biotechnology, firmer and more coordinated government oversight, and the need to restore public confidence in the national food supply. His remarks (penned by the Spaeth/Pitts team) calling for "moderation and sound science" were widely reported by the national press and "inside-the-Beltway" publications.

Result? Mission Foods was now firmly perceived as holding the role of responsible leader—a significant turn-around from the earlier days of the recall imbroglio.

Spaeth and Pitts also led a lobbying effort in Washington D.C., first contacting the 15 Congressional Representatives with Mission Foods factories in their districts, as well as members of the Agriculture and Science committees. The Mission Foods message was as consistent as it was powerful: "All parties must work together to solve the problem."

Mission Foods acted swiftly and smartly, receiving kudos from unexpected places, such as Friends of the Earth, who said that Mission Foods, "moved quickly and thoroughly." The FDA declared that the actions of Mission Foods were both "responsible and prudent." And customers voted with their pocketbooks—positively. Mission Foods is now regarded by its peers in the food industry as well as by advocates and regulators as the experts in dealing with the delicate issues of bioengineered food—from labeling to responsible testing and quality assurance programs.

In the meantime, in a bitterly negative counterpoint, Aventis—the firm that developed StarLink—chose to stonewall the media throughout the crisis, earning the enmity of the press and government regulators. Top executives were fired. Market share was lost. Industry confidence was eroded. Lawsuits began mounting.

The guiding principle throughout the crisis was to behave in an honorable and ethical manner. As Irwin Gordon said in his nationally covered speech, "The ethical decision is always the best business decision."

How's business for Mission Foods? It's never been better, and approval for the firm's ethical behavior is high among all of their target constituencies. And, rather than having a divisive impact among employees, the crisis served as a positive experience, teaching colleagues to work together and develop pride in their company's position.

For their counsel on the StarLink crisis, which could have had an explosive impact—but was resolved by swift and decisive crisis management—Spaeth and Pitts were awarded the 2001 Silver Spur from the Texas Public Relations Association.

Peter J. Pitts is president of Indianapolis-based Wired World.

Merrie Spaeth is president of Dallas-based Spaeth Communications.

A SEMINAR FOR PROFESSIONALS ON CRISIS COMMUNICATIONS STRATEGY

James E. Lukaszewski is one of American public relations' most quoted and prolific authors/crisis communications management consultants. In March 2001, Lukaszewski conducted a 2-day seminar for PR professionals sponsored by PRSA in New York on the subject Crisis Communication Strategy. Although newcomers to the industry will not be required to take responsibility for crisis situations, it is nevertheless important to understand the implications, response strategies, and practical applications of this vital component of PR practice.

Seminar Overview

Crisis means victims and explosive visibility. Bosses need trusted advisors who can offer focused, pragmatic, useful advice that helps them deal with difficult situations strategically and immediately, while limiting collateral damage. Using powerful case examples, participants will explore crisis communications management problems and strategies while immersed in the same management struggles, confusion, dilemmas, and moral challenges managers face. Case studies involve managing victims; reducing litigation; recovering reputation; healing corporate wounds; dealing with organized opposition; selectively engaging the media; Web attack survival; and influencing employee, community, and public attitudes.

Seminar Outline

> Defining crisis from management's perspective.
> Establishing a crisis communication policy.
> Setting priorities in crisis communication response.
> Understanding the patterns crises always present.
> Problem simulations:
>> Activist attack.
>> Web attack.
>> Local incident with national implications.
>> Product recall.
>> Workplace shooting.
>> Meeting with angry neighbors.
>> Organized professional anticorporate attack.
>> Criminal indictment.
>> Class action lawsuit.
> Response strategies:
>> Containment.
>> Control.
>> Preemption.
>> Counteraction.
> Practical application:
>> Avoiding the classic mistakes.
>> Indentifying the crisis management model that fits your organization.
>> Providing crucial counsel to senior management.
>> Dealing with the ethical dimensions of crisis.

THE MOST FREQUENT TYPES OF CRISES

A crisis such as the Columbine tragedy has deep emotional impact and, for the students and their parents, a slow recovery. Yet there are other crises, perhaps less grave for individuals, but of serious consequence to corporations and other groups. We list a number of examples:

Aquisitions
Age discrimination
Alcohol abuse
Bankruptcies
Boycotts
Bribery
Contamination
Controversial legislation
Drug abuse, drug trafficking
Earthquakes or natural disasters
Economic espionage
Embezzlement
Explosions
Fatalities
Fires
Floods
Government investigations
Hostile takeovers
Hurricanes
Industrial accidents
Insider trading and corporate mismanagement
Kickbacks
Kidnapping
Labor/management strife
Lawsuits and legal challenges
Layoffs and plant closings
Mergers
Murders
Negative media reports
Negative or controversial legislation
Nuclear accident in an energy plant
Oil spills
Product failures, tampering, and recall
Protest demonstrations
Racial issues
Reduced earnings
Riots and civil unrest
Robbery
Sex discrimination and harassment
Suicides

Tax problems
Terrorism
Toxic waste
Transportation accidents or failures
Workplace violence

According to Bill Cantor in his book *Experts in Action: Inside Public Relations*,[1] the recent emergence of crisis management as a recognized specialty field within public relations suggests that crises are occurring more frequently than in the past. He offered these reasons chiefly responsible for the phenomenon:

- The technological revolution ushering in the age of instant communications.
- The resulting preeminence of the electronic media as the main source of news for most of the industrialized world.
- Changes in the manner of news coverage, largely related to the electronic media's insatiable demand for drama.
- The rise of citizen activist groups and coalitions that have stimulated public investigation of institutions and government regulation of their activities and operations.
- Greatly increased access to the media by these activists organizations.

What Happens When Crisis Management Fails

Cantor listed some of the potential results of mismanaged emergencies and crises:

- Long-term damage to the organization's reputation with resulting loss of confidence in its management by investors, customers, and employees.
- Continuing employee morale deterioration, labor relations problems, and recruitment difficulties.
- Adverse impact on stock prices and investor relations.
- Waste of management time and financial resources by prolonged preoccupation with crisis issues.
- Political intervention resulting in excessive government regulation, increased scrutiny of other activities and operations, and punitive actions.

- Costly litigation (even if ultimately successful!).
- Involuntary bankruptcy or reorganization.
- Community relations problems.

Other Prominent Crises

Prominent crises we have witnessed in recent times include:

Bhopal, India, 1984: Thousands died from a gas leak in a Union Carbide plant.

Chernobyl, 1986: The explosion of a nuclear reactor in the former Soviet Union, resulting in many deaths and the spread of radiation throughout Europe.

Los Angeles, April 1992: The looting and arson following the verdict on the Rodney King police brutality trial, causing the deaths of more than 50 people and property loss of more than $750 million.

World Trade Center, February 1993: A terrorist bombing that killed 6 people and injured 1,000.

TWA Flight 800, July 1996: Plane crash off coast of Long Island, New York, killing all 230 people on board.

Brown & Williamson Tobacco, 1999: Whistle-blower Jeffrey Wigand's exposé, the "60 Minutes" coverage, and "The Insider" movie.

A CRISIS OF EPIC PROPORTIONS

On March 24, 1989, the *Exxon Valdez*, an oil tanker more than three football fields in length, with a cargo of 11 million gallons of crude oil, was headed from Prince William Sound in Alaska to Long Beach, California, when it struck a reef and ran aground. The spill would become the worst environmental disaster in U.S. history, killing 2 million animals in its aftermath.

Exxon Valdez created a public relations crisis of massive proportions. An investigation determined that the captain of the *Exxon Valdez* was drunk at the time the ship hit the reef. Exxon's CEO used bad judgment in not taking charge and visiting the site of the accident immediately.

The operators of the oil terminal in Alaska moved sluggishly in dealing with the spill. Exxon's official response to the media was criticized for not being forthright in addressing all the issues. Press statements were contradictory, and, as a result, the company's reputation was tarnished. It would take years and billions of dollars for Exxon to finally settle the case with the State of Alaska, Alaska fishermen, and other Alaskans. We recommend Kathleen Fearn-Banks's book *Crisis Communications: A Casebook Approach* for consummate coverage of this momentous crisis.

DOW CORNING'S HARSH LESSON IN CRISIS MANAGEMENT

In 1992, Dow Corning was a $1.8-billion-a-year corporation whose primary business was the development of space-age silicone materials for the aerospace and electronics industries. In total, the company made about 5,000 silicone products, one of which was a breast implant.

Although it had been on the market since the 1970s, problems didn't erupt till the 1990s when women who had the implant began having medical problems cause by leakage of the silicone gel that had seeped out of the implant's envelopes.

When Dow Corning stonewalled the issue, and appeared inadequately concerned about the users' complaints, lawsuits proliferated, and the U.S. Food and Drug Administration began its own investigation. What made things worse for Dow Corning was the release of documents showing that it had known about the leakage for 20 years, but believed that it would not cause health problems.

And, of course, media and the investment community were well aware that Dow Chemical, the parent company of Dow Corning, had had similar predicaments with its Agent Orange, a defoliant that caused serious health problems in Vietnam veterans.

Finally, in March 1992, Dow adopted a proactive stance. It appointed a new CEO who set up advisory groups of women who have the implants, and considered that Dow Corning should pay for the removal of the implants for women who couldn't afford it. Many observers felt that the company moved too late for effective damage control.

For further information on this case, the reader is directed to the chapter "Crises of Deception" in *The Crisis Manager* by Otto Lerbinger.[2]

DEALING WITH CRISES

When confronted with disasters like these and others discussed in this chapter, an organization must be prepared to institute crisis management practices. Part of that management consists of communications with the media, stockholders, and the organizations various publics.

Companies and institutions with crisis communications programs generally deal with crises as follows:

- A crisis communications team is identified.
- The crisis team assesses the situation.
- Spokespersons, usually people specifically trained in this demanding function, are chosen.
- Key messages, such as "We will provide the media with updated information as soon as it is available," are identified.
- Communications methods are determined.
- The company rides out the storm.

The PR personnel on a crisis team may come from the organization's media relations staff, its PR counsel firm, or both. In a corporation, a select group of senior executives heads the team with the CEO as the quarterback calling the signals. The firm's top PR executive and legal counsel serve as the CEO's chief advisors.

The CEO's seat is "closest to the flames," and the CEO ultimately must make the big decisions and then face the public, shareholders, employees, customers, and the board of directors to explain the wisdom of those decisions. These actions become more significant when a company is facing a ravenous press.

Not all corporate crises involve accidents or disasters. A company going into bankruptcy needs the good will and understanding of its stakeholders if it hopes to survive.

Calling in the Big Guns

At the top 10 public relations firm Hill & Knowlton, crisis counselors provide strategy, planning, and advice in crisis communications and issues management in every U.S. office and around the globe. Because the firm respects the confidentiality of its clients, we cannot give actual names, but offer the situations instead.

Hill & Knowlton's work has included dealing with racial charges against managers of a national restaurant chain and responding to a Supreme Court decision on a landmark age discrimination case.

The firm has helped a company involved in the largest inland oil spill in U.S. history and the January 1994 oil spill off the coast of Puerto Rico. And in another case, Hill & Knowlton counseled a national clothing store chain responding to false shoplifting allegations against minority youth and store picketing by special-interest groups.

In addition to typical crisis services such as reviewing relevant client preparation and communications procedures, Hill & Knowlton presents a detailed plan to the client that will identify likely crises and includes step-by-step procedures for handling possible scenarios.

One of the firm's training and simulations services is *The Virtual Crises,* a ready-made simulation for every company. This proprietary CD-ROM-based crises exercise uses a sexual harassment scenario. Hill & Knowlton crisis specialists challenge the participants on what they decide to do and how they communicate it.

In addition to various media and Internet monitoring services, the firm has a Rapid Response Web site. It is a "dark" Internet site that downloads "go live" during a crisis situation and is designed to centralize and control information flow, providing immediate, accurate, and comprehensive information. As the crisis unfolds, digital photos, streaming audio, or streaming video (as necessary) can be added to ensure that the company can accurately and effectively communicate.

Finally, Hill & Knowlton offers its 10 "Rules Of The Road" for crisis situations:

- Rule One: Take ownership—it's not the same as taking blame.
- Rule Two: Recognize the difference between bad publicity and a crisis, then calibrate your response accordingly.
- Rule Three: Get the confirmed facts, and base your response only on them. When possible, use research to help determine how to respond.
- Rule Four: Recruit and use third parties to speak on your behalf.
- Rule Five: Treat the media as conduits, not enemies.
- Rule Six: Assume you'll be sued.
- Rule Seven: Watch the Web as closely as the traditional media.
- Rule Eight: Demonstrate concern, care, and empathy.

- Rule Nine: Take the first 24 hours very, very seriously.
- Rule Ten: Begin your crisis management program now by building your reputational assets.

THE ODWALLA APPLE JUICE RECALL

The handling of a massive and fatal product contamination in the United States won the Silver Anvil Award in 1997 for Crisis Odwalla, Inc., and Edelman Public Relations/San Francisco, a firm hired to handle crisis communications. Here is a transcript of the award citation.

Odwalla, Inc., Crisis Management

Crisis Odwalla, Inc., with Edelman Public Relations

Silver Anvil Awards '97 Category 11B—Crisis Communication

Overview

Late in the evening of October 30, 1996, health officials in Washington state alerted fresh juice maker Odwalla, Inc., that a link had been discovered between *E. coli* 0157:H7 and several cases of Odwalla fresh apple juice. Odwalla immediately recalled its apple juice and all juice blends containing apple juice, amounting to 70% of its product line and affecting more than 4,600 retail accounts in seven states and British Columbia. On October 31, Odwalla hired Edelman Public Relations/San Francisco to handle crisis communications. Daily, proactive crisis communications continued through December 17, when Odwalla made a presentation at an FDA hearing on the necessity of mandating the pasteurization of apple juice. Odwalla remains a client of Edelman Public Relations/SF.

Research

- The first step taken was an extensive briefing on the incident and the company from Odwalla management, revealing a company that highly values health and nutrition. It became clear that managers and employees were devastated that a company that prides itself on "nourishing the body whole" had caused illness.
- Edelman conducted an exhaustive audit of initial print, broadcast, and online coverage of the recall for tone and content, and reviewed media coverage of a recent *E. coli* outbreak in apple

cider in New England. We learned that when *E. coli* "jumped" from meat to juice, public fear and confusion mushroomed.

- We reviewed all materials provided by the Seattle Department of Health, reviewed research on *E. coli*, and were briefed by Edelman/DC on past FDA actions regarding product recalls.
- Previous Edelman crisis work was reviewed, including work done by the San Francisco office on an *E. coli* contamination in dry salami; reports and articles on high-profile contamination cases were reviewed; and the agency was briefed on local market perceptions by Edelman's Denver affiliate, Johnston Wells, and independent Seattle agency Elgin Syferd.
- Internet chat rooms and newsgroups were monitored for discussion of the Odwalla situation, and we continuously reviewed consumer calls to the Odwalla 800 number to help evaluate daily consumer response to our messages.
- We analyzed media coverage daily throughout the crisis to evaluate how Odwalla messages were received and to note changes in media attitude. We also searched for and reviewed analyst comments.
- Quantitative telephone research was conducted two weeks into the crisis and also in January 1997 to understand consumer response to company actions. Consumer attitude focus group research was conducted in December 1996.

Planning

The plan was developed in concert with Odwalla's public relations and marketing directors. It incorporated findings from the research, as well as the business and personal objectives of Odwalla's management. The plan was reviewed daily based on new developments.

Communication Objectives.

- Communicate the effective product recall and neutralize potential press criticism.
- Express the company's genuine sorrow that Odwalla products caused serious illness.
- Communicate with and reassure trade partners and consumers about the incident, product availability, the company's long-term viability and Odwalla's response and industry leadership.
- Protect Odwalla's position in financial markets to rebuild stock value.

Strategies

- Be honest and immediately responsive to all requests for information and interviews.
- Humanize Odwalla through its officers, values, and all communications.
- Focus on Odwalla's responsible recall actions and changes made to ensure safety.
- Establish a dialogue directly with consumers and financial analysts.
- Establish Odwalla as the preeminent authority on fresh juice.
- Use product reintroductions and ongoing new product introductions to showcase company stability and future promise, and to maintain dialogue with retail trade.

Target Audiences. Media, consumers, retail trade partners, employees, families of afflicted persons, health departments, investment community.

Materials and Resources Used. Newswires and press releases, fax list database of reporters following the story, Website, online newsgroups, 800 number, in-store communication, retail trade partner information packets, employee and investor conference calls, express clipping service, video monitoring recap reports, on-site media center, and Internet monitoring of media coverage.

Budget. $90,000 Over 2 months: $75,000 in fees and S15,000 in expenses.

Execution

Two agency teams, one in San Francisco and one at the company's Half Moon Bay headquarters, managed the overall crisis response alongside Odwalla's public relations and marketing directors, and coordinated activities in Denver and Seattle. The San Francisco team responded to more than 200 media calls the first day and maintained contact with 225 local and national broadcast and print reporters throughout the crisis. We developed a media track response and interview information request relay system; set up a daily interview schedule with executives; prepared daily briefing kits for Odwalla senior management; developed daily message points to respond to new developments; and prepped executives. A media center was set up at Odwalla to monitor local and national television and radio coverage. We coordinated the company chairman's trip to Denver and Seattle to visit media and affected families, and immediately expressed company grief when a child in Denver died. Edelman/SF also:

- Managed communications, including daily press releases, in Odwalla's seven-state territory.
- Created a Web site within 48 hours to allow Odwalla to communicate directly with consumers and receive feedback. We updated the site daily; updated consumer, 800 number script daily or as needed.
- Created a news bureau on the Web site to advise media, expanded site awareness with hyperlinks.
- Prepared communications with Odwalla's trade partners.
- Kept employees informed via regular e-mail, and conducted telephone media training for employees in outer markets.
- Held conference calls with the investment community.
- Helped develop the Nourishment and Food Safety Advisory Council made up of food safety and nutrition experts.
- Prepped Odwalla to participate in a Seattle FDA press conference on the contamination.
- Set up a press conference for Odwalla's CEO, chairman, and council members to clarify initial FDA plant findings.
- Helped prepare Odwalla for presentation to the FDA on mandatory pasteurization.
- Helped reintroduce recalled products as well as new products throughout crisis.

Evaluation

Objective 1. Communicate the effective product recall and neutralize potential press criticism.

- Consumers read or saw Odwalla's messages in more than 5,000 newspaper/magazine stories and 850 broadcast stories.
- Media coverage of the recall was neutral to positive in tone and factual in content. Media praised Odwalla actions and intentions via headlines, editorials, and third-party expert quotes.
- The web site informed approximately 50,000 visitors about the recall, another 15,000 called the 800 number.

Objective 2. Express the company's genuine sorrow about illness.

- Numerous headlines expressed company grief—"Odwalla apologizes for outbreak."

- The company's message of sorrow that its products had caused serious illness was illustrated by praise from attorneys of affected families. "This company has done everything right," one attorney said in a television interview.
- Focus groups expressed "heartfelt support" and respect for Odwalla's responsible handling of the crisis.

Objective 3. Communicate with and reassure trade partners and consumers about the incident, product availability, the company's long-term viability, and Odwalla's response and industry leadership.

- Odwalla retained 80% of its accounts; lapsed accounts continue to reactivate. Safeway, Odwalla's largest account, supported Odwalla's decision to pasteurize apple juice; and while other unpasteurized apple juices were forced out of the stores, Odwalla's position was secure.
- Calls to the 800 number jumped from an average of 30 a week to more than 3,000 the first week. The Web site received 19,000 hits in the first 48 hours; approximately 50,000 hits by January.
- Odwalla has expanded its crisis site into a permanent presence on the web.
- An independent AOL survey showed that 86 percent of online respondents supported Odwalla and would return as consumers. Other surveys showed 94% of those polled were aware of the *E. coli* outbreak; 96% of those aware approved of Odwalla's handling of the crisis.
- FDA characterized *E. coli* in apple juice as an industry problem. Odwalla was asked by the FDA to make a presentation at a December meeting on mandatory pasteurization, underscoring recognition of the company as an authority on fresh juice.
- Odwalla successfully reintroduced products after the recall, and continues to introduce new products at a normal rate.

Objective 4. Protect Odwalla's position in financial markets to rebuild lost stock value.

- Financial markets responded to the communications effort; stock price was $19 prior to the crisis, dropped to $9 immediately after, and has risen to $13.

- Analysis commented positively to media about Odwalla actions and company future.

One important element in this crisis management situation is that even as early as November 1996, Edelman and Odwalla took full advantage of the Internet to give reporters and consumers immediate access to information about the recall. Although Odwalla did not have a corporate or promotional Web site, the company's crisis-related site was up and running within 48 hours.

Based on its experience in the Odwalla case, Edelman PR has developed an online response product that enables clients to establish crisis preparedness sites on their Intranets. The PR company has even developed an online version of the traditional crisis manual.

The online manual contains information about the crisis team, fact sheets, mission statements, frequently asked questions, and various scenarios. Edelman has its own domain name (www.enw.com) and can instantly create a subdomain to host a client's site when crisis strikes. With that technology, a crisis-specific Web site can be online in a matter of hours.

One aspect of the Odwalla site that drew plaudits from the media was the links it offered to other sites of interest, particularly to the Food and Drug Administration and the Centers for Disease Control and Prevention.

Crisis sites are of great importance to the media, but are also beneficial in taking the company's message to stakeholders such as vendors, franchisees, customers, employees, and the investment community.

In a new media environment, information travels the globe in seconds, and the effect of a crisis is immediately felt in financial markets.

Here's a hypothetical situation that will explain an important element of crisis management, the *crisis dark site*. A large nuclear power installation has an accident in the middle of the night. The press finds out about it immediately and contacts the power plant's Web site. Now if the installation has taken a proactive stance about such a crisis, it will already have prepared a "crisis dark site" template. Once the facts of the accident are discovered, that information is plugged into the Web site so the press can have immediate access.

Crisis communications and crisis management present great challenges to the public relations practitioner, particularly because these situations constitute threats to corporations, organizations, governments, and governmental agencies. Each crisis requires its own set of strategies and tactics.

FIGURE 17.1   Left/right and center: Restoring confidence in Egyptian tourism; counseling Odwalla, Inc., on an outbreak of *E. coli* with a program that now serves as a model for crisis management, responsible action, fast response and the use of Internet communications. (Courtesy Edelman Public Relations Worldwide)

CHAPTER 18

New Media High-Tech Public Relations

The headline in *Advertising Age*, September 25, 2000, was big and bold: "From the basement to the penthouse." The subheads for the piece were equally optimistic:

"PR's new status: Thanks to high-tech and dot-com plays, public relations is hitting heights as marketing's power tool."

"PR is in its golden age today. You've got to be almost dead not to be successful in PR today."

The article goes on to say, "The era of digital communications and the hype and buzz surrounding high-tech and dot-com companies have ushered public relations into the limelight—so much so, the industry believes, it can never again be considered the Rodney Dangerfield of marketing communications."[1]

High-tech PR today is not only about breaking news in *The Wall Street Journal* with a story about a dot.com's prospects—it's about influencing the consumer, the high-tech community, and the venture capitalists, as well.

PR firms are riding the high-tech boom big-time. It is not uncommon for a top-line PR firm to charge its high-tech client a monthly minimum fee of $30,000 to $50,000. Large tech companies also have formidable in-house departments to spread their PR message in conventional media and online.

HOW HIGH-TECH PUBLIC RELATIONS IS PRACTICED AT THE TOP PR FIRMS

All the top firms we looked at in chapter 4 are deep into the practice areas of high-tech. Let's look at examples.

Fleishman-Hillard

Fleishman-Hillard, the number one U.S firm, represents giant companies like Dell Computer. In 2000, Fleishman-Hillard won a Cipra 2000 award for client SBC Communications in the category of new service introduction. That same year, the firm and SBC won a Silver Anvil Award in the category of technology for the campaign "Bringing Broadband to the Masses... Pronto." The culmination of this effort was a massive $6 billion Project Pronto initiative.

The project was eminently successful. In 1 year, SBC's DSL (digital subscriber line) service had 169,000 subscribers.

Burson-Marsteller

Technology is one of Burson-Marsteller's largest practices. Sun Microsystems is one of its leading clients. The Java platform is Sun's programming language. Since 1996, once a year Sun sponsors a JavaOne Developer Conference in San Francisco. The conference draws luminaries, visionaries, and celebrities from around the globe, as well as hundreds of media folk eager for interviews, briefings, and questions about technology. And, oh yes, 25,000 people attend the conference.

Burson-Marsteller account managers are responsible for media training for spokespeople, the writing of press releases, orchestrating press conferences, interviews, media luncheons, and panel discussions. In order to carry out these voluminous specialized media tools, Burson-Marsteller people must understand the nuances of the technology presented at the conference.

Shandwick International

Shandwick is one of the world's largest PR groups working in the technology sector. The firm has been a pioneer in the new media of the Internet, interactive communication, and Web monitoring services.

One Shandwick nuance is Brand Protection, which involves monitoring Web publications, chat forums, and sites to keep track of a client's reputation on the Internet. Media relations for the firm's clients comprise Webcasts, virtual presentations, online press kits, and virtual press rooms.

This Interactive Marketing program includes site submission campaigns, search engine positioning, and "must-see" Web animations, in addition to viral e-mail campaigns.

Shandwick Broadcast has innovated in the digitizing of video materials for use on an external or internal corporate site and using digitized clips of video material for CD presentations.

Hill & Knowlton

More than 200 professionals make up Hill & Knowlton's technology practice. By 2000, the practice's revenues reached more than $50 million. And, under the theory that in technology today's emerging company can be next year's hottest brand, H&K represents both ends of the spectrum.

One H&K success story is E*Trade, the leading online trading company. H&K operates its tech practice out of more than a dozen offices worldwide. The practice also includes Silicon Valley-based Blanc & Otus Public Relations, a leading technology brand and pioneer in high-tech PR, and SocketPR, a high-tech information technology and e-business PR firm with offices in Atlanta and in Austin, Texas.

Edelman PR

Edelman Global Technology Practice serves clients like NCR, AT&T, Ericcson, Microsoft, and Apple Computer. At this writing, technology represents more than 25% of Edelman's overall agency portfolio and continues to expand.

FIGURE 18.1 Left to Right: Launching Reflect.com, an independent company funded by Procter & Gamble, as the first interactive, customized beauty service; securing global industry support for a new wireless communications technology code–named "Blue Tooth," positioning NCR as a leader in professional hardware and software solutions. (Courtesy Edelman Public Relations Worldwide)

Ketchum

Here's how Ketchum won a Silver Anvil 2000 award for its client Levi Strauss & Company.

In 1998, during the "Dark Ages" of e-commerce, Levi Strauss took the risk of launching the Levi's Online Store. This was at a time of declining company sales, and when shopping online was still considered risky.

To get back "in" with the in crowd, and to reposition Levi's as a hip brand, Ketchum created an "in"-teractive program to "expose" (not sell) young consumers to the brand in a discreet, cool way.

Armed with a weekly allowance and media training, three students were featured in a branded, weekly MTV Real-World-esque Internet show, showcasing their shopping sprees (Levi's products included). The Online Challenge worked. Traffic on Levi.com went from an average of 3,000 visitors a day before the experiment to 130,000 visitors per day after the experiment. It was a prime example of how Ketchum does technology business.

BSMG Worldwide

Monster.com is a pioneer in the online career category, although dozens of direct competitors appeal to the same audience via the Internet. BSMG helped to position Monster.com as a slightly irreverent but consistently innovative and potent change agent for individuals seeking career opportunities and growth.

BSMG raised Monster.com's profile; monitored the Web for feedback; engineered important site enhancements, directory and search engine placements and critical link agreements. Add a few mega-dollar Super Bowl commercials, and Monster.com was on its way as one of the most well-known and successful brands to originate on the Web.

BSMG also performs technology tricks for clients like Hewlett-Packard, Toshiba, and Unisys.

Porter Novelli Convergence Group

In January 2000, Copithorne & Bellows, the world's foremost PR agency focused on technology, merged with Porter Novelli International to form the San Francisco-based Porter Novelli Convergence Group. The new entity had $50 million in annual revenues and more than 500 employees worldwide. It is a model for technology public relations that integrates all critical client services into a single global service organization.

The Porter Novelli Convergence Group offers an excellent definition of convergence:

> "Convergence" is the most powerful and evocative word that describes the technology-driven changes revolutionizing every aspect of the way business is done across the world. Convergence—of entertainment and computing, of computers and communications, of analog and digital, of traditional and new forms of media, and of different types of people, societies, and organizations—is the driving force of the New Economy. The World Wide Web and other technology changes are forcing virtually every organization to redefine its business model and reconfigure its means of interacting with customers, investors, employees, and other important audiences. And this transformation is forcing companies—and their public relations firms—to change the way they develop and deliver the messages they must communicate.

Ogilvy Public Relations Worldwide

In 1998, Ogilvy acquired Alexander Communications, one of the Silicon Valley's top tech PR firms, with offices in San Francisco and seven other cities. Alexander, renamed Alexander Ogilvy, focuses on emerging and high-growth technology market segments such as Internet tools and technologies, electronic commerce, and interactive media and information appliances. Ogilvy's technology practice includes such heavyweight clients as IBM, Automatic Data Processing, and the global cellular phone provider Nokia.

Key Alexander Ogilvy clients are Nortel Elastic Network, NCR, and major technology conference and trade-show organizers. Pam Alexander, who founded Alexander, is one of the new digital entrepreneurs. She was featured as one of "the E-gang" in *Forbes* in its July 26, 1999, issue, and as one of the "e 50" in *Vanity Fair*'s coverage of the Eestablishment in its May 2000 issue.

Golin/Harris

As do many large PR firms, Golin/Harris owns several other firms that operate under different brand names. The MWW Group specializes in Internet and technology marketing. Mindstorm Communications services several e-business, telecommunications, and digital entertainment clients. TSI Communications Worldwide offers an Internet Practice area through its offices in New York, San Francisco, and London.

What PR Firms Look For in New Hires

Alicia Fogelman Beyer is president of the ProMarc Agency, a Washington, D.C.-based high-tech firm with 22 employees. In the May 2000 issue of *TACTICS*, she discussed the hallmarks of a great high-tech hire:[2]

- Missionaries for success. People who can work well with the top executives of a startup company.
- Tightrope walkers. Staffers who have a high tolerance for risk, and can get from one side of the tightrope to the other, knowing that the wind could switch direction any minute.
- Complexity theorists. Those who are not afraid of a challenge say, "digital imaging technology."

- Big-picture generalists. Not techies, but instead employees who excel at "de-geeking the message"—loving the client for its bottom-line solutions, not just its technical proof points.
- Sponges for business, technology, and media knowledge. Outside training at this firm is critical. ProMarc spends an average of $10,000 per person per year on conferences, seminars, and other forms of education, and even employs a dedicated director of media intelligence and a director of business and technology intelligence.

Conferencing Techniques for Audio, Video, and the Internet

In the June 2000 issue of PRSA's *TACTICS*, Richard Weiner discussed conferencing techniques, an increasingly important tool for PR professionals, particularly those in a high-tech practice.[3]

The largest category of conferences is still the *audio conference*. A standard telephone or speaker phone is used. A typical meeting involves six people and lasts for an hour.

Each participant is alerted to the time of the conference in advance. A conference coordinator usually makes the arrangements with the phone company, greets the participants, and handles instant polling, if necessary, as well as other procedures.

Videoconferencing is still not widely popular, although it is used for news conferences, seminars, stock analyst and sales meetings, conventions, and other events. A recent development is desktop videoconferencing, which is used for the transmission of charts, documents, and other stationary visuals.

Internet conferencing is the hot ticket today because it is the cheapest, fastest, and most flexible type of meeting. With AT&T's new on-line service, AT&T Click2Dial Conferencing, the conference can be set up over the Internet, but then everyone talks to each other on their regular telephone.

Learning Communities for Internet Professionals

The rapidly growing Internet universe has dramatically changed public relations, thereby creating an ongoing need for an increase in the knowledge and skills of its practitioners. These subjects and more are tackled in the Internet Public Relations Discussion List (I-PR). This free twice-weekly e-mail discussion list features news, tips, and resources for developing and implementing successful Internet PR campaigns. Topics covered in I-PR include:

- PR strategy and implementation for the Internet.
- Online media relations.
- Internet PR tools and resources.
- Industry articles.
- News from major trade shows and seminars.

Many leading Internet public relations experts are members of the I-PR community and are generous in sharing their knowledge with others on the list.

Jobs at a Hot High-Tech PR Firm

Niehaus Ryan Wong has been around high-tech PR for a long time by industry standards—since 1986. The company focuses on three interrelated market segments: people and technology, new commerce, and e-business. NRW offers clients the added benefit of specific expertise in the areas of broadcast PR, interactive communications, and speaker placement through its bureaus:

NRW Broadcast Bureau
NRW Interactive Bureau
NRW Conference Strategies and Events Promotions Bureau

By specializing, the firm has gained depth in areas such as the Internet, networking, electronic commerce, online communities, object software, enterprise client/server development, and collaborative computing.

NRW has offices in San Francisco, New York, and Austin, Texas. At the time of this writing, the firm had 21 clients, of whom six were dot.coms.

NRW is always looking for a few good men and women who know both technology and consumer media and "like to evangelize how our clients are leveraging the Internet to change the way the world works and lives." E-mail your resume to jobs@nrwpr.com.

NRW has a hip but practical new internship program. The firm offers fast computers, free juice, and cool clients. Want to learn more? Send an e-mail to internship@nrwpr.com.

Media Placement Tips for Online Media

The headline in the January 2001 issue of *Media Relations Insider*, published by Bulldog Reporter, reads "Pitching Online Media—Determine If It's a Land of Opportunity or a Waste of Time."[4] The article points out that there are now 6,000 news Web sites, and people are getting nearly a third of their news online. Internet users spent more than 93 billion total minutes online in September 2000, and the numbers are growing exponentially.

So is this a vast new market for media relations people? Maybe. The *Insider* offered a few guidelines on which stories fit best on the Web:

1. If the story is aimed at Gen. X and Gen. Y'ers, pitch them online.
2. High-tech clients crave online exposure.
3. Online stories often find their way on to traditional media.
4. Rejected print stories may make it online.

How heavy is online usage by those committed to the medium? Media Matrix offered these online stats:

- By the end of 2000, more than 39 million people went online in an average day.
- Users viewed an average of 50 different Web pages per user day.
- Each user spent an average of over 19 hours online in 1 month.
- Users averaged just over 1 minute per unique page.

What are the top news sites? MSNBC.com, CNN.com, Time.com, NYTimes.com, and ABC News (various domain names).

The top business and financial sites at this writing are Time.com, Marketwatch.com, Quicken.com, Fool.com, and Onmoney.com.

CHAPTER 19

Colleges, Extension Programs, and Summer Institutes

A t the University of North Carolina, Chapel Hill, public relations students learn the basic PR skills of media relations and
the dozen or more practice areas of the trade. To improve their
visual literacy skills, students also take a corporate video communications class.

As we have already seen, PR professionals use video in many ways.
Companies use it for videoconferencing for executives, video news
releases for the media and the public, employees' video newsletters,
and satellite news conferences.

Although some large corporations and PR firms prepare video services in-house, most use outside companies. But whether video is done
in-house or out, PR professionals need visual literacy and a total
comprehension of visual images in an active effort to determine and
create patterns.

At the University of North Carolina, most students at the School of
Journalism and Mass Communications get an introduction to visual
literacy through the school's basic graphic design course. They are
also exposed to the use of visual media to communicate to various
publics. Because the school didn't have the necessary equipment for

advanced video training, Professor Dulcie Murdock Straughan and her colleagues came up with an innovative solution to the issue. Her department worked out a cooperative arrangement with an area company that had a large corporate video department. The course was taught by two journalism school professors and the head of the company corporate video department. The company's facilities and some of its staff members were made available to the students in the class. So that there was no commercial benefit in the student training program, pro bono community public service projects were produced.

By the fifth week, students had learned how a video was put together from the problem-solving stage, to developing a concept, writing a script, blocking the shots, working with camera and sound people, doing a rough edit, and overseeing the final edit of the project film. The program was so successful, it became a regular part of the school's curriculum.

We discuss this teaching experience as an example of how college mass communications programs are meeting the needs of students in the rapidly developing discipline and profession of public relations.

Public relations is today's media favorite in the whole sphere of mass communications. That's why many colleges that formerly grouped PR with advertising are now offering public relations as its own major.

As we noted in chapter 4, large advertising agency organizations have purchased PR firms because public relations is getting the communications job done more efficiently and more effectively than advertising.

HOW COLLEGES SPECIALIZE THEIR PUBLIC RELATIONS PROGRAMS

In August 2000, I attended the 83rd annual convention of the Association for Education in Journalism and Mass Communications. This convention brings together hundreds of academic professionals in the public relations discipline. Here are some of the subjects of sessions conducted at this convention. They indicate the scope and sophistication of today's public relations education.

- Talk the Talk, Walk the Walk: Advancing Measurement in Public Relations.

- Making Health Communications Meaningful for Women: Factors That Influence Involvement and the Situational Theory of Publics.
- Web Site and Database Pitfalls.
- An Exploration of Integration of the Public Relations Function in International Business Operations.
- The Postmodern Public Relations Practitioner as Organizational Activist.
- Check Out Our Web Site at . . . The Public Relations Content Characteristics of Fortune 500 Companies.
- Use of World Wide Web Sites as Marketing and Promotion Tools: A Pilot Study.
- Ethics in a Crisis.
- Lockdown on Learning: Public Relations and Media Response to School Violence.
- Ego Involvement and Practitioners' Attitudes Toward Integrated Marketing Communication.

Postgraduate Education and Training

If public relations was not your major in college, you can still take evening or summer courses at a number of colleges. Here are two fine programs.

New York University's Summer Institute in PR. New York is the nation's media communications capital. If you can afford about $4,000 plus living expenses, we recommend NYU's summer PR program, held each June.

The summer institute has a faculty of 15 to 20 leading industry professionals who bring their expertise to play in the 3-week program. This faculty is drawn from the evening certificate program in PR at the Management Institute of NYU's School of Continuing Education, another fine training source. In addition, many special guests are invited to speak, conduct workshops, and act as panelists and judges.

The summer institute is a total immersion program with daily lectures, demonstrations, field trips, practice, and feedback that guide the students through the history, theory, and techniques of public relations. Students prepare news releases and use other tools. They make field trips to PR agencies, corporations, and video production facilities. The general approach is to learn by doing.

Classes meet Monday through Saturday, 9 a.m. to 6 p.m. Saturdays are reserved for independent team project review and planning.

Several evenings are scheduled for team assignments, guest speakers, and social events.

In the program students learn how to write press releases and proposals, conduct research, plan press conferences and events, and work with print and electronic media.

The staff also helps students with career planning, resumé writing, interviewing techniques, and portfolio development.

The program is limited to only 30 people. For information, call the institute's office at (212)790-3212 or write to: New York University, School of Continuing Education, Management Institute, 11 West 42nd Street, Room 401, New York, NY 10036. The program's e-mail address is rlh1@is2.nyu.edu. The Web site is www.scps.nyu.edu/summer.

UCLA's PR Program. The University of California at Los Angeles (UCLA) conducts a comprehensive course of study for students, working professionals, and those in entertainment, corporate, nonprofit, and other organizations for which public relations plays an important role. Students may take three kinds of certificate programs in public relations: public relations (general), public relations with entertainment publicity concentration, and public relations with nonprofit public relations concentration.

Within these three concentration there are more than 25 individual courses, including such specialized subjects as:

Sports public relations
Political fund raising and public relations
Publicity in the music industry
Publicity for the entertainment industry (film and television)
Public relations for nonprofit organizations
Reputation and crisis management

Most courses are taught evenings by working professionals. Contact UCLA Extension at (310)825-0641 or e-mail at jrprfr@uclaextension.org.

Graduate Programs in PR

Many fine graduate programs in public relations are conducted by colleges and universities. Ten colleges grant a doctorate in PR. About 25 offer master's degrees in this discipline. Among those rated best are the University of Maryland, Michigan State University, the University of Florida, San Diego State University, Boston University, San Jose (California) State University, the University of Texas, Syracuse University, Northwestern University, Ohio State University, and the University of Georgia.

Preparing for a Job Public Relations

According to a survey of prospective employers on the West Coast conducted by Dr. Dennis Wilcox of San Jose State University, the ideal applicant for a PR job has:[1]

- A 4-year undergraduate degree.
- Experience with courses in news writing, business, and the social sciences.
- An outstanding personality and a willingness to work.
- The ability to write well.
- Work experience in a related field.

CHAPTER 20

The Alphabet Organizations of Public Relations

In this chapter we discuss a number of professional organizations that may be helpful to newcomers seeking employment, information, training programs, internships, and professional development.

PUBLIC RELATIONS SOCIETY OF AMERICA (PRSA)

Way back in 1947, when the PRSA was first chartered, corporate public relations was in its infancy. At that time there were no large PR counsel firms, only a few colleges had courses in the subject, and most people who worked in this field were called "press agents."

The PRSA, headquartered in New York City, is the leading professional organization for PR practitioners, with more than 20,000 members in more than 100 chapters throughout the United States. The principal service of the PRSA to its members is to increase their opportunities in the field through professional development, communications, networking, and peer recognition programs.

Let's look next at some of the PRSA's services and professional development programs.

Public Relations World Congress

This annual event offers PRSA members an opportunity to interact with public relations professionals worldwide and to share knowledge and network.

Members can participate in dozens of seminars, professional interest section programs, general sessions, roundtable discussions, and professional development workshops. Here are highlights of some of the seminar subjects from Public Relations World Congress 2000 cosponsored by PRSA and the International Public Relations Association (IPRA):

- New Rules in High Tech PR—How to Build a Public Relations Program that Rocks.
- Writing That Sells . . . Products, Organization, Ideas.
- Navigating Your Career in a Dot.com World.
- Integrating Public Relations into the Marketing Mix.
- Crisis Communications in Internet Time.
- How to Get a Raise.

It is interesting to note the diversified background and affiliations of PRSA members and lecturers at the Public Relations World Congress 2000. Some examples include:

E. Ronald Culp, Senior Vice-President Public Relations & Government, Sears Roebuck and Company.

John Edelman, Global Director–Human Resources, Edelman Public Relations Worldwide.

Susan Nathanson, PhD, Executive Director, National Breast Cancer Organization.

Robert Grupp, Director Corporate Communications, Eli Lilly and Company.

James Grunig, PhD, Professor Department of Communications, University of Maryland.

Patricia Rose, Chair, Department of Advertising and Public Relations, Florida International University.

In addition to PRSA's World Congress, the organization conducts seasonal seminars. For winter 2001, there were six 1- or 2-day seminars, held in New York, San Francisco (two), Atlanta, San Diego, and Dallas. These seminars dealt with a single subject, such as strategic public relations planning, writing that sells . . . products, services, and ideas, and crisis communication strategy.

Home Study Conference Courses

Top-quality home study courses have been developed from sold-out PRSA seminars to provide comprehensive skill development and guidance from personal instructors.

Audio and Video Libraries

Speeches, presentations, and other training tools are available to members. In addition to material on practice areas, subjects like creativity and public relations law are also covered.

Publications for Members

PRSA publishes *STRATEGIST* quarterly and *TACTICS* monthly, both of which are covered in chapter 21.

The Blue Book is a listing of PRSA members.

The Green Book is a guide to public relations service organizations.

The Red Book is a directory of the PRSA Counselors Academy, cross-referenced by geography, practices, and industry.

Member Job Search Assistance

A bimonthly newsletter lists available positions at or above $35,000 a year. Members can subscribe to it at a discount.

PR Power is a source for temporary positions. The Web site, www.prsa.org, serves as an online career reading room, classified job list, and links to related public relations resources. Members can post their resumés under specific job titles or practice areas.

PRSA Professional Practice Center

PRSA maintains a research information center that can be reached online or by fax-on-demand, which furnishes up-to-date industry trends, research fundings, and other resource material.

Professional Interest Sections

Sixteen professional interest sections conduct seminars, workshops, and conferences. They provide newsletters, Web sites, listservs, and monographs for members' professional use.

Awards and Recognition

Throughout the book we have noted various winners of PRSA's prestigious Silver Anvil Award and Gold Anvil Award. The Silver Anvil is PR's equivalent of the Academy Awards. It is issued annually to practitioners for excellence in PR programs in the judgment of their peers.

The Bronze Anvil recognizes outstanding public relations tactics, and the individual components of programs or campaigns.

PRSA also awards the Gold Anvil to an individual for his or her accomplishments to the profession and grants an award to an outstanding educator and to a member for public service achievement.

PRSA's Nationwide Network of Chapters

Members don't have to come to New York for PRSA meetings. They can attend them at a convenient local chapter. The individual chapters conduct seminars, special events, and search services.

Accredited in Public Relations—APR

Members who have demonstrated knowledge, experience, and judgment in planning and managing public relations activities are eligible for this voluntary certification program. By 2001, more than 5,000 public relations professionals had achieved the APR designation, and over 400 qualified members take the examination each year.

The Public Relations Student Society (PRSSA)

PRSSA has 6,500 members in 220 chapters on college campuses across the country. PRSA members often interact with their local PRSSA chapters by volunteering to be professional advisors, mentors, or guest speakers at events. Members also help support scholarship programs and give financial assistance for students to attend the International Conference cosponsored by PRSA and IPRA.

FIGURE 20.1 Winning the "Oscar" of the PR industry, the Silver Anvil, is a democratic process honoring not only the big guys with megadollar campaigns, but also smaller companies with modest budgets. (Courtesy PRSA's *THE STRATEGIST*)

INTERNATIONAL ASSOCIATION OF BUSINESS COMMUNICATORS (IABC)

IABC members almost never use the words "public relations." In the organization's literature and publications, members are referred to as "communicators" who are engaged in "strategic business communications management."

The role of IABC is somewhat similar to that of PRSA, dealing with communication that is "strategic, interactive, integrated, and international." Members in 55 countries are employed by large and small corporations, foundations, educational institutions, dot.coms, and, yes, even the same PR counsel firms described in chapter 4.

Here are some of the things IABC does:

- Operates a knowledge center dispensing expert advice, step-by-step instruction, case studies, and proven models that members can tailor to their own needs.
- Supports the IABC Research Foundation as a research and development arm for new findings, knowledge, and understanding of the profession.
- Conducts an international conference bringing together communicators from around the world.
- Publishes *Communication World*, a magazine with editorial features on research, technology, trends, and interviews.
- Maintains *CW Online*, a members-only interactive resource on IABC's Web page with industry news briefs and tips and current and archived articles.
- Conducts IABC seminars and district/regional conferences.
- Gives Gold Quill Awards for excellence in communications.
- Accredits member recognition with an ABC (Accredited Business Communicator).
- Publishes a career planning workbook and holds career-related workshops—also available online.
- Supports various recognition and award programs.
- Organizes student chapters at colleges and universities throughout the United States and Canada.

IABC/PRSA Compensation Survey

The IABC and PRSA jointly published *Profile 2000*, a survey of the profession that presented an overview of job satisfaction, workplace trends, and roles and responsibilities of those employed in this field. It also included the salary and compensation of the 40,000 professionals represented by the two organizations.

Here are some of the highlights of the survey:

- The average annual base salary for communicators in the United States is $72,000.

- It's higher in New England ($96,000) than in the South Atlantic, East Central, and Mountain regions. But it's highest in the Mid-Atlantic ($113,000).
- Consultants' salaries are significantly greater than those with a corporate position ($110,000 vs. $63,000).
- If you have *vice-president* in your title, your average salary is $149,000.
- A senior account executive at a PR counsel firm averages $36,000. It's much higher in New York.
- You won't get rich in academe. The average professor who teaches public relations or communications makes $52,000 a year.
- Finance and banking communications people average $82,000, while medical/health care is $79,500 and cultural/travel/tourism is only $48,000.
- Women in communications still earn less than men. If you're an Accredited Business Communicator (ABC) or Accredited Public Relations (APR) professional designated by PRSA, the average male makes $89,500 and the average female $82,500. Nonaccredited males average $88,000 and females drop to $56,500.

These are not huge salaries overall; however, they do match those in advertising and other areas of mass communication. The average bonus for communicators in the joint ABC/PRSA study is $10,000.

THE COUNCIL OF PUBLIC RELATIONS FIRMS

The Council of Public Relations Firms membership is made up of 122 PR firms, including all the top 10 and 65% of the top 50 firms. Its mission is to build the business of public relations by advocating to business professionals the value of public relations as a strategic business tool, promoting the benefits of careers in public relations to prospective employees, and assisting members and their clients in setting the standards for the profession.

The council divides its role into three programs.

Business Programs

- Works with an advisory board of clients to identify strategic research that it will fund.

FIGURE 20.2 The Council's valuable booklet on jobs in the industry.

- Promotes the strategic value of PR to business executives and students and professors in MBA programs.
- Assesses seven reputation management systems that members will follow in their reputation programs.
- Commissions commercial research to develop a methodology for predicting and measuring the outcomes of public relations programs.

- Conducts annual review of corporate communications spending at Fortune 500 companies, and correlates this information with *Fortune*'s "Most Admired Companies" list.
- Helps companies streamline the process of PR agency selection.

Talent Programs

- Recruits at top liberal arts and minority colleges and holds career fairs. Develops internship programs for member firms.
- Develops a curriculum for universities to use in courses that prepare students to work in agencies.
- Produces workbooks, recruiting publications, and seminars that enable members to learn best practices for successful recruiting.

Management Programs

- Conducts an annual Industry Documentation and Ranking of Public Relations firms by size, location, and specialty. Publishes a comprehensive report, *The Impact of the Internet on Public Relations and Business Communications*, as a guide for member firms in developing innovative sources and making strategic and financial decisions for the New Economy.
- Publishes *M & A Reports* as an insight to acquisition strategies, motivations of sellers, and post-merger lessons learned.
- Develops *Benchmarking Surveys* to assist members in improving their businesses.
- Makes *Business Consulting Services* available free or at reduced rates for members. A "consultant's corner" is provided on the Council's Web site.

CAREER TIP

Log on to the Council of Public Relations Firms Web site, www.prfirms.org/student, for its Career Resources section. In it you'll find such links as:

> Find a Firm—a database to help you identify potential employers who meet your specific needs.
> Post Your Résumé—edit or delete it.
> PR Career Information—articles and publications produced by the council, as well as relevant resources to build a career.
> Public relations job sites and recruiting assessment tools.

THE INSTITUTE FOR PUBLIC RELATIONS

Formerly known as the Foundation for Public Relations Research and Education, the Institute for Public Relations engages in a comprehensive program of publications, lectures, awards, symposia, and professional development forums to promote and encourage academic and professional excellence.

The institute has supported more than 200 separate research projects covering everything from what PR students should study to an analysis of how new technologies are affecting the profession.

The institute also produces practice-oriented programs and publications on the effectiveness of public relations in profit-making and nonprofit institutions.

The institute offers awards and competitions as incentives for students and scholars to build the body of knowledge in the field.

INTERNATIONAL PUBLIC RELATIONS ASSOCIATION (IPRA)

Founded in 1955, IPRA today has more than 1,000 individual members in more than sixty countries worldwide.

IPRA publishes a number of publications and is involved in organizing professional development seminars.

The group works closely with the United Nations on such projects as "Cartoonists Against Drug Abuse." IPRA is also active in environmental issues, sponsoring programs like the project to arrest the degradation undermining the Alpine ecosystem.

ASSOCIATION FOR EDUCATION IN JOURNALISM AND MASS COMMUNICATIONS (AEJMC)

The AEJMC is a national organization of colleges and departments offering undergraduate and/or graduate programs in journalism and mass communication. Public relations is one of the divisions of the AEJMC; the others are newspaper, magazine, advertising, radio–television, and mass communications. Each division has its own publication and maintains contact with its own membership during the year.

Once a year, in August, the AEJMC holds its annual convention, in a different city each year. At the convention, members conduct presentations and hold workshop sessions relating to their specialization. In addition, the convention offers an opportunity for the individual divisions to hold business meetings on subjects of related interest.

Some typical presentation subjects from the 2000 convention are:

> Teledemocracy in the Age of the Internet.
> Newspaper Closings: Smart Business or Corporate Irresponsibility.
> Images and Portrayals in Magazines.
> Overcoming the Excuses: How to Make Newsrooms and Classrooms as Diverse as America.
> Preparing Public Relations and Advertising Students for the 21st Century.

CHAPTER 21

Important Publications, Web Sites, and News Services

PUBLICATIONS

Many excellent magazines and dozens of fine newsletters cover every facet of the burgeoning field of public relations. Some of these publications are available by subscription or may be found in university libraries. We discuss a number of them here.

Public Relations *TACTICS*

Published by PRSA, *TACTICS* is a monthly four-color newspaper focused on PR strategies. *TACTICS'* primary role is to help professionals do their job better with the latest news, trends, and how-to information ranging from the newest PR applications in technology to the most current PR research.

"Top of the News" is a regular feature in *TACTICS*. Typically, this page-one column delivers an in-depth examination of a widely publicized public relations crisis or issue. The section combines case studies, how-to information, and analysis that puts the issue in perspective. Recent articles from *TACTICS* include the following:

PUBLIC RELATIONS

TACTICS

SPOTLIGHT ON:
CAREER DEVELOPMENT

Portfolios are full of shining writing examples
that may or may not reflect a candidate's true
skills and talents. How do you make sure your
new hire can provide the writing support you
need? Also, several PR pros look back at their
first year in public relations. Our Career
Development section begins on page 14.

PRSA www.prsa.org   FOCUSED INFORMATION FOR THE PUBLIC RELATIONS PROFESSION $4/MARCH 2001

INSIDE THIS ISSUE

Train To Win
Whether the goal is increased
work proficiency or improved
recruitment, training programs
are the lifeblood of every organization. Page 10.

Establishing Priorities
Through technological
advances, organizations now
have a tremendous range of
resources to establish internal
PR as a critical priority. Page 12.

To Tell The Truth
Today, most people believe
there are clear-cut concepts of
"lying" and "telling the truth."
Yet the reality of modern communications is that PR pros
often find themselves delivering what can be called "controlled honesty." Page 27.

DID YOU KNOW...

Hail To The Chiefs
The principal communication technology
used by CEOs:

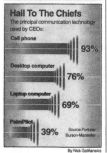

Cell phone — 93%

Desktop computer — 76%

Laptop computer — 69%

PalmPilot — 39%
Source: Fortune/
Burson-Marsteller

By Nick Galifianakis

COVER STORY

Survivors!

PR Pros Share
The Ups And Downs
Of Their Wild Ride
In Dot.Com Land

By Katie Sweeney

Just a year ago, many PR pros were still jumping at the
chance to work for a dot.com. And why not? Who
could pass up the opportunity to help build and brand
a new business in the New Economy – and pocket some
lucrative stock options along the way?

As it turned out, of course, many dot.coms' brush
with stardom turned into a mere 15 minutes of fame. In
2000 they came crashing back to Earth, closing their
doors or cutting costs – and staff – dramatically. In
December alone, recruitment firm Challenger, Gray &
Christmas reported a record 10,459 job cuts at Internet

Continued on page 16

FIGURE 21.1 *TACTICS*.

*"Survivors! PR Pros Share the Ups and Downs of Their Wild
Ride in Dot.Com Land."* Employees told of long hours, perks, and
promises unfulfilled. One comment from this article: Management
would say, "We're going to get X million dollars on this date," and it
never happened.

"Total Recall—Examining the Top PR stories of 2000." What were some of the top stories?

- Bridgestone/Firestone and Ford—A Troubled Road.
- Elian Gonzalez—Boy in a Bind.
- Airline Woes—Fly the Unfriendly Skies.
- The Emulex Hex—Newswires Under Scrutiny.
- Harry Potter and the Goblet of Fire—Promotional Wizardry.
- John Rocker [baseball pitcher]: Screwball?
- Dot.Com Crash—Here Today, Gone Tomorrow.

TACTICS also features "Trendwatch," a section of industry news and trends; "Talk From the Top," an insider's take on the issues facing business today; "Ask the Professor," a Q&A column on job-related questions; and "Hands On," how-to columns on improving tactical skills.

Public Relations *STRATEGIST*

This slick, quarterly PRSA publication is geared particularly to the issues facing senior management and public relations executives in business, government, and the nonprofit sector. Edited by author and industry leader Fraser Seitel, *STRATEGIST* contains well-reasoned debate and insightful commentary concerning the most demanding PR issues.

Highlights from recent issues are:

"Going to the Mat with the People's Governor (Jesse that is)."
"The New Reality for . . . Serving Public Relations Clients."
"Avoiding the Media At All Costs, Keeping the Media Satisfied."
"Integrating Communications on Internet Time."
"The Future of Public Relations Is On the Internet."
"Getting Along With Lawyers: A Primer for Public Relations."

One recent article in *STRATEGIST* was an interview with Murray H. Bring and Steven C. Parrish, top external affairs and corporate affairs officials at the Philip Morris Companies, the world's largest tobacco company. In the article they frankly discussed the issues the company faces in litigation, strategy, a hostile press, and the large amount of money the company gives away each year, a sum critics maintain is an attempt to balance guilt at selling cigarettes.

THE PUBLIC RELATIONS
STRATEGIST

VOLUME 7
NUMBER 1
WINTER 2001

ISSUES AND TRENDS THAT AFFECT MANAGEMENT

FIGURE 21.2 *STRATEGIST.*

Bulldog Reporter

Published semimonthly, with an eastern and a western edition, *BULLDOG REPORTER* is the media placement newsletter for professionals. It keeps track of editorial assignments so that media pitchers don't waste time with the wrong catchers. And it also tells PR people what kinds of stories various media are looking for.

It helps, for example, to know that a particular senior writer at the magazine *Fast Company* looks for stories like the one she did about multitasking. In it, she interviewed a renowned juggler, who spoke about keeping "all the balls in the air."

BULLDOG REPORTER even tells PR people how to pronounce difficult sounding names, such as the Associated Press's Tom Kirchofer (pronounced "ker cha fur"), a technology and Internet reporter.

Lifestyle Media Relations Reporter

Lifestyle is a publication of the Infocom Group, publishers of *BULLDOG REPORTER*. Its editorial focus is "insider reports on PR placement in consumer media." *Lifestyle* writes about job shifts in the media business, but also goes into depth about an important magazine editor or a broadcast producer's news needs.

For example, one recent issue of *Lifestyle* carried the head, "Wow Wallace with News, Trends for 'The Early Show.'"

Alex Wallace is the senior broadcast producer of the 3-million-viewers-audience CBS program "The Early Show." *Lifestyle* dispenses tips on how to break Ms. Wallace's show:

Pitch her early, on stories that are pegged to breaking news or a current trend. Example: "If there's something breaking—say there's a bombing somewhere and you have a terrorism expert—e-mail me *that* day."

Or, Wallace loves human interest stories, which, for her, are pieces that put a human face on a current trend, tragedy, or major news peg. "If, for example, you're pitching the growing problem of diabetes in children, give me the story of Fred Smith, a ten-year-old boy with diabetes," Wallace suggests hypothetically. "Give us a reason to cover a trend. Give us a human peg."

PR Agency Insider

In January 2000, Infocom Group launched the monthly *PR AGENCY INSIDER*. Here, the editorial focus is on PR agencies, or counsel firms, as we have referred to them. The publication's subhead is

VOLUME 22, ISSUE 22 / NOVEMBER 17, 2000

http://www.infocomgroup.com

BULLDOG REP RTER

THE MEDIA PLACEMENT NEWSLETTER FOR PR PROFESSIONALS WESTERN EDITION

FIRST BITES

➤ **U.S. News & World Report** assistant managing editor **Brian Kelly** (202/955-2630; bkelly@ usnews.com) advances to managing editor, overseeing the *Business & Technology* and *News You Can Use* sections. He replaces **Damon Darlin**, who moves to executive editor of **Business 2.0**. Senior political writer **Jodie Allen** (jallen@usnews.com) upshifts to assistant managing editor of *Business & Technology*. She replaces **Jim Impoco**, who joins **Fortune** magazine.

➤ **Dallas Morning News** hires **Wall Street Journal**/Dallas spot news reporter (Ms.) **J.C. Conklin** as healthcare reporter. She replaces **Charles Ornstein** (202/661-8410), who shifts to DC-based domestic policy issues correspondent. He still covers healthcare as well. Defense and GA reporter **Katie Fairbank** shifts to restaurant reporter. She replaces **Dianne Solis** (213/977-8701), who moves to assistant national editor, an addition. **Toni McCoy** joins as editorial assistant; contact the biz desk at (214) 977-8429. Deputy national editor **Mary Carter** (214/977-8088) shifts to political editor, an addition. **Sarah Campbell** (214/977-7671) is assistant national editor. Latin America correspondent **Tracey Eaton** (teaton@dallasnews.com) has been named bureau chief for the paper's new Havana bureau, due to open in Jan. Contact staffers at firstinitiallastname@ dallasnews.com.

➤ **Denver Rocky Mountain News** small business and workplace reporter **Erika Gonzales** (303/892-2631) shifts to healthcare, insurance, tourism and ski industry reporter. She replaces **Michele Conklin**, who leaves. **Heather Draper** (303/892-5456) boards as Gonzales' replacement. **Jeanie Stokes** joins as banking and personal finance reporter. She replaces **Guy Kelly**, who leaves. **David Wren** (303/892-2648) boards as assistant business editor, editing Sun.'s *Wall Street West* section, an addition. Staffer **Steve Caulk** (303/892-2744) shifts to stock market and GA biz reporter, an addition. They prefer faxes to (303) 892-2835; follow-up call O.K.

➤ **USA Today**/DC desk deputy managing editor **Mark Memmott** (703/276-6548) shifts to globalization reporter, an addition. White House assignment editor **Ed Foster-Simeon** (703/276-5849) replaces him. Congressional reporter **Wendy Koch** shifts to page one writer. Replacements for Koch and Simeon TBA.

➤ **Investor's Business Daily** correspondent **Ira Carnahan** leaves. Business reporter **Matthew Benjamin** leaves. At the Silicon Valley bureau, servers and net infrastructure reporter **Rex Crum**, software reporter **Lisa Wirthman**, and reporter **Michele Hostetler** leave. Direct SV pitches to bureau chief **Mike Krey** (408/720-2129). In LA, financial writer **Kinou Treiser** vacates. No replacements pending.

■ GENERAL BIZ, MANAGEMENT

Offer *Fast Company*'s Muoio Biz Strategies and Unique Insight

Since **Fast Company** has no particular beat list, targeting the right reporter for ink in the business solutions pub can often be a cumbersome task. But senior writer **Anna Muoio** (pron. "*moy* oh") offers some insight into her coverage: "I tend to write about leadership, change agents, e-learning, and model and mentor subjects—people outside the world of business who can offer insight into the world of business," she offers. Topics tend to be general, she adds, and she wants sources who can offer commentary on a broad scale.

INSIDE INFORMATION

Chart: Contacts at Fast Company **2**
USA Today's Media Reporter Alexander **2**
Inter@ctive Week's New Section B **3**
Chart: Inter@ctive Week Contacts **4**
PBS' Nightly Business Report **4**
PC Mag's Peripherals Section Editor Kaplan **5**
OC Reg's Telecom/Economics Reporter Berry **6**

FIGURE 21.3 BULLDOG REPORTER.

"What's New and What's Working For Growing Agencies," and its page-one Contents section defines its thrust:

- Idea Bank: "Brain Bang" for Creative Ideas.
- Retention Tip: Targeted Perks.
- Management: Keep Clients When AEs Leave.

A PUBLICATION OF
INFOCOM GROUP
http://www.infocomgroup.com

BULLDOG REPORTER'S

VOLUME 8 ISSUE 21
NOVEMBER 02, 2000

Lifestyle
MEDIA RELATIONS REPORTER
INSIDER REPORTS ON PR PLACEMENT IN CONSUMER MEDIA

FAST MOVES

■ **Country Living** hires **Cheryl Slocum** as associate food editor, an addition. Assistant home building editor **Emily Wolahan** leaves. Food editor **Cynthia LaGrone** has changed her name to **Cynthia Nicholson** (212/649-3514).

■ **Men's Health** editor-at-large **Denis Boyles** leaves. Associate editor **Matt Marion** advances to senior editor, nutrition. Associate editor **Ted Spiker** upshifts to senior editor. Assistant international editor **Mariska van Aalst** leaves. She is replaced by intern **Tracy Erb**. Intern **Lisa Jones** advances to assistant style editor, filling a vacancy. Contact the magazine at (610) 967-5171.

■ **YM** executive editor **Ellen Seidman** leaves. **The American Lawyer** managing editor **MaryAnn Saltser** (212/499-1682) joins as managing editor. She replaces **Mary Witherell**, who leaves. Senior editor **Chandra Czape** (pron. "*zah* pay") departs. Entertainment editor **Alyssa Vitrano** (212/499-1664) advances to entertainment director. Staffer **Patty Adams** (212/499-1666) upshifts to senior entertainment writer. Staffer **Danielle Raymond** (212/499-1663) advances to beauty and fitness director, filling a vacancy. **Vogue** market editor **Regina Teplitsky** (pron. "tep *lit* ski;" 212/499-1681) joins as fashion director. Replacements TBA.

■ **Ladies' Home Journal** senior articles editor **Pamela Guthrie O'Brien** (212/455-1052) upshifts to executive editor, replacing **Susan Crandell** (212/455-1053), who remains with **More** as executive editor. Senior entertainment editor **Melina Gerosa** leaves, replaced by new hire **Jim Brosseau**. O'Brien's replacement TBA.

■ **Redbook** senior editor **Christina Boyle Cush** (212/462-3314) joins **Modern Bride** as executive editor, replacing **Antonia van de Meer**, now editor-in-chief. Assistant editor **Patty Curtis** leaves to freelance. Associate editor **Rose Martelli** (212/649-3454) advances to associate health editor, an addition. **Emily Burton** (212/649-3417) joins as assistant managing editor. She replaces **Leslie Rhein**, who leaves. **Lisa Pilnik** (212/649-3423) joins as editorial assistant. She replaces **Sophie Sjoholm**, who leaves. Editorial assistant **Stefanie Marrone** (212/649-3433) advances to assistant articles editor, an addition. Replacements TBA.

CULTURE

Carvajal Craves Culture Stories for *New York Times*

If your pitch speaks to a widespread cultural trend, it may scream 'Story!' to **New York Times** reporter **Doreen Carvajal** (pron. "*car* va haul"). "A strong cultural angle is my main guideline," Carvajal says. "With just the right twist, I can turn a business pitch into

FIGURE 21.4 *Lifestyle Media Relations Reporter.*

BULLDOG REPORTER'S

PR AGENCY INSIDER

WHAT'S NEW AND WHAT'S WORKING FOR GROWING AGENCIES

VOLUME 1, NUMBER 12, DECEMBER 2000

Build Your Competitive Edge—And Stop Losing Business to Ad Agencies by Developing Your Own Advertising Strength

PR and advertising professionals have long offered services that cover common ground—enduring an uneasy alliance that has worsened recently as more PR firms find themselves losing clients to ad agencies with PR staff or departments. To regain competitive advantage, however, many PR shops have begun to fight back by supplementing their capabilities with advertising expertise to offer clients a more complete range of services.

MANAGEMENT

Here are four approaches used by PR agencies, to illustrate how you could offer full services and still keep your autonomy and professional standing:

1 **Form an alliance with an advertising agency or other specialists.** If you're a small agency—and especially a one- or two-person shop—you should think about forming an alliance with other sole

practitioners or small shops offering services you don't have. **Kim Gamel**, who offers PR under her company name **Catalyst Communications** in St Louis, has partnered successfully with **Compass Rose Marketing**. Actually, Compass Rose principals approached her because they were searching for PR competencies—and the relationship is working well after a year of multiple joint projects. Here are two ways to make this work:

• Keep the relationship seamless by incorporating staff from the ad agency into your creative team, and unifying the billing so that clients see a total cost rather than separate bills. Gamel does this and adds a 10 percent markup to the ad agency services.

• Take the client aware of the partnership, as sole practitioner **Carol Zahorsky** does in Olympia, Wash. She

continued on page 11

What's in a Name: How to Attract New Business Prospects and Stand Out from the Crowd by Choosing an New Agency Name

It's a jungle out there, and sometimes the race for a new client doesn't go to the swiftest, but rather to the one whose name everyone can remember. With high-tech PR now serving as a mainstay of agencies' client base, many firms—especially new ones—are selecting agency names that are memorable and serve to identify them with the market. A change from a bunch of principal names run together to a one- or two-word phrase that sparkles could win you the next big opportunity to get your foot in the door.

NEW BUSINESS

PRAI talked to several firms with new, distinctive and unusual names, to see how and why they did it and whether the efforts have been worth the costs. If you're contemplating this big step forward, check out these guidelines to stretch your creativity for maximum effect, to give your agency the competitive edge:

Stop Sounding Like a Law Firm

Look at any directory of PR agencies, and you'll see a

lot of eponymous names—which does nothing to explain what they do. More recently, however, many PR firms are abandoning legal-sounding monikers in favor of the innovative, "in your face" style that dot-coms and start-up high-tech firms are using.

continued on page 2

CONTENTS

FIGURE 21.5 *PR AGENCY INSIDER.*

- Staffing: Use Celebrations to Build Team Spirit.
- New Business: Keep Nonprofits in Line.
- Money: Divvying Up Profits With Employees.
- Bonus: Get Tech Savvy by Taking Quiz.

Infocom began publication of *MEDIA RELATIONS INSIDER* in January 2001 as a monthly dedicated to "what's new and what's working to increase your media coverage." It offers tips, news, and views for media relations professionals with articles such as these:

- Pitching Online Media—Determine If It's a Land of Opportunity or a Waste of Time.
- Experts Tell How to Respond When Your Company is Caught Red-Handed.
- The Nuts and Bolts of VNR Packages.
- PR Pros We Love—Journalists Reveal the Qualities They Most Respect.

All of Infocom's publications are practical, factual, and totally devoted to their mission of improving the skills and techniques of media relations people.

Bulldog Reporter publishes a *National PR Pitch Book*, which contains pitching tips, profiles, and contact data on more than 40,000 journalists from the nation's leading media.

You can search *BULLDOG REPORTER*, *Lifestyle*, *MEDIA RELATIONS INSIDER*, and *PR AGENCY INSIDER* at www.infocomgroup.com.

PRWeek

Long established in the United Kingdom, *PRWeek* divides editorial coverage into three areas: market focus or regional report, technique, and media.

The publication often adopts the light touch. A major feature of the February 19, 2001, issue was the "Top Ten Most Eligible Men and Women in PR," and the following week's edition covered "Fake Showbiz Relationships."

COMMUNICATION WORLD

COMMUNICATION WORLD is published six times a year by the IABC. Its editorial thrust is to provide information about the

BULLDOG REPORTER'S

MEDIA RELATIONS INSIDER

WHAT'S NEW AND WHAT'S WORKING TO INCREASE YOUR MEDIA COVERAGE

VOLUME 1 NUMBER 1
JANUARY 2001

TECHNIQUES

MEDIA UPDATES

ONLINE PR

Pitching Online Media—Determine If It's a Land of Opportunity or a Waste of Time

The statistics can be staggering—more than 6,000 news Web sites, people getting nearly a third of their news online and spending countless hours each week on the Internet. Some publicists have found that placing stories on the Internet gives their clients a sense of instant gratification. Yet, for many PR pros, the jury is still out on the true value of online media exposure and how much of your time it is really worth. The choice between trying to get your story on a Web site or into a tried-and-true newspaper or magazine can be a difficult one—especially when some clients are skeptical of the value of online publications.

Perhaps you haven't been pitching online media and are unsure of where to start, but are anxious to reach those information junkies and affluent consumers on the Web. We asked several PR practitioners with experience in placing stories online to provide some guidelines on how to determine which stories fit best on the Web.

1. If you're trying to reach a younger audience, pitching online may be the way to go. "I think it's fairly well accepted that with the Generation X and Generation Y crowds, those markets combined spend an increasing amount of time, whether at

continued on page 2

MEASUREMENT

Prove Your Value—New Study Compares the Effect of Public Relations Versus Advertising

A recent study has found what many PR pros have long known but could not prove—public relations can be more potent in promoting awareness of a product than placing advertisements. Until PR researcher **Bruce Jeffries-Fox** conducted the groundbreaking study for AT&T last year, no one had ever looked at how news coverage interacts with advertising. PR was viewed as an intangible commodity compared to ads, which give people artifacts they can see, hold and more readily measure. As a result, advertising usually gets a bigger piece of the budget pie.

Now that could change. The study's conclusions—that PR is often a better investment than advertising when it comes to changing people's opinions and behavior—can be powerful ammunition when you try to convince your upper management to boost your budget.

Jeffries-Fox, currently executive vice president of **InsightFarm**, a joint venture between Burrelle's and Video Monitoring Service, says that with PR now in its heyday, there is a greater need for accountability to justify larger budgets. He shared with **Media Relations Insider** the results of his study that won the CIPRA and PR Week Proof awards for best PR research:

• In "normal" timesperiods where there is little controversy either positive or negative—news coverage and advertising

continued on page 10

FIGURE 21.6   *MEDIA RELATIONS INSIDER.*

PRWEEK

October 22, 2001

20 years and counting
In a business world where loyalty is a rare commodity, companies like the Fabulous Fox Theater have enjoyed long relationships with their PR agencies. PRWeek looks at the ties that bind Page 20

How does fashion PR look?
The September 11 attacks forced the fashion industry to cancel its crucial New York Fashion Week. In turn, the entire sector has had to design truly creative concepts to stay on the runway Page 23

Heightened alert
Taking every precaution to ensure safety is paramount at present, the Sears Tower has heightened communication with all tenants as part of its overall crisis preparation plan Page 4

Quote of the week

> **Communications schools need to teach more business, and business schools need to teach more communications**
>
> Paul Argenti, professor at Tuck School of Business, explains the role MBA schools might play in giving the corporate world a better understanding of the value of PR
> Page 18

$4.00
Periodicals

Neely is the likely pick for Office of Homeland Security's top PR pos

By Douglas Quenqua
WASHINGTON: Susan Neely, SVP for communications at the Association of American Medical Colleges, has emerged as the likely nominee for the director of communications position in the newly created Office of Homeland Security, according to White House and industry sources.

Tom Ridge, director of the new office and former governor of Pennsylvania, reportedly met with Neely early in the week and gave his approval. A White House source confirmed that she was being "looked at closely," and was indeed the top person being considered for the position.

Neely, who declined to comment for this article, has long been a fixture on the Washington PR scene, and was recently elected chairwoman of the Public Affairs Council (PAC) effective 2003.

Doug Pinkham, president of the PAC, said Neely's experience as a communications executive in the medical and insurance industries make her uniquely qualified for the homeland security position, as she has a "great ability to understand how public policy and communications work together."

The Office of Homelan Security was created President Bush in response the attacks of September 11. is charged with coordinatir the intelligence and activiti of 46 federal agencies in a attempt to protect again future terrorist attacks o American soil.

Kodak switches its focus to Ketchum for global PR

By Eleanor Trickett
ROCHESTER, NY: Ketchum has emerged triumphant in the three-way battle for Kodak's giant PR account, put into play in August after a split with Weber Shandwick Worldwide.

The business encompasses global brand PR strategy for the Kodak Professional, Customer Imaging, and Digital & Applied Imaging divisions, coupled with full implementation of that strategy in the US initially.

Fleishman-Hillard and Ogilvy PR also competed for the business. Ogilvy's failure to convert the pitch will be keenly felt, as many had thought it would be a shoo-in. Not only does Ogilvy handle the PR business for a number of markets in Europe and Asia, but many of Kodak's other marketing requirements are handled by sister WPP shops. Ad agency Ogilvy & Mather, media planning and buying shop MindShare, direct-marketing agency OgilvyOne, and new-media shop Ogilvy Interactive all work for the photo giant.

Kodak... *Ketchum will be key to integrated marketing plans*

Charles Smith, director of worldwide PR and VP for Kodak Consumer Business, explained that he was now looking to have "fewer agency relationships" across the globe, and was gradually replacing

WSW on a "pan-regional basis," suggesting that further account reviews worldwide were to be expected.

While contractual arrangements are still being hammered out, Ketchum would not disclose how many staffers would be assigned to the business, nor would Kodak disclose a budget for competitive reasons. The account will initially involve the New York office, as well as Atlanta (where Kodak's consumer sales and marketing operations are headquartered) for consumer and digital expertise, relying on Ketchum/CTC in Chicago for b-to-b technology input. But both parties stressed that this arrangement was "for now," suggesting that the relationships would spread globally as the account takes hold.

Smith explained that Ketchum would be working closely with Kodak's other agencies – the result of an effort on Kodak's part to integrate all marketing activity under the tagline "Share moments. Share life."

"In the past, we have had separate advertising and marketing campaigns and spoke with multiple voices to the consumer," said Smith, "but now it is all aligned. Kodak's message is all about getting better pictures and finding ways to share them."

Ketchum secure coveted Panam tourism accoun

By Robin Londner
ATLANTA: Ketchum has scored second win this week, this tin with sister ad agency BBD beating out three other ad-P teams to represent the Panam tourism board.

For the past two year Interpublic's McCann-Eric son ad agency represente Panama in a $1 million deal wi little PR work. This win has bee cited as a $10 million accour

The new program will invol 15-20 international Ketchu staffers, as Panama targets aud ences in the US, Canada, Chil Columbia, Argentina, Cos Rica, France, Italy, German and Spain. Ines Rodrigue. Gutzmer, VP/GM of Ketchum Latin America group, will lea the account from Atlanta.

Rodriguez-Gutzmer said sh plans limited media relation "Panama is not for every one," she said. "We're going t focus on key influencers in tar get audiences such as ec tourism, adventure, an historical travel."

To win the account, Ketchur bested teams from BVK/Pume Imagen 10 with Fleishman Hillard, Diaz/TBWA wit Roberto Gaudelli y Asociado and incumbent McCannErick son World Group/Panama.

Workers fear loss of job over safety, suggests survey

By Robin Londner
NEW YORK: Job security is a bigger concern to employees than personal security, suggests new research from the Council of PR Firms.

Council president Jack Bergen said findings show the increasing importance and sensitivity of internal communications, and encourage companies to ramp up these efforts.

The survey of 1,013 employees nationwide found that 36%

were concerned about being laid off or their company going out of business, more than twice the 16% who were anxious about their physical security at work.

In evaluating communications since September 11, 59% rated their companies' communications to them about worker fears, concerns, and business outlook as excellent or good. However, 31% rated it fair or poor, and 7% said there had been no communication at all.

Bergen credited companies with stepping up communications with workers since September 11, and for creating dialogue with a new tone of openness and sensitivity.

Ex-Chase exec to lead Oracle global PI

By Julia Hood
REDWOOD CITY, CA: Oracle has named former Chase Manhattan exec James Finn as its new VP of worldwide PR.

Finn will spearhead a vastly beefed-up in-house team, and will cast his net far and wide to recruit more talent. He will also scrutinize Oracle's PR agency relationships with an open mind. "Everything is on the table," he explained.

Last month, Oracle ended its eight-year relationship with agency of record Applied Communications. Oracle continues to retain PR21 to work on the applications side. Finn said he will start discussions with PR21 soon. "I'm going to be looking at the whole situation. The goal is to communicate as one company with one voice, and I have an open mind about how we achieve that."

The position was previously held by Margaret Lasecke-Jacobs, but has not been filled for

Oracle... *Finn will run global PR from Redwood City campus*

a year. Oracle currently has an in-house PR team of about 25 people.

Finn will report to Mark Jarvis, chief marketing officer. Jarvis said filling the job was not easy. "It was very hard to find people in PR who have global experience," he said.

"In talking to Mark, it became

very clear to me that we shar the same brand of aggressive PI thinking," Finn said.

Finn was previously SVP fo PR at Chase Manhattan, and a executive with the New York based treasurer's office of Gen eral Motors. He also worked in IBM's Europe, Middle East, an Africa operations.

FIGURE 21.7 *PRWEEK.*

FIGURE 21.8   COMMUNICATION WORLD.

profession of organizational communication and news of IABC, its members, chapters, and activities.

One recent article was titled "Getting It, the Making of a Dot-comer." A lamentable accompanying piece was headed "Downfall of a Dot-comer."

Another article in the same issue, "The Annual Report Isn't What It Used to Be," afforded practical tips on producing the report, while another informational article, "Gather the GURUS, Then Get Them Into Global Teleconferencing," discussed the near future of this Internet convergence.

PR Reporter

PR Reporter, a weekly newsletter, covers public relations, public affairs, and communication strategies. A highlight of *PR Reporter*'s editorial concept is its in-depth case studies in which the editors interpret a situation and the strategy chosen, the tactics employed, and the results of a PR campaign.

A recent feature, "Earning Public Relations a Seat at the Boardroom Table," had tips for gaining this important access. One was "don't wait to be asked," two, "know what keeps the CEO up at night," and three, "get involved in the company's policy-making process." Reach *PR Reporter* at www.prpublishing.com

Ragan Communications

Ragan publishes more than 16 targeted newsletters in the areas of employee communications, Web PR, organizational writing and editing, sales and marketing, media relations, motivational management, and investor relations.

In addition to these services, Ragan produces several communications conferences, workshops, and senior-level forums throughout the United States. Ragan's Web address: www.ragan.com

INTERNET SERVICES AND RESOURCES TO BOOST PUBLIC RELATIONS CREATIVITY

PR professionals use dozens of Internet tools and services to move their messages to media sources. We discuss a number of them here:

PR Newswire (www.prnewswire.com)

PR Newswire (PRN) is the leader in the electronic delivery of news releases and information directly from companies, institutions and agencies to the media, financial community, and consumers. Let's look at some PRN services.

Tyson Foods is the world's largest fully integrated producer, processor, and marketer of chicken and poultry-based food products. PRN conducted a conference call on the Web (CCOW) to announce Tyson's fourth quarter financial results.

When Federal Reserve chairman Alan Greenspan addressed the American Council of Life Insurance, PRN Webcast the speech via live streaming video on the Internet in real time.

PRN Video takes clients' commercials, B-roll, movie footage, trailers, or company background footage and delivers them on the Internet.

Among PRN's numerous targeted products and services are:

Newslines	Information services
Photo services	Database services
Fax services	Small business tools
Multimedia services	Journalist profiles
Broadcast services	Agency links

Tracking Media

Many services track media coverage. Started as clipping bureaus, these services sent clients "clips" of articles that appeared in a newspaper or magazine.

As media became more advanced and included broadcast and other outlets, a need developed for electronic clipping services to track the dissemination of this information. One such firm, Burrelle's Information Services (www.burrelles.com), monitors electronic newspapers and magazines; broadcast networks, both TV and radio; specialized cable networks; and news and wire services such as the Associated Press.

Burrelle's NewsAlert is a combination of technology and editing expertise, delivering custom-filtered stories daily from thousands of online publications. It also tracks network news broadcasts, Web pages, news groups, and chat rooms.

With NewsAlert, Burrelle's is able to search for all mentions of a company and its products or services, monitor competitors, keep tabs on public opinion and the organization's reputation, and monitor crisis situations.

Luce Online (www.luceonline.com)

Luce is an automatic, electronic news clipping service provider delivering up-to-the-minute stories from more than 7,000 print publications, newspapers, wire services, magazines, trade publications, and Internet/online newsites.

Lexis-Nexis (www.lexisnexis.com)

The Lexis-Nexis research service contains more than 1 trillion characters and 1.4 billion documents in more than 8,692 databases. It adds 4.6 million documents each week. Lexis-Nexis is an electronic clipping service that offers database research that may be accessed via computer.

PR Infofinder (www.prsa.org/ppc)

PR Infofinder navigates quickly and easily to high-value public relations and marketing information, services, and resources. Built-in content analyzer, relevancy ranking, and summary features eliminate wasted time.

Online Public Relations (www.online-pr.com)

This is an easy to navigate online catalog of public relations, media and marketing sources.

PRPlace (www.prplace.com)

This site features a free guide to 700 major U.S. media, and hot-linked lists of PR publications and PR organizations, news sources and news services, and journalism interest groups.

About.com (www.about.com)

About.com is a network of comprehensive Web sites for over 500 topics, run by About.com Guides, from across the Net and around the world.

Corporate Information (www.corporateinformation.com)

This is actually a list of other sites that offer information about private or international companies that is otherwise hard to find. It is organized by country with a simple search feature.

InfoSeek (www.infoseek.com)

A search of Infoseek can yield the most relevant matches, topics to explore, and news from popular magazines, TV networks, and the best online experts. The InfoSeek Guide makes it easy to find e-mail addresses, stock quotes, company profiles, and more.

Excite (www.excite.com)

This unique concept is based on navigation technology. It covers over 11.5 million pages and is updated weekly. A team of journalists reviews sites. Excite also offers Usenet newspaper groups, hourly news, and commentary.

AJR Newslink (www.newslink.org)

This site links to newspapers, magazines, and TV sites. It couples statistics on Internet sources.

Federal News Service (www.fnsg.com)

Want to read Vladimir Putin's latest speech verbatim? Federal News furnishes same-day transcripts of the actual works spoken by Russian and American leaders on matters of official government policy and other issues.

Bacon's Media Directory (www.bacon's.com)

Bacon's comprehensive media directory maintains a list of nearly 300,000 contacts at 60,000 media outlets, plus thousands of editorial calendars.

CHAPTER 22

The Job Search

In 1993, when the first edition of this book was published, I wrote in the job search chapter that getting a job any time is difficult. When times are bad and companies are downsizing, or even worse, going out of business, finding a job in PR is a Promethean task.

I also said, "It is as difficult getting a job at one of the large PR counsel firms as it is at the top advertising agencies. These firms have their pick of outstanding graduates."

Well, 8 years later the task is not quite Promethean; let's just call it formidable. Much has changed in public relations in this short time span. Corporations that spent huge sums on advertising have redirected their spending and turned to public relations as a potent promotion and marketing medium. Many advertising agency groups have purchased public relations counsel firms, and the largest firms have gone global in a big way.

In 1993, I wrote that Edelman Public Relations Worldwide, then the sixth-largest PR firm in the world, employed 500 people. In 2001, Edelman is still the sixth-largest firm worldwide and employs more than 1,000 in the United States alone and 2,000 worldwide.

Another major development is the relationship of high tech and PR. Most of the top firms have substantial high-tech divisions, and today, there are many firms whose practice is exclusively in this area.

An article in the booklet of the Council of Public Relations Firms, *A Student's Guide to Public Relations Education*, notes that the new century marks the golden age of public relations. Professionals are employed at an estimated 6,000 PR counseling firms, thousands of corporations, more than 500 trade associations, and at the media relations departments of hundreds of colleges and universities. In addition, PR people are working at the federal, state, and city levels of government, and at hospitals, social welfare agencies, religious institutions, cultural organizations, philanthropies, and many other nonprofit organizations.

With the globalization of business, both on the corporate and the PR counsel firm side, comes a need for trained PR personnel to spread the word about products and services to a world population.

The U.S. Bureau of Labor Statistics estimates that PR is one of the fastest growing professional fields in this country. PR firms are constantly looking for new people as their businesses grow. But many candidates don't fill the bill. Why? They didn't learn to write well, they didn't pursue the right courses in college, and they didn't work at internships. There are a dozen reasons. We'll discuss them here.

FINDING THE FIRST JOB

No task is harder than finding a job, particularly your first. Success in this endeavor requires planning, preparation, energy, and enthusiasm—all in large doses. Here is some basic advice. We'll go into specifics later.

- Research the field in which you have the greatest interest. Use libraries and the Internet. Journalists are also useful sources.
- Prepare a good résumé.
- Learn about possible job openings in advance of contacting employers. Scan the list of Fortune 500 companies. Chances are these companies have large PR departments. Write to the top PR executive, as well as the head of human resources. Follow up your letter with a phone call.

- Use personal contacts for referrals. They are your best sources for job leads.
- Use business directories for company names. Two important ones are *O'Dwyer's Directory of PR Firms* and *O'Dwyer's Directory of Corporate Communications*.
- Contact all the large PR firms in chapter 4 of this book.
- Prepare for an interview by learning as much as you can about the corporations or organizations you are visiting. Read their annual reports and look for articles about them in trade journals.
- Show samples of any press releases you have written and include copies of any press coverage these releases have generated. Your portfolio should contain this material, as well as any other writing you have done, particularly if it has been published. Writing for college publications can be used, but only if it is your best effort and is clear, concise, and informative.
- Take the initiative in the interview by describing your qualifications and what you believe you can accomplish on the job.
- Don't fret about rejection; it is no cause to suppose that you will not qualify elsewhere. Consider your job hunt as a learning experience. Perseverance will win you the opportunity to begin your PR career.
- Read any current books you can find about public relations and its related fields.
- Contact your college's alumni association. This will enable you to track people from your school who have gone to work at a company in which you are interested.
- Attend job fairs in which PR firms are participating. Ask specific questions about hiring procedures and company policies.
- Make sure you are adept at cold calling, letter writing, and networking, because these are the ways you will probably get your first job.
- Don't lie or exaggerate on your résumé. Your prospective employer will undoubtedly check references, education, and job experience.

TIPS FROM INDUSTRY PROFESSIONALS

The PRSSA asked a group of seasoned professionals what they valued in people seeking to break into the field. Their answers offer insight into the experience and characteristics needed to get started in PR. Asked, "If I were planning to enter the field again today, I'd," they replied:

"Earn an advanced degree, perhaps an MBA [and] learn more about the social sciences."

"Improve my writing skills and learn more about business."

"Study liberal arts and work in the college PR office."

"Study economics, history, sociology. As vacation preparation I'd get a job on a daily newspaper or a business news magazine."

"See about a foreign job in PR in Hong Kong, London, or Geneva, then return to the U.S. in a year or two."

"Get a few years' writing experience in print or broadcast."

"Join a counseling firm in any capacity whatsoever."

"Study economics and speech; force myself to join debating groups, etc."

"Have a better understanding of techniques of writing and a broader knowledge of report writing."

What Employers Look for in Job Candidates

In a survey conducted by Dr. Dennis L. Wilcox at San Jose State University, 90 top-level employers were asked about the traits, qualities, and educational background that are desirable in public relations candidates. Sixty-five replied. Highlights of their answers indicate that the ideal applicant will have:

A 4-year undergraduate degree.
Courses in news writing, business, and social sciences.
An outstanding personality and a willingness to work.
The ability to write well.
Work experience in a related field.

The respondents also said that a bachelor's degree is a minimum, and a master's degree, particularly an MBA, is helpful.

An applicant's attitude is important to 97% of the employers, and writing ability got a 95% vote. Other significant traits were growth potential 88%, poise 71%, cooperativeness 69%, and speaking ability 65%.

In the Council of Public Relations Firms booklet, a paragraph titled "Writing Classes" merits particular consideration. We quote it here:

Even in this digital age when the computer and the Internet have become a more popular source of information than traditional media (such as newspapers), the ability to write well is still a critical public relations function.

The Top Ten Characteristics for Entry-Level Practitioners

John Milkereit, APR, Fellow PRSA, manages his own PR and marketing consulting business in Charleston, South Carolina. In an article in the March 2001 issue of *TACTICS*, he highlighted the most important qualities that a new-to-the-field PR practitioner should possess. Here is his top 10 list:[2]

1. Strong sense of empathy.
2. Being a good listener.
3. Critical thinking skills.
4. Willingness to start at the bottom.
5. Skill in writing and a mastery of English usage.
6. Maturity in self-expression and oral skills.
7. Ability to organize and edit information.
8. Maturity in grooming and appearance.
9. A good manager of personal time.
10. Experience in community service.

THE RIGHT STUFF ABOUT THE JOB SEARCH

Some students wait for graduation to begin hunting for a job in public relations on the theory that they are better prepared at that point to tackle this daunting assignment. Most authorities disagree with this approach, maintaining that an internship is a more practical way to get started. In either case, there are steps to follow in the job-seeking process.

One of the most important tools to landing your first job is your résumé.

It's the vehicle you use to market yourself to potential employers, and it should distinguish you from all other candidates. A well-written résumé is the key to securing an interview. Write your cover letter and résumé so that your accomplishments, not just your experience, are emphasized. That way, you're more likely to convince an employer that it would be in the company's best interest to hire you.

Because your résumé is often your first chance to make a good impression, write it in such a way that will make you stand out. You'll want to highlight your skills and strengths in a simple but polished format. Here are some do's and don't's about the résumé-writing process:

Do:

- Write the résumé as a one-page account of yourself.
- Include all of the following: name, address, phone and fax numbers, e-mail, position desired, summary statement, education, practical experience, pertinent internships or part-time work while at college, and extracurricular and voluntary activities reported chronologically or in terms of the types of skills demonstrated or the work accomplished.
- Be persuasive and honest. Pay attention to the impression your résumé makes by its layout and the way you express yourself. Remember to use action-oriented words, and check and recheck your résumé, particularly for typographical errors.
- Include names, addresses, and phone numbers of two or three references. Don't say "References available."
- List all your computer skills and competence.
- If you've won any awards for educational excellence or leadership, detail them.
- If you have writing ability, be prepared to show samples.
- If you have already been in the job market, show the internal promotion you had. The lack of progress on a job suggests that you're on the job market because you can't get ahead in your present job.

Don't:

- Address the résumé package to "Dear Sir."
- Create a gimmicky or cutesy résumé.
- Include self-defeating comments such as, "Please don't misconstrue my fourteen jobs as job hopping. I have never quit a job" or "Work skills: strong on interpersonal relations, typing, filing, and reproduction."
- Omit dates of past jobs or college degrees. It looks like you are hiding something.
- Use a highly ornamental résumé. Avoid slick paper and bright colors that might imply you emphasize appearance over content.

Is Your Résumé a Joke?

Robert Half is the founder and president of Robert Half International, the world's largest staffing service. In an article in *The Wall Street Journal's* "Managing Your Career," Half contributed from his collection of résumé bloopers.[1]

"Some of the worst," said Half, "come from college grads seeking their first jobs." Here are some favorites with Half's comments in parentheses.

- Graduated Magna Cum Loud.
- No degree due to school refusing to give it to me.
- Have taken repeated courses constantly (Could you repeat that).
- A job in the financial sector commiserates with my education (And someone to commiserate with in the event she doesn't find that job).
- To work for a strong, growing company in a professional environment with opportunities for advancement and the union of inculcated academic ideals with practical objectivity (Doesn't everyone?).

Half ended the article with this piece of advice:

> "There are thousands more examples of what happens when students fail to pay proper attention to their résumés before dropping them into the mail. Through scrupulous proofreading (ask a trusted friend to help), you can avoid earning the wrath of overworked, impatient résumé readers. I wish you good luck in your chosen career, and hope that your résumé will never land in my blooper file."

Don't Overlook the Cover Letter

An article in the *Yale Daily News Guide to Internships 2000* by the staff of the *Yale Daily News*, published by Kaplan and Simon & Schuster, stresses the importance of the cover letter that accompanies the résumé. Here are a few do's from this excellent book:

- To a potential employer, both the cover letter and the résumé are like "hearing your voice on paper." Try to stay away from the form-letter mentality; make it original but keep it brief.
- Before you begin to write, think about these basic questions: Why are you interested in this position? What do you have to offer the company? What do you have that helps you stand out from the other candidates?

- Clearly state what job you want and why you are qualified.
- Make your cover letter brisk and upbeat.
- Match your personal interests with those of the company.
- Show enthusiasm about the job to which you are applying.
- Keep it to the point and not longer than one page.
- Demonstrate some knowledge of the company.
- Type your cover letter.

The Director of an International Career Marketing Firm Talks About Résumés and Cover Letters

Steve Stromp is the director of client services for Bernard Haldane Associates, an international career marketing firm. He manages Haldane's career advising staffs in 16 U.S. and Canadian markets. Here are some questions and answers on the subject of résumés and cover letters taken from an online interview on Washingtonpost.com: Live Online:

Columbia, Maryland: *Should your cover letter summarize your résumé or should it give more of a personal overview?*

Steve Stromp: Consider the cover a mini résumé. Tailor it to the position and highlight relevant portions of the résumé.

Washington, D.C.: *Is it true that most employers now screen résumés by computer?*

Steve Stromp: Yes, and this requires that you prepare your résumé accordingly in ASCII format, 60 characters wide.

Bethesda, MD: *Should you create several forms of your résumé to target different types of jobs, e.g., training, management, and research?*

Steve Stromp: A résumé is really an ad describing a product—you. So I'd suggest one résumé that allows you to cover the market. If you have the résumé on your computer, you can make slight changes to meet specific jobs.

Ft. Washington, MD: *Is there some unwritten rule that says a résumé should be one page in length?*

Steve Stromp: You will get different opinions. Mine? I feel a two-page résumé is effective. Why compress your qualifications into one page? If you're early in your career, a one-page may be OK, but for most people I'd suggest two pages.

Washington, D.C.: *Can you advise a "good" résumé program or guideline? One that would be within current standards for today's job searcher?*

Steve Stromp: Most résumés I see from the general public are historical in nature. You want an action-driven, results-oriented résumé that highlights what you can do. Don't focus on your job responsibilities; stress what you've accomplished. Employers want to know what you can do, not what you were required to do.

Fairfax, VA: *Can I write a general cover letter to send to many different places?*

Steve Stromp: No. If you expect results, take the time to tailor your letter to the company's requirements. The Haldane system provides special techniques on how to do this.

Washington, D.C.: *I'd like to know more about automatic résumé screening. Are there certain magic words that always work? Also, does this mean no one will read that letter I labored over?*

Steve Stromp: An increasing number of employers today use computers to scan résumés into a database and search for key words. If your résumé lacks such information, you may get few hits. Scan the classifieds and notice what skills employers are seeking in your field. Build those key words into your résumé—if they apply. If you're still not getting results, continue to play with the word mix.

Washington, D.C.: *What are the rules for submitting résumés via e-mail? Do hiring managers prefer to receive attachments of MS Word documents, or should the résumé be included in the body of the e-mail? Do cover letters need to follow any special formatting rules in e-mails?*

Steve Stromp: Don't send employers an e-mail with the résumé attached. Because of viruses, companies try to avoid opening attachments. Write a cover letter in the e-mail and paste a 60-character-wide ASCII version of your résumé.

Bethesda, MD: *I've sent out a number of letters–résumés over the past month but have not yet heard back from the companies. Is it a good idea to call them and ask for an interview directly?*

Steve Stromp: You're a reactive job-hunter waiting for companies to call. Be proactive. Where there is opportunity, call the HR office before you mail; talk to the specialist who will be screening résumés. Direct your letter to that person by name. Include an action close in the letter. Rather than writing "I can be reached at (000) 000–0000, state, "I will call you November 22 to discuss my qualifications in greater detail and schedule an appointment." I guarantee you'll get improved results this way.

Résumés Go on a Trip Into Cyberspace

By the end of 2000, there were more than 2.1 billion available Web pages for companies to dig out talented job prospects.

Today's job seekers are a sophisticated bunch. They prepare their résumés in several different formats: producing one in traditional hard copy for use in interviews and mailings, and a plain text résumé they can send out in the body of an e-mail.

Job candidates may also fill out online questionnaires and post them directly to an employer's Web site, where they are stored. The employer then searches the database using relevant keywords that will pop up information on the kind of candidate he or she is looking for.[2]

In a popular technique called "flipping," recruiters can search the entire Web for employees who have worked for, or even attended, a conference held by a particular employer, provided a link is listed back to that company on their electronic résumé.

Here are some tips for getting your résumé noticed on the Internet.

> Post a digital version of your résumé with examples of past work experience on your own home page. Many colleges and professional associations offer free or low-cost Web space and resources for posting résumés.
>
> Place the word "résumé" in the Web site address to increase your chances of being caught by Internet recruiters.
>
> Place plenty of links to Web sites of present and former employers, colleges, professional associations, and publications on your digital résumé.
>
> Create a simpler version of your résumé to send to a recruiter or potential employer and let them know a longer version is available.
>
> Read the privacy policies on online job boards to prevent unwanted eyes from viewing your résumé. Some companies have "Web scavengers" who check for their own employees' résumés online. In turn, some job boards let users "block" certain companies from seeing their postings.
>
> Use niche job boards in your field. Smaller, targeted boards can sometimes be more effective than the big brand-name sites. (Source: CareerXroads, RISE Internet Recruiting Seminars, Advanced Internet Recruiting Strategies)

What about the numerous job sites that compete aggressively for the attention of employers, as well as candidates? Opinions differ on the efficacy of online job applications. A study from Forrester Research in 2000 concluded that the quality of jobs offered on the Internet is below average and that online résumé databases generate little response.

The success rate among job seekers is telling. The Forrester study found that only 4% of respondents found their latest job using the Net, compared with 40% who landed a job from a referral and 23% from a newpaper ad.

In the Forrester Research study, Monster.com had the highest number of users, more than 10.1 million registered, but Craigslist.com, a tiny, Bay Area nonprofit organization, scored highest for efficiency in finding employees.

Some college career centers further the job-seeking process by having prospective graduates fill out an online form that includes courses, activities, and work experience. A center then e-mails the completed form to companies, online job boards, and on-campus recruiters. Job candidates may find themselves being courted by major firms without ever putting ink to paper.

A STUDENT'S GUIDE TO PUBLIC RELATIONS EDUCATION

The best college programs in PR will prepare students for skills in the following areas:

- Research, including methods, analysis, recommendations, reporting, environmental and social assessment, and understanding research statistics.
- Management of information, including its role in the public relations process.
- Mastery of language, both written and oral.
- Problem solving and negotiation.
- Management of communication.
- Strategic planning.
- Issues management, including environmental scanning, issue anticipation, risk analysis, and change methodology.
- Audience segmentation.
- Technology and visual literacy (particularly Internet and desktop).
- Publishing and development of new media.
- Message strategies and the design and layout of messages.
- Managing people, programs, and resources.
- Sensitive interpersonal communication.
- Fluency in a second language.
- Ethical decision making.
- Participation in the professional public relations community.
- Writing and production of specific communications messages.
- Informative and persuasive writing for various audiences.

- Area of emphasis such as community relations, consumer relations, government relations, employee relations, investor relations, and media relations.
- Working within a current issue environment.
- Public speaking and presentation skills.
- Applying cross-cultural and cross-gender sensitivity. (Source: *A Student's Guide to Public Relations Education Council of Public Relations Firms*)

Not all college PR programs offer the same curriculum. PRSA and leading educators agree that the most important skills are the ability to communicate effectively in written and oral form and to be able to think creatively and quickly.

Do You Need an Advanced Degree to Make It in Public Relations?

If you're shooting for the corner office (a few still exist) in a PR firm or a corporation, it may be a good choice to attend graduate school. There, if you've chosen the right school, you'll acquire advanced skills and knowledge in research, problem solving, and issues, as well as management-level expertise.

Although many PR industry leaders agree that a degree in mass communications with a major in public relations is sufficient background for a career in this field, others build a strong case for an advanced degree.

Most advanced degrees call for 30 to 36 credit hours of graduate coursework in course areas such as:

Communication theory
Communication law
Research methods
Communications management
Communications processes
Programming and production
Management sciences
Behavioral sciences

Here are the comments of the well-known author and teacher Dr. Doug Newsom on the subject of graduate education[3]:

> Graduate education helps you work smarter. You learn research methods that enlarge your professional public relations "tool box."

Exposure to a broader range of literature makes you examine strategies carefully, ask "why" a lot more often and look for evidence that effort equals effects.

We add that a graduate degree is a great boost in the search for the first job.

ACING THE INTERVIEW

You've taken all the right public relations courses at college. Now, whether you're applying for an internship or a full-time job, you'll have to face the blue funk of an interview.

Here are the comments of a group of seasoned professionals on what impresses them most when interviewing an entry-level candidate:

"Personal attributes such as appearance, self-confidence, courtesy... ability to learn as well as respond thoughtfully... how well candidate has done homework about our company, etc."

"Articulateness, clear thinking, pleasant disposition, high energy, and good writing samples that stress ability to think, not just to string words together."

"Their knowledge of my company."

"Enthusiasm (but not phony), writing ability."

"Self-confidence, knowledge of the humanities, interest in business."

"Sincerity... the candidate's desire to learn from the bottom up."

"Breadth of interest—economic, political, social, philosophic."

"Ability to manage time."

"Brain power and intellect."

"Enthusiasm... candor... good work samples."

"Working experience in media or PR he or she had while in school."

"Crystal-clear and orderly speech—suggesting an orderly mind."

"Ability to listen, as well as converse... demeanor and dress."

"The gray matter he/she has, an eagerness to learn."

"The questions he/she asks."

"Evidence of intelligence, motivation, and interpersonal skills."

"Knowledge of what PR is and isn't."
"The preparation the candidates have made for the interviews."
(Source: PRSSA)

An article in Kaplan/*Newsweek*'s book, *How to Use the INTERNET to Choose or Change CAREERS*, puts a new face on today's interview process.[4] Overwhelmed by the need to hire the best people in an employee's market, employers are trying new techniques to sift for winners and sign them up. They're prescreening applicants with online interviews, telescoping a month's worth of meetings into day-long marathons, and administering psychological questions and skills tests. And in an effort to reclaim power in a job hunter's market, they're making "exploding" job offers: Accept within 48 hours or the deal's off the table.

If you think you're in the driver's seat in an interview situation, grab the initiative. Find out what you really want to know about the company. Ask about corporate culture, the clients, and the pace of work, with questions like, "How frequent are your staff meetings?" or "Could you describe what my typical day might be?" A question like "How is your new expansion in Europe going?" shows you've done your homework. "But," says the article, "don't ask about pay and retirement benefits. That discussion will come soon enough—maybe by the end of the day."

Why People Bomb in Interviews

An article in the spring 1997 issue of *Managing Your Career*, published by Dow Jones, offered an assessment of why job candidates fail interviews[5]:

- You can't translate the questions being asked.
- You fail to consider what the company wants in a new employee.
- When asked why you should be hired, you cited only values.
- When replying to the icebreaker, "Tell me about yourself," you started with where you were born and continue chronologically.
- You didn't research the company.
- You haven't a clue why you should be hired.
- You didn't prepare for a weak interviewer.
- You forgot that your ability to fit into the company's culture is important.

- You confused interviewing with psychotherapy or a gig at a comedy club.
- You failed to exude confidence.

These valuable tips are general, yet they are certainly applicable to jobs in public relations.

An article in *The New York Times*, on January 30, 2001, pointed to another important issue—"Finessing Interviews: Don't Ask, Do Tell." Its message was, complete candor in the interview process.[6]

"Your mantra," said David Kirby, author of the article, "should be anticipation and preparation. You want to anticipate the questions and prepare your answers in advance." Kirby went on to say, "Begin by studying your past very carefully. Short-lived jobs, abrupt departures, and gaps in your résumé almost always raise red flags."

Kirby also said that job placement experts recommend that you carefully respond to questions about gaps in your résumé, address why you haven't found a job by now, and offer candor about your weaknesses.

The PRSA Tips on Interviews

PRSA again weighs in with sound advice, this time on interviews:

Prepare for interviews by learning as much as possible about the organization beforehand. Financial information about major business corporations may be available from the company's financial relations office.

Show samples of your work, but keep in mind that they should represent your best efforts. Quality is more impressive than quantity.

If the interviewer does not choose to lead the discussion, be ready to take the initiative in describing your qualifications and what you believe you can accomplish on the job. Also, be aware of the fact that the quality of your questions about the company and the position can be as impressive and revealing of your potential as your background, particularly if your experience is limited.

Every candidate for a public relations position must remember that the number of persons hired for any particular opening is small compared to the number interviewed. Rejection is no cause to suppose you will not qualify elsewhere. Consider your job hunt as a learning experience. Through perseverance you can will the opportunity to begin your public relations career.

INTERNSHIPS: A STEP FORWARD TO GETTING AN ENTRY-LEVEL JOB

At the beginning of the 21st century, advertising has given way to public relations as the hot communications medium. As a result, PR firms are expanding their operations and eagerly looking for talented new people to sustain their growth. Yet there is still heavy competition for entry-level jobs at the large PR firms and at the major corporations.

For people seeking these select positions, an internship is often the ticket of admission. One professional gave this advice to those planning to enter the field of PR:*

> My advice: internships, internships, internships! There's nothing to beat practical experience. You can learn only the basics of PR in school. Building technique, strategy, even creativity comes on the job. This is a fast-paced, often high-stress field, and there is a lot of competition. You have to be confident in what you know and all that you do, so learning as much as possible before you begin your professional career is important.

The most productive internships are those involving assignments of one or more of the following duties:

- Writing, layout, and editing for external or internal publications, promotional material, and brochures.
- News gathering, and news release and feature writing.
- Research and report writing.
- Preparing lists of key personnel at various media.
- Preparing audiovisual presentations.
- Helping to arrange or take part in special events.
- Assisting in fund-raising programs.

In the opinion of management, most of these skills should have been learned by the candidate prior to the internship. However, for an internship to work, the management, or principals of an organization, must be available to supervise and teach. If they are not, the internship will be a waste of time.

"Internships are a great way to break into public relations," says Keith Greenberg.* "Companies learn a great deal about the candidate from this experience. They find it easier to evaluate a student or a prospect's work rather than try to predict potential through reading a résumé."

Ruder Finn's Standout Executive Training/Summer Internship Program

Ruder Finn is one of the nation's largest full-service, independent, international public relations agencies. The firm has offices in a number of U.S. cities and abroad.

Ruder Finn has a paid executive training program offered three times a year in its New York City headquarters. The program is for college graduates who have at least a bachelor's degree. Executive trainees work full-time and also attend weekly classes. Graduates of the program who are hired become assistant account executives. Ruder Finn also sponsors a part-time summer internship for college juniors. They are paid $10 per hour for the 20-hour-per-week program.

A Success Story in High-Tech Public Relations

Sue Bohle is president the The Bohle Company, a Los Angeles-based public relations firm specializing in technology. Bohle went from being a journalism graduate at Northwestern's Medill School to a job in PR at Burson-Marsteller's Los Angeles office, to becoming the first female vice-president at J. Walter Thompson's Los Angeles office, then to working for Bill Gates's new Microsoft company in 1981, and finally to owning her own agency in Los Angeles, specializing in technology public relations. Bohle is not only a success story, but also a tribute to the achievement of parity by women in this specialization.

Here are some excerpts from her interview with Dennis Gaschen, APR, in the March 2000 issue of PRSA's *TACTICS*:

Sue Bohle: From Backpacks To Bill Gates

Sue Bohle, APR, Fellow PRSA, is president of The Bohle Company, a Los Angeles-based public relations firm specializing in technology (www.bohle.com).

Bohle was one of the first women inducted into PRSA's College of Fellows and, in 1999, served as its chair. She is also past chairman of the Counselors Academy as well as past president of PRSA's Los Angeles chapter. This year, Bohle celebrates her 30-year anniversary in public relations. *TACTICS* contributor Dennis Gaschen, APR, talks with Bohle about the challenges of being a woman in the profession, her decision in 1979 to focus almost exclusively on technology, and her work in the '80s for a little-known start-up company called Microsoft.

How did you get your start in public relations?

It wasn't my first career choice. I graduated with my bachelor's degree from Northwestern University's Medill School of Journalism in the '60s. Both my parents were teachers and my father told me that teaching was a good career for a woman. "You can quit it to have a family and then go back when the kids are grown." I taught high school journalism for 3 years, but I knew that if I continued, my brain would atrophy. I went back to school, got my master's in journalism, and then headed West.

We arrived in Los Angeles in 1969, $20,000 in debt. I'd hoped to use my journalism skills at a local paper, but found no takers. One day, I got a call from Burson-Marsteller. They needed a female account executive to manage public relations for a feminine-hygiene product. Within three weeks I was traveling to New York to conduct my first media tour. I remember thinking, "Great travel, a secretary, and decent pay—this PR thing might not be half bad!"

What was it like when you first entered the PR profession?

Unlike today, the only career tracks open to women back then were cosmetics, fashion, and food. I had an interest in anything but those three, so I asked for more challenging assignments. Through persistence, I moved on to bullets, reloading equipment, and handguns. Later, it was backpacks and toboggans.

In 1974, I was recruited to help open J. Walter Thompson's Los Angeles office. Although there was still some resistance to female executives in the public relations business, I became the first female vice-president at J. Walter Thompson outside New York. Hearing about the promotion, a female reporter at *Business Week* asked, "Does this mean you don't have to pour the coffee anymore?" Despite these perceptions, the biggest challenge for working women during the '70s was finding dependable child-care.

When did you go out on your own?

In 1979, 10 days after I had my second child. I called the office the day I delivered and found it in a panic. A large client had fired the agency. Luckily, it was the ad side of the business. I was retained for public relations support, and I've had that first client, Eastman Kodak Company, ever since.

Have you always owned your own agency?

No, in the mid-'80s I sold The Bohle Company. I worked for the parent company for 18 months, but didn't want to focus solely on new business. I didn't feel I could ethically sign up a new client and then walk away. I started the present-day The Bohle Company in 1987.

When did you get into the high-tech field?

I've always had an interest in technology as a tool. From the day I first saw a PC, I steered my career and my business in that direction. I pleaded to a good friend David Simon, who ran one of the first high-tech PR firms in Los Angeles, "Call me if you ever have a client conflict." He referred my first technology account and the rest is history. In hindsight, getting into technology was one of the smartest things I've ever done.

When did you start with Microsoft?

I was introduced to Bill Gates at the 1981 Comdex. Ben Rosen, the chair of Compaq at that time, said there was a small startup that was looking for a high-tech PR firm. The company was Microsoft, and I worked directly with Bill Gates and Steve Ballmer [Microsoft's new CEO] for 3 years. We helped reposition Microsoft from a language and compiler company to a software company that produced operations systems. Presently, The Bohle Company works for Microsoft's Southern California Regional Office.

Can you tell us what working for Bill Gates is like?

Bill hasn't changed much over the years. He has always been super smart, in a hurry, and not willing to suffer any fools. You had to be well prepared for every meeting, efficient with his time, offer advice he respected, otherwise, he'd get up and walk out of the meeting. I found working with him extremely exhilarating. My only regret was that I didn't buy more Microsoft stock. [Laughs.]

How has high-tech public relations changed through the years?

The competition for a solid media placement is tougher today. The media used to be interested in concepts. Now they want real customers and alliances with strategic partners. The media strategy has also changed. You used to pitch publications with long leads [time] first, then medium leads and finally online publications. Now online publications carry the hard news and the rest cover trends or in-depth stories.

Where else is high-tech PR going?

The good news is technology has embraced the power of public relations. The bad news is that 75% of today's Internet companies won't be here tomorrow. For every good idea on the Internet, there are 30 competitors. Without capital, valid ideas can't succeed. We've turned away more business this year because the client wasn't ready or able to invest in success.

How is The Bohle Company preparing for the future?

We're only as good as our employees. I believe the secret to retention is frequent performance reviews and then recognizing that performance. We also must provide employees with the tools to grow. I want an employee to say, "I like to work here because I know you focus on my career."

Each employee receives 2 hours of training weekly. We also schedule two off-site seminars and, once a year, host a 3-day team building retreat somewhere fun. We've gone to Puerto Vallarta and Vancouver. But these trips are work too since they're entirely staff run. Employees do everything from making the travel arrangements to presenting. It's a great way to polish client skills.

As you enter your third decade in the profession, what's on the horizon?

I feel lucky to say that after 30 years in the business, the passion to go to work each day is still there. Now I want to pass along some of the knowledge. I sponsored my first internship in 1974 and it was the beginning of a life-long commitment to mentoring. Now, I'd like to combine the teacher in me with my other love—travel. If I can raise the reputation of the profession along the way, all the better.

Red-Hot Job Market in High-Tech Now Only Tepid

Until 2000, high-tech and dot.com companies were going public as fast as the regulatory agencies could approve their registration. Then, in late 2000 and early 2001, the markets cooled and the seemingly endless supply of venture capital dried up.

But, although there were fewer high-tech startups, the demand for PR people skilled in this sphere remained strong. Companies are still looking for the help PR can afford in bringing a startup to the public's and the industry's attention.

Another market for high-tech PR beyond new companies is traditional offline companies penetrating the online market.[7] As Katie Sweeney points out in another *TACTICS* article, offline companies, as well as the dot.coms, have a strong need to apply a total marketing approach to their efforts, one that combines messaging, branding, and positioning, as well as PR.

"But," says Sweeney, "employers are still choosy. They're looking for talent, people who understand the high-tech industry, how to use the Internet to its greatest advantage, and, finally, how PR fits into the whole picture."

Hands On: How-To Advice for Practitioner Skills You Need to Expand Your Counselor Role

Carole M. Howard, APR, is an author and frequent speaker on communications and global marketing. She is the retired worldwide vice-president of PR for the Reader's Digest Association.

In the course of updating her book *On Deadline: Managing Media Relations*, she asked 20 senior PR corporate officers, agency heads, and academics the question, "What are the most valuable skills for a

PR professional to develop in order to become an effective counselor to management?"

While much of this advice falls within the orbit of senior PR staffers, it does help put the entire PR role in perspective. Here is some of the response Ms. Howard received from her query:

> Some mention listening skills. Several mentioned the confidence and courage to speak the truth. Many mentioned strong communications skills. Yet every single one of them said the most essential qualification of all is a thorough knowledge of your organization's business.
>
> Top executives and other decision-makers will find it difficult to take advice from anyone who does not have a thorough understanding of the business. It's essential that you constantly update your knowledge of the organization you represent, its strategy, its position in the marketplace, its growth and expansion plans.
>
> Recognizing emerging issues is another key role of a PR counselor. Much like products, public issues also have life cycles. Your goal should be to identify new issues early enough so that your organizations can shape and manage them rather than merely respond.
>
> Though PR professionals generally are well informed, you can increase your chances of recognizing important issues early by paying careful attention to all media, traditional and new, not just which cover your businesses and industries regularly.
>
> Read a wide variety of media, not only business and trade press, but also "alternative" press and publications devoted to subjects and ideologies outside the scope of your industry. Do keyword searches on the Internet and visit opinion-leading Web sites.
>
> Read editorials and be alert to new subjects and shifts in the opinions of thought leaders.
>
> Monitor letters-to-the-editor sections in newspaper and magazines, especially in the more prestigious publications, as well as newsgroups, chat rooms, user groups, and forums on the Internet. Important new issues or changes in viewpoints on old ones often get their first public exposure in these arenas.
>
> Pay attention to better quality TV and radio talk shows and interview programs for good sources on issues.
>
> Maintain informal contacts with key media people. Seek their opinions.
>
> Build internal alliances in a strong informal network of sources in your organization. They can alert you to developing trends within your industry and markets, and changes that need to be made.
>
> When you do the counseling job well, you can become catalysts for change and make significant long-term contributions to your organization's success.

How to Achieve Fast-Track Career Success and Earn a Quick Promotion

Donald Asher writes books on careers. In the Dow Jones career supplement *Managing Your Career*, spring 1997, he discussed how to earn a promotion in 12 months or less[8]:

1. Don't lock into a particular industry or location too early.
2. Even if the money is great, be sure you're interested in the job.
3. To get ahead fast, always ask for more responsibility.
4. Volunteer for presentations and writing assignments.
5. Anticipate what you should know, then learn it on your own.
6. Always be looking for your next assignment, but make sure you have good results on your present one.
7. Develop mentors, someone you can talk to about job problems.
8. Create a wide network, outside and inside the organization.
9. Don't get involved in company politics, especially early in your career.
10. Take risks. Don't be afraid to fail.

THE 50 MOST POWERFUL WOMEN IN PUBLIC RELATIONS

In 1979, when I wrote my first book, *The Magazine: Everything You Need to Know to Make It in the Magazine Bussiness*, I commented that although women were making strides beyond editorial jobs on fashion magazines, there were few women publishers or even ad salespeople on general magazines. By the mid 1980s, one of the magazines that I published, *National Lampoon*, had a woman as advertising director and an all-female ad sales staff. A few years later, the issue of women in magazine publishing ceased being an issue. Women had become publishers of some of our largest magazines, including *Fortune, People, Ebony*, and *Self*.

Women are employed in public relations in greater numbers than men, but they head only two top PR counsel firms, APCO and Ruder Finn.

In the corporate world, women are a healthy percentage of the top professionals in the country. At General Electric, Beth Comstock is vice-president of corporate communications, and Marilyn Laurie holds that position at AT&T.

Other senior corporate women in PR include Mich Matthews of Microsoft, Elizabeth Krupnick of New York Life, and Kathy Fitzgerald of Lucent.

In the technology sector, Pam Alexander founded Alexander Communications and now runs Alexander Ogilvy Public Relations Worldwide, while Jonelle Birney heads Hill & Knowlton's global technology practice.

Again, in technology, Melissa Waggener is CEO and president of Waggener Edstrom, a firm she started in 1983 with two employees. At this writing, her firm has more than 400 staffers.

At high-profile AOL, before the merger with Time Warner, Kathy Bushkin was chief communications officer and senior vice-president. She had been head of the media relations practice at Hill & Knowlton before joining AOL.

So, is there a downside to this picture of women running the PR business? Yes, if we read the article, "The 50 Most Powerful Women in PR" in the August 1999 issue of *PRWeek*.[9] "It's 60 women to 40 men at the entry level," said Chris Komisarjevsky, (male) CEO of number-one worldwide Burson-Marsteller. "As you move higher into the organization, women decide there are other things they want to do and the proportions change. There are women starting families, deciding to make lifestyle changes." At Burson-Marsteller, by the way, there are only two women on the worldwide leadership team.

Clearly, although women are underrepresented in the boardrooms of large PR firms and their corporate clients, women are making giant steps, but not big strides.

ONE WOMAN'S CAREER PATH FROM LAW SCHOOL TO CORPORATE/FINANCIAL PUBLIC RELATIONS PRACTICE

Liza Olsen ran a circuitous route to her job as an account executive in the corporate/financial practice of Burson-Marsteller's New York office. There she works on such challenging assignments as the acquisition of the largest power company in Venezuela. I asked Olsen about her fast-track career.

What college training or major best prepared you for a career in the public relations industry? Do you think your college training gave you a sufficient business background?

Any course of study or experience that provides the opportunity to read, analyze, and synthesize a wide range of ideas, and then clearly write critical analyses, is beneficial to a career in public relations. As an English major, my academic courses were ideal training for me.

My college experience did not provide me with an in-depth business background, largely because I chose to concentrate on English and liberal arts courses. However, when I entered the business world, I found that reading daily newspapers and other business publications—and working closely with colleagues who had strong business backgrounds—helped me gain the insight and perspective necessary for the job.

What career path did you follow to your current position?

Immediately after graduating from college in 1989, I joined Senator Pete Wilson's (R-CA) staff as a press office intern in Washington, D.C. At the end of the internship, I obtained an entry-level staff position, responsible for monitoring and responding to constituent concerns. In 1990, when Senator Wilson became governor of California, I moved to Sacramento and worked for 3 years in his press office as an assistant press secretary.

In 1993, I left my position with Governor Wilson and enrolled at the University of Utah College of Law. During my law school years, I clerked for two summers—first in the public affairs division of the Utah Attorney General's Office, and then at a small law firm in Salt Lake City.

After graduating from law school in 1997, I studied for and passed the Utah and California state bar examinations. As I considered my next step, I looked at careers that would make the most of my communications training from the political sector, research and analytical skills from law school, and personality that is best suited to a people-focused industry. Because the public relations field offered the type of environment that was a clear fit for me, both personally and professionally, I accepted a position with Burson-Marsteller's public affairs practice in Los Angeles. After working in the Los Angeles office for two years, I joined the company's corporate/financial practice in New York City, where I have been working for more than one year.

How important are writing skills in your work as a PR professional?

Writing skills are one of the most important elements to a successful career in public relations. In my experience, written material is the major channel through which most clients' messages are communicated, and I believe that the quality of writing has a significant impact on how well these messages are received by both internal and external audiences. Public relations professionals need to be able to write in an organized, clear, and jargon-free way. And because audiences include employees, shareholders, members of the media, Internet/intranet users, and the general public, the ability to write in a variety of tones is a distinct advantage.

I believe that because of the variety of the work and the pace of the profession, the public relations industry offers writers a work environment and professional opportunities rarely found anywhere else.

What is the most important skill that an account person can possess?

There are a number of important skills that effective account people need to perform their jobs well—written and verbal communication, organizational and multitasking skills. However, I believe the most important skill an account person can have is to be curious, and possess the desire to learn and understand a client's business. These skills do more than enable an account person to respond to the client's current needs—they enable him or her to move beyond the tried and true and recommend new approaches.

Do you function in single or multiple practice areas?

As a member of Burson-Marsteller's corporate/financial practice, I am primarily involved in three of the Practice's subspecialties—global transactions and litigation, investor relations, and crisis communications.

How many accounts do you service?

I'm usually working on at least two client accounts simultaneously, and am continually involved in new business projects. However, because of the pace of the work and the degree of sensitivity that are so much a part of crisis communications and merger/bankruptcy projects, there are times when I only work with one client at a time.

What was the most creative and interesting project you've worked on since joining Burson-Marsteller? What was the nature of the situation and its resolution?

The most interesting and intellectually rewarding project I have worked on involved AES Corporation and La Electricidad de Caracas (EDC). Burson-Marsteller was hired to help AES make a tender offer for the Venezuelan company EDC, the largest power company in Venezuela and a benchmark stock on Venezuela's stock exchange.

AES launched a surprise tender offer for a 51% majority of EDC, at a premium over the current share price that represented the largest foreign direct investment in the Venezuela private sector.

Our objective was to help persuade the requisite amount of shareholders to tender their shares to gain a 51% majority by demonstrating that AES's investment was in the best interest of the shareholders. We also needed to reassure the Venezuelan public that a foreign takeover did not represent a political liability, a loss of local control of the local company, or a reduction in quality electricity service.

Burson-Marsteller's team played a pivotal role in the transaction. It provided strategic counsel, media relations support, financial communications, and positioning so that AES could best leverage its position as a global power company seeking to acquire the leading company on the Bolsa de Caracas Exchange.

Burson-Marsteller worked with the "Deal Team" to communicate the message that the tender offer was in the best interests of the shareholders. Press coverage in Venezuela and the United States reached millions of readers and viewers, and generated positive perceptions of the AES offer.

AES communications with the local business press, shareholders, and the financial community convinced a higher-than-expected number of shareholders that it was in their best interest to tender their shares of EDC to AES. After a months-long battle, AES acquired 81% of EDC for a total of $1.6 billion, the largest stock purchase in Venezuelan history. The stock offer was so popular with shareholders that AES gained control of 30% more stock than it originally hoped for.

With whom do you interact at your clients' organization?

My clients are usually vice-presidents and other senior-level executives, typically in the communications, public relations/public affairs, or investor relations departments. On occasion, I work directly with a company CEO.

How do you assure that there is a steady flow of ideas from your firm to your clients?

I believe that there are three elements to a productive agency-client relationship:

First, knowledge about the clients' business and industry, which I accomplish by reading newspapers, magazines, trade journals, and Web sites, as well as attending workshops, conferences, seminars, and other training and education programs offered by Burson-Marsteller and other organizations. Participating in these activities ensures that I remain strategically focused and that I can respond to, and anticipate, my clients' communications challenges.

Second, ability to anticipate the client's needs and provide valuable counsel. An important part of my job as a consultant is to identify opportunities, approaches, and solutions that my clients may not have otherwise considered or pursued.

Third, consistent delivery of the highest quality work possible.

Describe, in a few hundred words or less, your first year at Burson-Marsteller.

I joined Burson-Marsteller in January 1997. I worked exclusively with QUALCOMM, a digital wireless telecommunications company, providing strategic counsel and communications support to its corporate and legal office, and promoting its proprietary technology, code division multiple access (CDMA).

My greatest challenge was educating myself not only on QUALCOMM's business strategy but also on the intricacies of its technology. With a professional background focused primarily on law and politics, I was unfamiliar with the growing telecommunications sector, its audiences, its influencers, and the channels and processes for effectively communicating messages.

I spent my first year learning as much as possible about the telecommunications industry and the issues facing its members. In addition to my own research on the industry, I worked closely with a team of Burson-Marsteller colleagues who had strong telecommunications, technology and corporate positioning backgrounds. I also had to adjust to agency life, and for that I also turned to my Burson-Marsteller colleagues. They provided me with guidance on the procedures, work flow, and skills that are needed to thrive in the fast-paced, but never uneventful, public relations industry.

My first year was certainly a time for learning, but it also provided me with the opportunity to share with my new team members the unique skills that I developed in the political and legal arenas.

REAL JOBS IN PUBLIC RELATIONS

We scanned the "Marketplace" section of various issues of PRSA's *TACTICS* for a sampling of job offers:

- The Fortune 500 company Litton Industries, in sunny California, listed a job for an expert-level writer who can also write executive speeches for delivery to the financial community. The job pays $90,000 a year plus incentives.
- If you qualify as a marketing manager for a large law firm's Los Angeles office, the salary range is $90–120K, depending on your qualifications and experience.
- In late 1999, the technology powerhouse Brodeur Worldwide was looking for account executives in their Boston office. The jobs called for monitoring trends, writing press releases, tracking competition, arranging press tours, and utilizing the Web and other traditional means to reach the media and investment analyst communities. The jobs called for 3–4 years of PR or other communications experience.
- To qualify as a senior account executive with a Miami-based PR and marketing firm handling national accounts, you need to be a superb writer with 3+ years experience. The job pays an excellent salary and offers great benefits.

West Coast Public Relations Jobs (www.westcoastprjobs.com)

West Coast PR Jobs is an outstanding source for jobs in public relations and marketing. A search of its Web site yielded the following excellent offering:

Horizon Communications, a Silicon Valley high-tech PR agency, was looking for account people from within the high-tech industry with 2 to 4 years of strong experience. The responsibilities ranged from classic PR services to creating and implementing comprehensive marketing campaigns. One job requirement was a well-developed sense of humor. The company offered a full range of benefits that even included vitamin and chiropractic discounts. Salary was commensurate with experience and "probably a lot more than you're making now." To apply for this job with Horizon, the firm asked for a cover letter, résumé, salary history, and writing samples. Most of West Coast's account executive jobs called for 2 to 4 years of high-tech PR agency experience.

O.K. Already, We Love Public Relations, But How Much Money Will We Make?

In the first edition of this book, I reported the 1991 results of a salary survey conducted by Research & Forecasts, a division of the large PR firm Ruder Finn. Some of its findings indicated that the media salary for all PR practitioners at counsel firms was $47,000. Men made 15% more than women and received about twice the bonus.

The median salary for an account executive with a PR firm then was $28,132 and with a corporation $35,724. Well, the good news is that salaries are substantially higher now, but only about one-tenth the salary of the lowest-paid NBA basketball player, who makes about $550,000 a year and averages about 2 minutes playing time per game.

The Marshall Consultants 1999 Compensation Review

Marshall is a corporate and marketing communications recruiting firm. Its most recent available salary survey is based on 1998 figures. We can assume that these figures rise about 10% per year. Also, salaries are higher in the pharmaceutical and high-tech fields, especially for those with media relations skills.

One other positive and long overdue note: Kathleen DesRosiers, head of Marshall's Los Angeles office, commented, "Gender no longer makes a difference in hiring practices and compensation policies, certainly in the large cities that are centers for communications."[10] She predicted, "Since there are more highly qualified women than men entering the field, it should follow that in the future, more jobs will be held by women."

Large corporations in the Marshall study were defined as those having sales of $1 billion or more, mid-size corporations between $400 million and $1 billion, and smaller corporations as those with sales less than $400 million.

The study defined large PR agencies as those with fee income in excess of $5 million; mid-size, $1 million to $5 million; and small with less than $1 million. Here are the salaries found.

TABLE 22.1 THE MARSHALL CONSULTANTS 1999 COMPENSATION REVIEW

SPECIALIST	LARGE CORP.	MEDIUM CORP.	SMALL CORP.
Consumer products	$66,000	$54,200	$41,500
Healthcare	$79,500	$70,700	$61,500
High tech	$80,900	$68,700	$62,000

The IABC and PRSA Profile 2000 Compensation Survey

In 1999, the IABC and PRSA conducted a study of the salary and compensation of 40,000 professionals represented by the two organizations. The findings, published in June/July 2000, reflected a composite of both IABC and PRSA respondents. Here are some of the results of the study.

TABLE 22.2 SALARY BY JOB CLASSIFICATION

TITLE	MEDIAN	AVERAGE
Writer	$45,000	$50,000
Account executive	36,500	36,000
Sr. account executive	50,000	48,000

SALARY BY INDUSTRY

TITLE	MEDIAN	AVERAGE
Medical/health care	46,000	$79,500
Association/nonprofit	42,000	50,000
Consulting firm	61,000	79,650
Public relations	62,500	123,500

SALARY (AVERAGE) BY GENDER, ACCREDITATION STATUS

	MALE	FEMALE
Accredited[a]	$89,500	$82,500
Not accredited	88,000	56,500

[a] Accredited Business Communicator (ABC) is the designation for those successfully passing IABC's accreditation exam. Accredited Public Relations (APR) is the designation of PRSA.

Council of Public Relations Firms Salary Survey

In October 2000, the Council of Public Relations Firms conducted a compensation and benefits survey. Here are the results.

The council also noted that entry-level salaries in public relations firms ranged from $25,000 to $40,000, depending on location and specialty. New York, San Francisco, and Washington, D.C., paid the highest, as did the high-tech, health care, and financial specialties.

The council also pointed out that the industry offers the most advanced benefits, investment programs, and training and tuition reimbursement opportunities. Public relations firms are generous with benefits, quality-of-life enhancements, and bonuses, even for junior staff.

TABLE 22.3 AVERAGE SALARIES BY NUMBER OF YEARS IN INDUSTRY

	YEARS								
	1.3	2.7	4.4	6.2	9	12.3	13.9	16.1	OVER 20
Average	$29,000	$36,400	$47,500	$59,500	$80,900	$129,700	$174,200	$219,800	$275,600

A Young Public Relations Professional's Day

Again, the Council of PR Firms has furnished us with valuable inside information, this time the actual work day of a PR professional at a large counsel firm. It hastened to add that there is no such thing as a typical day, and, of course, all clients have different needs.

> **Background:** 2 years experience.
> **Education:** BA (History major, Psychology minor).
> **Position:** Account executive, New York office of an international public relations firm.
> **Clients:** Major beverage brand, pre-IPO Internet company, New York office of a French law firm.

8:30 a.m. Check wire services, Internet, newspapers, and magazines for client stories.

9:00 a.m. Call/e-mail clients to report news coverage and coordinate day's activities.

9:30 a.m. Conference call with Paris-based agency colleague and law firm's expert on new French law regulating U.S. biotech companies producing genetically engineered foods.

10:00 a.m. Call reporter at *The New York Times* to persuade her to interview law firm's biotech expert and New York office partner on new strategies for U.S. biotech firms seeking to do business in France.

10:30 a.m. Draft a press release and media list to announce Yahoo.com partnership for Internet client and submit draft to account supervisor for his review.

11:30 a.m. Review new product launch plans with beverage client and their advertising agency.

Noon. Lunch meeting at Web design firm to review Internet promotion and college campus sweepstakes sponsored by beverage brand.

2:00 p.m. Return calls from reporters: The *New York Times* will interview law firm partners, *The Industry Standard* needs information on Internet client, and *Advertising Age* inquired about Internet college contest.

2:30 p.m. Call Internet client to obtain data necessary to respond to *The Industry Standard*; send contest details and Web page design to *Advertising Age* call reporter to provide additional information about the beverage brand strategy.

3:00 p.m. Incorporate account supervisor's changes into Internet company press release and post on newswire; call *InfoWeek* reporter to discuss news and propose interview with vice-president of business development about Yahoo partnership before publication's deadline tomorrow; and provide talking points to Vice President of Business Development.

4:00 p.m. Respond to calls from two high-tech publications, providing details on Yahoo partnership announcement.

4:30 p.m. Conference call with Internet company human resources director to discuss impending layoffs; client public relations officer and agency account team discuss sharing responsibilities—client will handle employee communications and agency will communicate with the media and investors.

5:00 p.m. Discuss biotech story with New York law firm partner; send e-mail to Paris, setting time for phone interview tomorrow with *The New York Times* and providing sample questions and answers.

5:30 p.m. Attend welcome reception for new staff.

6:00 p.m. Head home.

Working on three accounts, this account executive must do a balancing act. Clients often feel underserved in such situations. The keys to success are persistence, creativity, and establishing relationships with the media that can be mined for other clients.

GOING TO WORK FOR A TOP PUBLIC RELATIONS FIRM

It is hard to get hired at a top public relations firm, but the situation has changed in many respects. For one, advertising is losing dollars as corporations find that they can accomplish their objectives more effectively and at lower costs with public relations.

As a result, there are more jobs at business corporations and other organizations, or at one of the large PR firms, which pay higher salaries than smaller agencies. They also have internships and training programs, and some include opportunities to work abroad. We offer here a general look at jobs at a number of top PR firms.

Fleishman-Hillard

Among the many advantages in working for this number one U.S. PR firm is an ongoing professional development curriculum. The program includes training sessions, company-wide meetings and events, the support of all the firm's 49 offices in 16 countries worldwide, and interoffice collaboration.

You can make it into Fleishman-Hillard's internship program as a college junior or senior or as a recent college graduate. As an intern, you will be involved in all types of projects, including research, writing, event coordination and staffing, media pitching, and brainstorming. Internship candidates must have at least a 3.0 grade point average. The firm favors applicants who have excellent writing and critical thinking skills, as well as a commitment to the challenge of public relations.

The internship selection process includes interviews with a team of account professionals plus a writing exercise. Send your résumé with a writing sample to the intern program coordinator and say at which Fleishman-Hillard office you would like to intern.

Once hired at Fleishman-Hillard, you will receive a comprehensive benefits package that includes health coverage, financial incentives, employee assistance, and a sabbatical program.

Burson-Marsteller

What's it like working for the world's largest PR firm, an organization with more than 2,000 professionals in 35 countries? For answers, I sought out Mischelle Leathers, the firm's human resources director.

What is the best college training for someone choosing a PR career?

While public relations courses are helpful, we have also found that the best training includes courses and extracurricular activities that strengthen written and verbal communications skills. Experience working in a team-oriented environment is also very helpful. We also look for someone with a wide range of interests that demonstrate intellectual curiosity.

What is the extent of Burson-Marsteller's internship and scholarship program?

The Harold Burson Summer Internship (HBSI) program is a 10-week, paid internship at one of Burson-Marsteller's U.S. locations. Each intern is assigned to a client team, or specialist group, guided by an experienced professional. Interns have the opportunity to do real work while learning our proprietary perception management methodology and other critical communications skills. Representatives from different areas of the company conduct seminars for interns during the course of the summer. Interns are grouped into teams to work on a special HBSI project, which they present to a senior management panel for review. By the end of the summer, interns will have been exposed to some of the challenges and opportunities facing our clients and our company. As part of the annual Harlem YMCA Black Achievers Award program, Burson-Marsteller offers scholarships to high school students who are entering college. In some cases, we offer scholarships to students who are already attending college.

Burson-Marsteller has a 6-week Discovery Journal and the B-M Learning Center for new people. How are they implemented?

Each region of the world has translated and localized information in the Discovery Journal, which is a 6-week, self-paced orientation program. The Discovery Journal as well as other online courses and materials can also be found on the Learning Center Web site. Some courses require management approval due to related costs. Other courses have no fee attached and may be taken by employees who may need specific training in order to move to the next level.

What technology training does Burson-Marsteller offer for new employees?

New employees receive instruction on desktop applications as well as on InfoDesk, the company intranet. In addition, all employees are given access to briefings on technology and the impact of technology on public relations, and those colleagues who are working with clients in the technology sector are giving ongoing training as relevant.

In hiring, do you favor people with MBAs or those with communications and journalism backgrounds?

It depends greatly on the level of seniority and practice/specialization. For the most part, Burson-Marsteller favors candidates who have journalism and communications backgrounds, but it depends on what business we are staffing. A business background is far more attractive for the corporate practice (although here again, an MBA is valuable but not required). Our employee population boasts a wide variety of backgrounds and academic credentials, which adds to the diversity of experience and expertise we are able to offer our clients.

What qualifications do you look for in an A-list candidate?

Burson-Marsteller looks for candidates with superior writing skills, strong client focus, intellectual curiosity, self-sufficiency, and strong business skills (growth and development). The more senior the level, the more important prior public relations agency experience and the ability to lead and develop teams become.

What do you think is the advantage in working for a PR firm over working in public relations for a client organization?

Clearly the most obvious advantage is the diversity of client assignments, and the role you can play as an outside "expert."

What is the typical career path of a new Burson-Marsteller employee?

Based on motivation and professional competence, a variety of experiences awaits new employees. Individuals can enter Burson-Marsteller at any level of seniority and take on increasing levels of responsibility within their original area of specialization; across a range of practice groups; across types of roles such as client leadership and key areas such as knowledge and insights; and in different parts of the world in telecommunications or e-business.

What does a Burson-Marsteller team look like?

Every client has a clearly defined client leader, who assembles teams based on the demands and opportunities of the client assignment. The client leader invariably reaches into a variety of practice groups to assemble the best team.

Which practice areas have the most opportunities?

Our industry and our company in particular are all enjoying significant growth opportunities. All our practice groups and specialist teams offer opportunities to learn and advance.

Where do you look for new people?

We find candidates through employee referrals, Internet sites, associations specific to the open position, local schools; media outlets, trade associations, networking, news releases, and PRSA.

In the first edition of this book, I wrote that 75 people in Burson-Marsteller's U.S. offices speak at least two languages, and that the staff of the firm's European offices is 99% bilingual, with more than half speaking at least three languages. What are the respective numbers today?

Currently, 260 people in Burson-Marsteller's U.S. offices speak at least two languages and the European offices are 99% bilingual, with approximately 60% speaking at least three languages.

A 1999 Marshall Consultants study concluded that account executives at PR firms in New York City earn $42,200 on consumer products accounts and $56,000 on high-tech accounts. In Los Angeles or San Francisco the corresponding figures are $31,200 and $49,700. Do you agree with these results, and do they prevail at a Top Ten PR counsel firm such as Burson-Marsteller?

Our titles do not exactly correspond to traditional agency designations, but this seems generally accurate.

Do you attract talented people by paying them more money up front than your competition, or do you make clear to them that they'll make more money and receive promotions faster than at other firms?

Neither. We attract them by offering them the best career assignments and opportunities for professional growth; we keep them by living up to that commitment, which involves rewarding and recognizing them for the contributions they make.

In hiring people for New York, how do you help them survive when a walk-up on the Lower East Side can cost $1,500 a month?

We generally suggest that there are other great places to live outside of the city with a reasonable commute.

Ten years ago, a top PR person said that the best-paid people "are those who've mastered the skill of helping to engineer wins in Washington." Is this still the case?

Not necessarily. A great deal of importance is placed on our ability to represent our clients' interests in Washington, but we place equal value on those professionals who in other ways provide our clients with the best in strategic, integrated communications counsel—effectively implemented—in order to help achieve the business results they seek.

Most of the 10 largest PR agencies we cover in this chapter offer similar recruiting advantages. Check them out carefully when you apply for employment. Burson-Marsteller has an online applications center where you can submit your résumé.

Weber Shandwick International

In chapter 4, we wrote about Miller/Shandwick Technologies, the parent firm's technology arm. Here are excerpts from an article in the company's promotional literature by Jodi Boyle, a Miller/Shandwick account executive, based in New York:

> My supervisor has encouraged me to jump right in and try all aspects of client work, including writing releases, meeting with the clients, and pitching the media. I doubt that other agencies would have allowed me the freedom to get so thoroughly involved. The result is that I am developing core PR skills even faster than I had imagined.
>
> I think that the key to growth in a PR agency is trying new things, which we do all the time. Everyone works closely together and the senior people set a great example. When we are crunching a deadline for a project or a presentation, titles don't mean a thing. Everyone rolls up their sleeves and does what it takes to complete the job no matter how long it takes.
>
> We have the best of both worlds. We are a part of a large global organization and yet we have a very close team that works together in an open and supportive environment. And, best of all, we are all friends who enjoy spending time with each other outside the office.

Doesn't that say it about Weber Shandwick?

Hill & Knowlton

In a June 2000 report to all Hill & Knowlton employees, Thomas Hoog, president and CEO, wrote proudly of the firm's achievements, with such gains as 7 accounts that billed in excess of $1 million and 12 or more who reached that level by the end of 2000.

One highlight of the CEO's report detailed the firm's training, mentoring, and career *pathing* (a word I'll be sure to borrow.)

A condensed version of some of his comments follows:

- The Employee Handbook was updated and more detailed training will be given in the first 30 days of employment.
- A new career path book would lay out initial goals between employee and supervisor, job descriptions and promotion process, performance evaluation procedures, and training programs.
- Training modules were produced through video conferencing.
- The firm's Spring College was a great success. It focused on PR skills and media in the new millennium and had outside speakers talking about what client satisfaction and leadership mean.

Perhaps the most encouraging sign for readers is this comment from the CEO: "Hiring continues at a brisk pace in all offices, and our biggest problem is finding enough qualified new staff to help us achieve all the plans we have in place."

Hill & Knowlton also attends job fairs, visits colleges, and works with the Council of PR Firms to increase career interest in the profession.

Edelman Public Relations Worldwide

Edelman looks for "Type E" personalities. What makes an "E"? Intellect, openness, respect for the individual, commitment to excellence, and courage are some of these attributes. Add to this list team players and ability to manage multiple projects.

Unlike some large PR firms where account people only work in one or two practice areas, at Edelman staffers are involved with multiple clients and a diverse range of assignments. Even with assignments for a single client, Edelman people may function in employee communications, investor relations, media relations, public affairs, and interactive communications.

We explored career opportunities at Edelman at the time of this writing.

To qualify as an account supervisor in the health care and science and technology strategies group, the candidate needs a bachelor's degree and 5 years of experience, preferably in these specializations.

For a job as assistant account executive in the corporate reputation group, a bachelor's degree and a minimum of 2 years of experience is required.

Edelman's internship program is open to college students completing their junior or senior year, as well as to recent college graduates and graduate school students. Proficiency in Microsoft Word is a must.

Ketchum

Two opportunities at Ketchum stand out: Camp Ketchum, a training program for midlevel employees offering continuing professional development, and Ketchum College, the firm's global training program held regionally to hone the skills of its employees at many levels. In addition to the two programs, Ketchum has on-site training programs in its offices with courses on writing skills, media relations, and even cyberspace.

Since the mid 1990s, Ketchum has conducted the Ketchum Boot Camp to orient college students into the world of public relations. There, students tackle a "real" client problem and experience, a program development competition between student "agencies," and a new brand image/logo for the program. It's a real-world opportunity to work with Ketchum people and even with agency clients. To view the most current job postings, contact Ketchum's local human resources representatives and post résumés.

BSMG Worldwide

In this chapter we've written about employee training, benefits, and growth opportunities. Each of the firms offers them with some variations. BSMG has a rather unique professional development program called Career Destinations. Its mission is to improve individual and organization performance and deliver quality education and training programs.

The seminars with Career Destinations are segmented into a well-rounded curriculum that includes:

- Leadership and management development.
- Agency fundamentals.
- Professional skills.
- Computer training.
- Personal development.

Courses in the seminars are led by BSMG executives, as well as outside consultants. In their first year, new hires are required to attend most sessions.

Some representative program titles are:

- Presenting with Confidence.
- Tips on How to Increase Client Budgets.
- New Media Technology and Its Impact.

- Visual Media Production.
- How to Be One Step Ahead of Your Boss.
- You Can Have it All: Achieving Work/Life Success.

Public relations won't always be the hot job ticket it is in the early 21st century, but meanwhile the pickings are great. BSMG employment opportunities at this writing include dozens of offerings in six different locations.

The firm talks of success stories. BSMG's Chicago office had 40 full-time employees who were once interns, 3 London interns who became permanent staff members, and a former intern in Dallas who became managing director.

Want to go to work for BSMG? Here are some typical recent employment opportunities at the firm:

Chicago.

    Assistant account executive
    Executive public relations associates
    Internships (October through April)

London.

    Web designer and web producer
    Marketing assistants
    Freelance designers and programmer

New York.

    Junior associate
    Associates
    Account executive

San Francisco.

    Account coordinator
    Media relations executive
    Account executive

What are the requirements for entry-level jobs at BSMG Worldwide?

Administrative Assistant. Seeking high-energy administrative assistant for the financial and professional services marketing group. Solid problem-solving skills, organizational excellence, extreme attention to details, and the ability to multitask with a sense of urgency essential. Articulate phone presence, strong administrative skills and proficiency in Word, Excel, and Internet savvy necessary. Must have previous office experience and excellent communications skills. College degree and an interest in public relations or finance a plus.

Internship. These paid assignments run about 3 months. Account projects include compiling a client clip report, media and market research, pitching, vendor relations, writing, and editing. BSMG's Chicago office has 40 full-time employees who were once interns.

Porter Novelli International

A look at Porter Novelli's job openings on its Web site at this writing shows a broad mix of opportunities:

- Internships in Atlanta.
- Account executive in Chicago.
- Assistant account executive in Ft. Lauderdale.
- Account executive in New York.
- Summer internship in San Francisco.
- Social marketing in Washington, D.C.
- Human resources manager in Silicon Valley.
- Account manager in consumer technology in Singapore.

Porter Novelli's acquisition of Copithorne & Bellows, a titan in technology, makes the agency a formidable force in this key practice area.

Ogilvy PR Worldwide

In keeping with the informality of today's office environment, Ogilvy's dress code allows for "business casual" for Monday to Thursday and "dress down" on Friday.

Another attractive offering is the firm's Work-Visit program. Employees spend from 2 weeks up to 3 months in other offices to get to know firsthand the capabilities and skills in these locations in order to share experiences.

Finally, Ogilvy offers a recruitment bonus for an employee who refers a candidate that is hired for a professional staff position.

A recent search of Ogilvy job listings came up with these choices.

Assistant Account Manager–Los Angeles. Become an integral part of the team. Participate in media outreach, press tours, grass-roots initiatives for companies like Listen.com and Discovery.com.

Assistant Account Executive–New York. Join a fun, interesting, and challenging women's health account.

Account Executive–San Francisco. Looking for healthcare staff at all levels.

GCI Group

GCI has a summer internship program. Apply to Sarah Garlinghouse at Sgarlinghouse@gcigroup.com.

A look at GCI's job openings at this writing yielded these opportunities:

Account Exec/Senior Account Exec–Los Angeles. Work on existing accounts. Need 2 to 3 years of experience.

Senior Account Exec, Health Care–Atlanta. Need 5 to 7 years of relevant health care experience.

Account Coordinator/Assistant Account Exec–Chicago. Work on health care PR; strong writing skills needed, and an understanding of PR strategies and tactics (preferably through previous internships or work experience).

This can be an entry-level job for a PR major. What are the duties of someone who gets this job? To name a few: draft news releases, collateral materials, and business correspondence; create media lists; and contribute to the execution of successful communications campaigns. As with most jobs like this, the firm requests a cover letter, résumé, and salary history.

For a job at this top company, contact the head individual: Dan Relton, Vice-President of Human Resources, North America GCI Group, 777 Third Avenue, 38th floor, New York, NY 10017. Phone: (212) 537-8030. Fax: (212) 537-8091. E-mail: joinus@gcigroup.com.

Brodeur Worldwide

Brodeur Worldwide is a power in technology PR. Headquartered in Boston, it is the world's largest public relations and communications consultancy focused exclusively on technology-driven companies.

Although the firm's broad focus is technology, it works with these clients on traditional areas such as investor relations and other corporate communications services. Its core communications services include online communications, product reviews, and media relations.

Brodeur has 9 U.S. offices and offers a global capability of more than 750 employees in 55 offices in 32 countries.

As do many of the top firms, Brodeur has an internship program for college students, usually in their junior or senior year, or for graduate students who are interested in a career in PR, marketing, corporate communications, or journalism.

Interns work with an account team and prepare and distribute press releases, update media and security analyst lists, coordinate press kits and other PR materials, help organize trade shows and other events, and more.

If interested, send a copy of your résumé and cover letter to: Brodeur Intern Coordinator, 855 Boylston Street, Boston, MA 02116. Phone: (617) 587-2800. Fax: (617) 587-2828. E-mail: hresources@brodeur. com.

At this writing, Brodeur had full-time job opportunities for account executives with 2–5 years of experience. A job as an account supervisor in the firm's San Jose (Silicon Valley) office called for 4 to 6 years of technical PR experience.

Interested in a job with *PRWEEK* Magazine's 1999 Agency of the Year? Send a letter and résumé to: Arlene Moynihan, Brodeur Worldwide, 855 Boylston Street, Boston, MA 02116. Fax: (617) 587-2027.

LEONARD MOGEL'S TIPS AND SAGE ADVICE ON LAUNCHING A CAREER IN PUBLIC RELATIONS

1. A common misconception is that during an interview you will be evaluated on the basis of your background and not on the way you present yourself. When an interviewer first meets you, he or she will judge you by how you look and act. The first impression is usually lasting. Grooming, facial expression, and body language all affect your personal image.

A broad, friendly smile puts across an image of trust that will serve you well. Always look at the interviewer directly.

Watch out for nervous habits. Although you may not be aware that you are drumming your fingers on the desk or jiggling your knee, such actions are a dead giveaway of nervousness and a lack of confidence.

2. There are five stages to getting a job:
  • Preapproach—deciding where to apply.
  • Approach—making initial contact and/or sending a résumé; "flirtation."
  • Pitch—meeting and talking; "the first date."

Once you successfully get past these stages, then it's time to:
  • Negotiate—talking seriously; courtship.
  • Close—saying "I do!"

It takes 6 months.

Anyone who waits till he or she could scream has waited too long.

Learn how a company you're interested in hires. Then be politely persistent, and when you've done something new the company might be interested in, send it there.

Most people think getting a good job is a matter of luck and timing. But there are ways to beat luck and timing, by beating the rush.

3. What are the biggest mistakes most job applicants make?
  • Not researching the job they're applying for.
  • Addressing résumé package to "Dear Sir."
  • Poorly written letters accompanying résumés.
  • Failure to clearly state what job they want and why they are qualified.
  • Gimmick or cutesy résumés.
  • Calling when an ad clearly states "no telephone calls."

4. If you're responding to a help-wanted ad and it says "no calls," don't!

5. Keep your résumé out of the wastebasket by using an effective one-page cover letter and a one-sentence first paragraph.

6. It is often difficult to get to the interviewer; don't blow it when you get there. It only takes the interviewer 5 minutes or less to gain a first impression of the candidate. Interviewers say that about 85% of the candidates they see should be better prepared. Bring two extra copies of your résumé. Be on time. Dress for success, but not like a fashion model.

7. You may be asked why you left your present job. Acceptable reasons are challenge, location, advancement, money, pride/prestige, security.

8. What will your references/coworkers say about you? Ask them before you use them.

9. If you were fired, don't lie about it. Never bad-mouth a past boss.

10. Follow up an interview with a thank-you letter within 24 hours, and keep it to one page.

11. Don't be disappointed if you're not hired after the first interview. In the broadcast business, a survey found that only 1% hired applicants during the first interview, and 55% after the second.

12. A common mistake in interviews is to discuss salary first, then the job description. Ask about overtime, benefits, chances for advancement, and even parking privileges.

13. End the interview on an upbeat note. Be gracious. Leave the interviewer with a positive impression of your demeanor and personality.

14. Be yourself on an interview. Don't try to alter your personality to what you believe the interviewer is looking for. Most interviewers are suspicious of a candidate who comes on too strong.

15. If the interview is going well, propose another meeting to further discuss the job.

16. If you are offered a job and the offer doesn't fulfill your expectations, don't be afraid to say, "May I think about it?"

17. Personnel expert Robert Half calls it "Résumania," referring to the irrelevant self-defeating comments candidates include in their résumés. Some don'ts:

"Please don't misconstrue my fourteen jobs as job-hopping. I have never quit a job."

"Work skills: strong on interpersonal relations, typing, filing, and reproduction."

18. In a study of top-level executives conducted by Korn-Ferry (with the University of Southern California), it was determined that one of the single most important traits for making it to the top was the ability to get along with others. That's true in life as well.

19. When you phone a prospective employer, do not open the call by telling him/her about yourself, your résumé, goals, and so on. All that information should be communicated in a brisk, upbeat cover letter, concise résumé, and an effective in-person interview. Plan your telephone call.

20. What to do if you don't get the job: Ask what you can do to be their first choice the next time. Ask where else you might apply. Write a thank-you note or letter. They'll file it with your résumé.

21. Let the local college in your area be a research tool, even if you didn't attend that school. Go to lectures and seminars to improve your knowledge and assist you in your job pursuit.

22. Read the PR trade publications listed in chapter 21.

23. Although we've said it before, it bears repeating here: Exploit any personal contact, whether or not the person is on top. A college friend or a relative who works at a PR firm or in advertising at a large corporation may be a good source for ideas and leads about jobs.

24. Contact your college alumni association. There you can track people from your school who have gone to work at a company that interests you.

25. You'll probably get your first job by cold calling, letter writing, and networking. Make sure you're adept at each.

26. A graduate degree in business is important if you want to reach for the gold. It may, however, be a good idea to first work in a particular field and then take a leave of absence with your company's permission. Many companies encourage this practice.

27. Be prepared, even on the first interview, to speak to an individual at a much higher level than the first interviewer. At one very large publishing company, with almost 3,000 employees, the president insists on personally interviewing each sales candidate for an hour and a half, after he or she has been interviewed by four or five other people.

28. Be prepared to ask hard questions about the job and all its duties.

29. Don't be afraid to ask about perks, benefits, tuition reimbursement, and vacations.

30. When applying for a specific job, ask about the pecking order in that department.

31. When negotiating for a job, keep your mind open and be flexible. Take note of your job priorities and be prepared to compromise on nonessentials.

32. Expect that the interviewer will go down the line on your résumé and ask specific questions about your education and previous jobs.

33. On your résumé include names, addresses, and phone numbers of two or three references. Don't say "References available."

34. Be sure to list all your computer skills on your résumé, particularly if you have special desktop training.

35. Your résumé should have eight parts:
   - Name, address, and phone number.
   - Position desired.
   - Summary statement including your background; tie your immediate job hunt to your long-range career goals.
   - Education.
   - Practical experience.
   - Professional affiliations.
   - Awards and honors.
   - References.

And keep it concise.

36. The hiring process may include written tests in spelling, grammar, and usage. Make sure you know the right spelling of Rwanda, Forrest Gump, and Afghanistan, the difference between affect and effect, and the difference between who and whom.

37. The top media companies are in many communications businesses: newspapers, magazines, broadcasting, and books, as well as fields closely related to public relations. There's a great deal of mobility for a talented individual in these organizations.

38. Read *The Wall Street Journal's National Business Employment Weekly*. It lists regional as well as national job opportunities. Pick up a copy at your newsstand.

39. Study, explore, and read about new media. It's the medium for the 21st century.

40. Check out National Public Radio for "Marketplace," a nightly program with ideas and job leads. Surf the Internet for job opportunities.

41. If you're looking for your first job, you'll probably need to use an employment agency. Once you have experience, go the executive-recruiter (headhunter) route. You will still have to do cold calling, letter writing, and networking.

42. Interviewing is a fine art. Some college placement offices set up role-playing situations to give you experience in handling an interview.

43. Before you go on an interview, do your homework about the company's products and services.

44. If you can't attend an MBA program full-time, many are given at night, weekends, and online. It takes longer, but it will pay off in the big picture.

45. Add to your computer training all the time. Night courses may be the best approach.

46. Be sure to use attractive personal letterhead stationery.

47. Many companies are now conducting job interviews via video conferences. Executive recruiters use them as well. How do you think you would fare in a video interview?

48. Some of the finest companies in an industry have paid summer internship programs. Seek them out early in your college career.

49. The top recruiting firms reject résumés fast. If you want your résumé to be taken seriously, pay attention to these two "don't's" and one "do."

- Don't omit dates of past jobs or college degrees. It looks like your are hiding something.
- Don't use a highly ornate, unprofessional résumé. Avoid slick paper and bright colors that may imply you emphasize appearance over content.
- Do show internal promotions. Lack of progress on a job suggests that you're on the market because you can't get ahead in your present job.

50. Where to go first? Identify the dominant and growth-oriented companies in your geographic area.

51. If you're still in college, check out the *Managing Your Career* publication put out four times a year by the *Dow Jones National Business Employment Weekly*.

52. Shortly after you've started a new job, plan to have a conference with your employer to redefine the objectives of your department and how your responsibilities can help to meet those objectives.

53. On the first day at a new job, arrive a half-hour early and plan to stay a half-hour late. Observe communications preferences at the company: memos, voice mail, e-mail, one-on-one, daily conferences, small group meetings, and so on. Note how people dress, how long they take for lunch. Adapt to the style of the new job.

54. Don't discuss salary (yours or theirs) with your coworkers. It's unprofessional.

55. Remember to thank the people who were instrumental in helping you get the job. A note or phone call is always appreciated.

ACKNOWLEDGMENT

I am indebted to Holland Cooke for some of the information in this section. Unfortunately, he no longer publishes his excellent newsletter, *Broadcast News Career Monthly*.

CHAPTER 23

The Future Face of Public Relations

THE FUTURE FACE OF PR—BEYOND THE BASICS

Now that knowledge of how the Internet is used in the business of public relations is considered an entry-level skill, what will future PR professionals need to develop their careers? Charles Fremes, president and CEO of Edelman Public Relations (Canada), offered the following in an article for *Strategy Magazine*.

> An advertising pal of mine was complaining over lunch recently about how the list in the paper of key advisers to ONEX, Canadian Airlines, and Air Canada included lots of public relations people, lots of lawyers and lobbyists, "but not one ad guy." He went on to lament that as little as 5 years ago, the CEO would have lunch with the president of his advertising agency at least once a month, just to gain another perspective on his competition and his business. "Today," he said, "he's having lunch with the PR guy or gal."
>
> The role of the public relations practitioner in North American business has changed dramatically over the past 5 years. This change

has been driven by most of the same external drivers that have affected every aspect of our lives. The ones that have had the most impact on the public relations discipline are: the pace and application of *new technology*, including the "virtual" workplace, the increased speed of information transference, teleconferencing, satellite media tours, and the arrival of new media, including the Internet, specialty channels, and e-commerce; the *globalization* of business and its impact on competitiveness; the *restructuring* of corporations and governments and its impact on employees, services, and consumers; and the rediscovery of the importance of *customer service*.

All of these drivers have combined to help shape the redefinition of the PR practitioner's role, and the skill set required to perform and excel in that role. In a relatively short period of time, senior public relations officers of corporations and their outside counsel have been called upon as never before to apply their analytical and strategic skills, their lateral thinking ability, their knowledge of a business and its competition, and their understanding of how issues become crises and how both can be successfully managed.

The senior PR practitioner is now required to work on a cross-functional basis to help protect and enhance corporate reputation (e.g., with human resources on a plant closing to sustain employee morale, or the heads of marketing and sales to protect shareholder value and customer loyalty on a product recall).

With these changes, in both the outside societal drivers and the PR professional's role, has come the consensus (it must be a consensus because it is now taught in our business and management schools) that in well-managed and respected companies, the public relations function is contributing significantly to the overall success of the business. PR can frequently make the difference between the perception that a CEO is performing well and is respected by her employees, or out of touch with the business and the work force; that a company's stock price is under- or overvalued; that a brand's equity with consumers is about to erode or is justified through signs of a true affinity; or that a donation to a charity or cause is perceived by employees and shareholders as important to the community and good business for the company, as opposed to a shallow attempt by a corporation to polish its image.

But looking ahead a bit, into the foreseeable future, what will PR and communications professionals need beyond the basics, and how can they develop these qualities? The short answer is, I don't know; the pace of change and the inability to truly predict the future suggests that no one knows. But here's a cut at my seven best guesses.

Beyond the Basics: Seven Career Success Factors for the PR Practitioner

1. The knowledge of the way business and government work, the way each sector is influenced and makes decisions, and the way each uses its communications function to competitive advantage.
2. The ability to analyse problems, help generate ways to fix them, and participate in and communicate their solution.
3. The knowledge of the way values, attitudes, and opinions work and interact to influence behavior, and how to design measurable communications programs based on market and public opinion research.
4. The ability to use communications to help manage change in a manner that at least protects, if not contributes to, employee morale and the company's reputation.
5. The knowledge of how different cultures react to communication, and how best to use communication to achieve transborder or multinational results for an organization.
6. The knowledge of how corporate reputation influences shareholder value, and the ability to use communications to protect and enhance a company's reputation.
7. The ability to take complex information arriving in greater volume at a faster pace than ever before, and translate it into something that people can truly understand.

Some of these keys to success can be learned in formal courses at the undergraduate and graduate level; others can only be mastered through experience and learning on the job.

At Edelman, we have a mentoring program, as well as Edel-U, a structured and continuous internal training program with curricula offered at the junior, intermediate, and senior levels. The courses vary from presentation preparation and delivery, to the use of the Internet for media relations, to an intense week of learning through our International Summer School.

We use technology to deliver courses taught by our own internal experts throughout the global network and hold regular CEO online chats with our offices around the world. For leadership training at the most senior level, we have enlisted the help of an outside resource, and are now starting to cascade this program throughout the organization and in all of our 43 offices.

Summary

The societal trends and technological advances that have driven the most significant changes for business and the media have affected all of the professional services, including public relations. The PR professional now fills a vital role in the management of successful companies and organizations, by being brought in earlier and having more influence than ever before upon strategic business decisions.

With this increase in responsibility has come a need for a new set of skills and knowledge, that go well beyond the basic accepted tools of the PR trade. Some of these new skills and knowledge can be learned and acquired through formal courses, others through experience, and still others through on the job training and mentoring.

Finally, as our world becomes more and more complex and the pace of change accelerates, the importance of clear and concise communications programs will increase, as will the need for consummate public relations professionals to design and deliver them.

Clients will continue to benefit from all of their communications and marketing suppliers working cohesively to achieve their strategic business objectives.

As for the ad folks, they shouldn't worry too much. They still get the lion's share of any budget, and the importance of paid media in the marketing mix will continue. In the meantime, the advertising guys will have to forgive those of us who work in the earned media category if we take a moment to enjoy just a little of our time in the sun.

ENDNOTES

Chapter 2

1. Philip Lesly, *Lesly's PR Handbook* (Worthington, OH: Publishing Horizons, 1983).
2. John F. Budd, Jr., "When Less is More," *Public Relations* Quarterly, Spring 1990, p. 5.
3. Fraser P. Seitel, *The Practice of Public Relations* (Upper Saddle River, NJ: Prentice Hall, 1987).
4. Ibid.

Chapter 3

1. Creativity in Public Relations Awards (CIPRA), conducted by PR Central.
2. Leslie Wayne, "Lucrative Lobbying Jobs Await Many Leaving Government Service," *The New York Times*, Dec. 16, 2000.

Chapter 7

1. Sunshine Janda, "Not-for-Profits: A New Ballgame," *PR Journal*, Jan. 1990, p. 22.

Chapter 8

1. Howard Mitchell III, *What Every Account Executive Should Know About Public Relations* (booklet), American Association of Advertising Agencies, 1989.
2. Philip Lesly, *Lesly's PR Handbook* (Worthington, OH: Publishing Horizons, 1983).
3. Joel Pomerantz, "The Media and PR: Pride and Prejudice," *PR Quarterly*, Winter 1989–90.

Chapter 10

1. "Clout and prestige in being a speechwriter," *IABC Communication World*, Oct. 1990.
2. Timothy J. Koranda, "Writing Speeches with Impact," *PR Journal*, Sept. 1990.

Chapter 11

1. "Spheres of Influence Grow in Washington," *The New York Times*, Oct. 16, 1999, C1.
2. "State of Corporate Public Affairs Survey, 1999–2000," *Public Affairs Council*, Washington, DC.

Chapter 13

1. Paul S. Forbes, "Applying Strategic Management to Public Relations," *Public Relations Journal*, March 1992, p. 32.

Chapter 14

1. Bill Cantor, *Experts in Action: Inside Public Relations* (White Plains, NY: Longman, 1989).
2. Cynthia Clark, "What Every Public Company Must Know About Disclosing Information," *The Strategist*, Fall 2000, p. 32.
3. Stephanie Zschunke, "The Annual Report: Corporate Compass," *Reputation Management*, June 2000.
4. "Managing the Annual Report," *Public Relations Journal*, August 1992, p. 24.

Chapter 15

1. Bernard Weinraub, "Gatekeeper to the Stars," *The New York Times*, May 3, 1999, p. B1.
2. Catherine Seipp, "The puppet masters," *The American Journalism Review*, Oct. 1999, p. 22.
3. Daniel Akst, "Legendary Hollywood Flack Ready for Next Starring Role," *Los Angeles Times*, June 30, 1992.

Chapter 16

1. Melody Petersen, "Pushing Pills With Piles of Money," *The New York Times*, Oct. 5, 2000.
2. Chris Adams, "FDA Scrambles to Police Drug Ads' Truthfulness." *Wall Street Journal*, Jan. 2, 2001.
3. Don Hyman, "Pharmaceuticals: Balancing the Demands of Diverse Publics," *Public Relations Journal*, Oct. 1990, p. 22.

Chapter 17

1. Bill Cantor, *Experts in Action: Inside Public Relations* (White Plains, NY: Longman, 1989).
2. Otto Lerbinger, *The Crisis Manager* (Mahwah, NJ: Lawrence Erlbaum Associates, 1997).

Chapter 18

1. Laurie Freeman, "From the basement to the penthouse," *Advertising Age*, Sept. 25, 2000, p. 40.

Chapter 22

1. Robert Half, "Is Your Resume a Joke," *Managing Your Career*, Spring 1997, p. 19.
2. *How to Use the Internet to Choose or Change Careers* (New York: Kaplan/*Newsweek* 2000).
3. Douglas Newsom, Scott A., Van Slyke Turk, J., *This is PR: The Realities of Public Relations*, 5th ed. (Wadsworth, 1993).
4. *How to Use the Internet to Choose or Change Careers* (New York: Kaplan/*Newsweek* 2000).
5. Donald Asher, "How to Earn a Promotion in 12 Months or Less," *Dow Jones Managing Your Career*, Spring 1997.
6. David Kirby, "Finessing Interviews: Don't Ask, Do Tell," *The New York Times*, Jan. 30, 2001, p. E2.
7. Katie Sweeney, "Dot.Com Frenzy Fuels Red-Hot Job Market," *Tactics*, Oct. 2000.
8. Donald Asher, "How to Earn a Promotion in 12 Months or Less, *Dow Jones Managing Your Career*, Spring 1997.
9. "The 50 most powerful women in PR," *PRWEEK*, August 9, 1997, p. 16.
10. Marshall Consultants 1999 Compensation Review.

GLOSSARY

Account executive: The individual employed by a PR firm, corporation, or organization charged with the general responsibilities of coping with present problems and anticipating future ones. These duties often encompass media relations and new products and may also include monitoring trends, organizing trade shows, and arranging press tours.

Accredited Business Communicator (ABC): Granted by the International Association of Business Communicators (IABC). An accreditation for high achievement and competence in business communication management.

Accredited in Public Relations (APR): A title conferred by PRSA, the Public Relations Society of America, designating that the individual is "accredited in public relations," in having completed written and oral examinations and served at least 5 years in this field.

Ad-Pub: In the movie and entertainment business, refers to the department responsible for advertising, promoting, and publicizing a film or theatrical production.

Advisory: An announcement or notice that serves to advise the media of the holding of a press conference. May also be used as a guide for securing media credentials for an event.

Advocacy: falls into the general sphere of issues management and may involve the relationship of a corporation or organization to its community, and include issues of contributions and volunteerism.

Angle: Also known as slant, peg, or hook. It relates to the point of view from which a release or news story is written, to interest a particular audience.

Audio conference: The modern counterpart of the old telephone conference, but today is considered an element of teleconferencing. A conference coordinator usually makes the arrangements.

Backgrounder: A briefing or report for the purpose of providing background information on a governmental agency, organization, or corporation.

Beat: The particular news source or activity covered by a reporter or correspondent in the media.

Branding: Relates to a corporation or other organization's effort to maintain the primacy of its image identity and reputation.

B-rolls: Used in broadcast and online. It is raw video footage, not scripted, about a new product, development, or even a competition and must be edited before use.

Byliner: The recognition received by the writer of an article in a newspaper or magazine.

Case history: Refers to the relevant information or material gathered about an individual, group, or company.

Cause-related marketing: A promotional technique in which a company is linked with a nonprofit organization, a public service, or another cause.

Change management: The setting of objectives, strategies, and policies as to where an organization wants to go and how to get there.

Chat forums, chat rooms, and sites: Media relations tools often used to reach the new E-fluentials.

CIPRA: Creativity and Excellence In Public Relations Awards. Given annually by PR Central for outstanding achievement in various practice areas.

Clip book: A collection of stories in the media about a client. Usually maintained by a PR firm.

Clipping bureaus: Research services that measure print and electronic press coverage.

Community relations: The practice area that encompasses a corporation or other organization's activities in education, philanthropy, and culture.

Components: Also referred to as practice areas. They include health care, public affairs, technology, public interest, and media relations.

Computer-aided research: Accesses the Internet for information about a corporation or other group, or its publics.

Consumer affairs: Addresses the subjects of consumer attitudes and purchasing practices. Also deals with product marketing and safety issues.

Convergence: A most powerful and evocative word that describes the technology-driven changes revolutionizing every aspect of the way business is done across the world.

Corporate communications: The department responsible for many activities within the organization. May include strategic planning, resource allocation, employee communications, public affairs, community development, government relations, event management, and issues management.

Crisis communications and management: The practice of PR that deals with an organization, corporation, or government agency's response, tactics, and communications when a crisis or disaster strikes.

Crisis dark site: A template that is plugged into a Web site during a crisis in order to provide immediate access for the media and other publics.

Databank services: The uses of computerized collections of information.

Daybook: A listing of upcoming news-making events fed by wire services, such as AP and UPI, to broadcasters and other media. PR people feed the events and items to the wire services.

Desktop videoconferencing: The transmission of charts, documents, and other stationary visuals.

Development: In fund raising, the cultivation of prospective donors. The fund-raising executive at a university or other organization is called the development director.

Diversity marketing: The marketing of goods and services to minority groups.

Double planting: The "unethical" practice whereby a media relations specialist sends the same "exclusive" to more than one news source at the same time.

E-commerce: New technologies and capabilities to create financial portals and Web-enabling businesses, and implementing more Internet payment options.

Electronic media monitoring: Used by PR people to monitor TV, radio, and wire services coverage. This service is often provided by the same companies that monitor press clippings from print media.

Electronic press kit (EPK): A video presentation containing graphics and other information about a film, product, or service.

E-mail: A means of conveying messages, information and news electronically to various media sources.

Employee communications and relations: The strategic PR practice that communicates issues, events, programs, and changes within an organization.

Exclusive: A piece of news sent to a newspaper or other medium, along with the privilege of using it first.

Fact sheet: A listing or statement of details about an individual or group, often included in the press kit sent to the media.

Flacks: The disparaging term once used for press agents. The name derives from Gene Flack, an old-time movie publicity agent.

Image building or image program: Advertising and other techniques to enhance goodwill or achieve other objectives, not directly to promote or sell.

Integrated communications: Public relations, advertising, direct marketing, promotion, and other disciplines coordinated through a single planning system.

Integrated marketing: Combines advertising, public relations, and other activities in a coordinated strategy using messages and media.

Interactive marketing: A practice most often employed by a PR counsel firm for a client. Its functions include site submission, campaign, search engine positioning, "must-see" Web animations, and viral e-mail campaigns.

International Association of Business Communicators (IABC): The professional association for public relations professionals and other communicators.

Internet conferencing: A conference set up over the Internet where everyone talks to each other on their regular telephone.

Internet marketing: A leveraging of the Internet to create identities and build brands.

Interviews: The most often used technique in public relations for a dialogue or conversation between an individual, perhaps a CEO, and a member of the media for the purpose of press coverage. Interviews are also used for focus-group research.

Intranet: The online tool that serves as a communications link within a large organization.

Investor relations: The practice that deals with a corporation or other organization's financial communication with its publics.

Issue backgrounder: A media relations technique that explains to the media all the facts about an issue.

Issues communications and management: The practice that falls within the purview of public affairs departments, primarily in corporations, but in other organizations as well. It deals with matters affecting the corporation in the present and potentially affecting it in the future.

Lobbying: A strategy that involves interaction between an organization's representatives and government officials. Often it takes the form of influencing legislation or, in some cases, introducing new legislation affecting the organization's interest.

Media alert: An announcement of a media event, speech, or presentation.

Media analysis: The evaluation of the available media sources for a campaign, or the results of a media effort.

Media brief: A specific announcement sent to the media about a speech or presentation.

Media database: A computerized directory of individuals and departments within the media to whom publicity solicitations are made.

Media kit: A packet of material containing information about an organization, publication, network, or even a TV show.

Media relations: The vital function of public relations dealing with the preparation and identification of news and information for use in the press and other media.

Media training: The educational process for those who face the media frequently to learn good communications technique, including subjects such as message development, speech and presentation skills, and media simulations.

New media: The broad term that encompasses high tech, the Internet, interactive communications, CD-ROMs, and online publishing.

Online media: The affinity sites, webzines, activist sites, and other online communities applied in media relations practice.

Pitch: An oral or written solicitation by a PR person on behalf of a story or event.

Placement: The acceptance and appearance of a news item, feature story, or other release in a newspaper, magazine, or broadcast medium. Also relates to "getting ink."

Position paper: A detailed, written statement about a single political or other issue that articulates a position, viewpoint, or policy.

PR firm or PR counsel firm: An organization retained by a corporation, organization, or individual to assist its clients in marshaling public relations and public affairs resources. In this respect, it is involved in both planning and execution.

Practice area: The specialization of public relations practice, such as public affairs, crisis management, health care, or media relations.

Press agent: A term often used negatively in public relations to refer to individuals whose approach is solely to gain favorable publicity or media attention in almost any way possible. Used frequently in the entertainment industry.

Press conference: The coming together of heads of corporations, organizations, and individuals with the press regarding news developments.

Press kit: A package of media tools that may include a press release, advisory, booklet, backgrounder, speech reprint, and press clippings.

Press release: Also called news release. Serves as a guideline for the media for their suggested coverage of a situation, event, or news story.

Public affairs: The practice of public relations that deals with lobbying, issues management, grass-roots activity, advocacy, and government relations.

Public interest service: The public relations component that encompasses community relations, corporate philanthropy, corporate image, and social responsibility.

Public policy: The position of a corporation or other organization on issues or policies. Is considered an adjunct of public affairs.

Public Relations Society of America (PRSA): The leading professional organization for PR practitioners.

Public speaking training: The skills, techniques, and nuances of delivering speeches, interviews, and press conferences.

Publics: The entities whose attention is sought by a corporation, individual, governmental agency, charitable organization, and others.

Rapid-response Web site: In crisis situations, this "dark" Internet site downloads to "go live" and is designed to centralize and control information flow, providing immediate, accurate, and comprehensive information.

Reputation management: Also known as image management. It refers to an organization's or corporation's continuing efforts to protect its reputation.

Satellite media tours: Where a CEO or other spokesperson is interviewed in a single location by many TV and cable broadcasters.

Silver Anvil: The coveted annual award bestowed by the PRSA for excellence by practitioners in various practice areas.

Social marketing: The efforts of a corporation to promote social issues and other initiatives.

Special events: A PR strategy used to expose a large, visible, and influential audience to a product, an issue, or an individual.

Spin: The term most often used in journalism for the manipulation of public perceptions. Also relates to "image fixing."

Spin doctors: The purveyors of spin.

Spokesperson: A person designated to speak for another or for a group.

Stakeholder: A term used synonymously with "a public." Relates to an individual or group that impacts on a corporation or other organization.

Strategic communications: The focusing and directing of a corporation's or organization's public relations and marketing plans involving its internal problems, future opportunities, customer concerns, employee relations, and public opinion.

Talking points: Facts, features, or short sentences that sum up an organization's position on the issues. Used often by a spokesperson in accenting or highlighting an issue.

Video news release (VNR): A news release transmitted to TV stations via satellite or videotape, or for use online.

Vision, mission, and values: A standard for large organizations to evaluate their reputation and image.

Webzine: A Web magazine that may also serve as an organization's employee publication.

REFERENCES

Chapter 1

1. Tye, L., *The Father of Spin: Edward L. Bernays & The Birth of Public Relations* (New York: Crown) Book review in *Columbia Journalism Review*, Nov./Dec. 1998, p. 67.

Chapter 2

1. Nolte, L. W., and D. L. Wilcox. (1979). *Fundamentals of Public Relations* (Elmsford, NY: Pergamon).
2. Lesly, P. (1983). *Lesly's PR Handbook* (Worthington, OH: Publishing Horizons).
3. Budd, Jr., J. F. "When Less is More," *Public Relations Quarterly*, Spring 1990, p. 5.
4. Seitel, F. P. (1987). *The Practice of Public Relations* (Upper Saddle River, NJ: Prentice-Hall).
5. "Projected Growth of Public Relations," U.S. Dept. of Labor, in *2000 Occupational Outlook Handbook*.

Chapter 3

1. Creativity in Public Relations Awards (CIPRA) 1998, conducted By PR Central.
2. Wayne, L. "Lucrative Lobbying Jobs Await Many Leaving Government Service," *The New York Times*, Dec. 16, 2000.
3. Ad for Philip Morris Companies, *The New Yorker*.
4. Philip J. Webster, "What's the Bottom Line?," *PR Journal*, Feb. 1990, p. 18.
5. Article on Coca Cola, *The Wall Street Journal*, Oct. 17, 2000.

Chapter 4

1. Council of Public Relations Firms, 2000 Industry Ranking, U.S. Revenue Breakout.
2. Award-winning campaigns of Ten Largest PR firms from various Silver Anvil winners, conducted by the Public Relations Society of America (PRSA) annually. Also, CIPRA (Creativity and Excellence in Public Relations Award, presented annually by *Inside PR*, a New York publication.
3. Much of the research for this chapter was supplied by the ten largest PR firms and accessed from their Web sites.
4. "Interpublic Group to Acquire True North Communications," *The New York Times*, March 20, 2001, p. C1.
5. "Is 'Flack Whacking' Good Public Relations?," *The New York Times*, Oct. 2, 2001.
6. "PR on a Roll," *Advertising Age*, Oct. 2, 2000.
7. "The 100 Most Influential PR People of the 20th Century," *PR WEEK*, Oct. 18, 1999.
8. "PR Gains Revenue—and Some Respect," *Advertising Age*, March 12, 2001.
9. "A Chill Hits Madison Avenue," *The Wall Street Journal*, March 19, 2001.
10. "Why did PR Firms Have Their Best Year Ever?," *Advertising Age*, March 24, 1997.
11. "The Agency of the Decade," *The Wall Street Journal*, March 2, 2000.
12. "Burson Runs for Olympics," *Advertising Age*, Sept. 11, 1990.
13. "A Good Man to Know in a Crisis," *The Times, London*, Aug. 16, 2000.
14. "PR Plans: IPG Revamps," *Advertising Age*, Sept. 25, 2000.

15. "Every Spin Control Couldn't Lighten '91," *Crain's New York Business*," March 23, 1992.
16. "Who's Who in Agency Healthcare PR," *PR WEEK*, Oct. 30, 2000.
17. "The E-gang," *Forbes*, July 26, 1999.
18. "Who's Hot and Who's Not," *Inside PR*, Winter 1999.
19. "The eESTABLISHMENT 50," *Vanity Fair*, May 2000.

Chapter 6
1. Facts About the Corporation. www.bankofamerica.com.
2. Bank of America's *Global Financial Markets Outlook*, Mar./Apr. 2001.
3. Bank of America Foundation Annual Report 2000.
4. Bank of America Summary Annual Report 1999.
5. Bank of America Summary Annual Report 2000.

Chapter 7
1. Annual Report 1999, Newspaper Association of America (NAA).
2. *Presstime*, publication of NAA, various issues.
3. Web site of the American Psychological Association (APA): www.apa.org.
4. Janda, S., "Not-for-Profits: A New Ballgame," *PR Journal*, Jan. 1990, p. 22.
5. CIPRA 2000 Competition, Dept. of Health, Administration for HIV/AIDS campaign.

Chapter 8
1. Mitchell III, H., *What Every Account Executive Should Know about Public Relations*, American Association of Advertising Agencies (booklet), 1989.
2. Program Guide, Public Relations World Congress 2000.
3. American Heart Association press release, Nov. 13, 2000.
4. Lesly, op. cit.
5. Mitchell III, H., American Association of Advertising Agencies, *What Every Account Executive Should Know about Public Relations* (booklet), 1989.
6. Pomerantz, J., "The Media and PR: Pride and Prejudice," *PR Quarterly*, Winter 1989–90.

7. Weiner, R. (1996). *Webster's New World Dictionary of Media Communications* (New York: Macmillan).
8. Ruberry, B., "E-mailing Media: A Primer," *Public Relations Tactics*, May 2000, p. 6.
9. *Ogilvy Public Relations Practice Book* (booklet), Ameritrade Case history.
10. "Soaring with Sabre," Vollmer PR's CIPRA 2000 entry.
11. Howard J. Rubenstein interview from *Creating Your Career in Communications and Entertainment* by Leonard Mogel, (Sewickley, PA: GATF Press, 1998), p. 242.
12. "The World's Fastest Press Conference," Meltzer & Martin Public Relations for client Sprint Business, CIPRA 1998 Award-winner.
13. Jay Kordich press tour, *ABA Newswire*, April 1992.
14. Peter Pitts on effective communications. PRSA's *The Strategist*, Winter 2001.
15. Mike Lynch, American Medical Association, interview.
16. Tips and Tactics from the *Media Relations Insider*, premiere issue.
17. American Heart Association press release, Nov. 13, 2000.

Chapter 9

1. "A 'Tank' Rolls Through CNN Before Merger," *The New York Times*, Dec. 4, 2000.
2. Bobo, C., "Gaining Support For a Strategic Emphasis On Employee Communications," *Tactics*, Feb. 2000.
3. Khan, J., "Internal Communications: Ensuring Strategy and Measurement Coexist," *Tactics*, Feb. 2000.
4. Davis, A., "Communicating Change in a Brave New Way," *Tactics*, July 2000.
5. Solution Engineering Case Study. "We Are One," Boxenbaum Grates PR, 1998.
6. The Boeing-McDonnell Merger. CIPRA 1998.
7. Bank of America Employee Bonus, *PR Journal*, Nov. 1990.
8. "The e-IBMer," CIPRA 1999.
9. "Diverse Service and Industrial Companies Use Innovative Employee Communications," *PR Journal*, Nov. 1990.
10. "Reaching Out to the TV Generation," *PR Journal*, Nov. 1990.
11. "Creating a Shared Focused Future," Edelman PR Worldwide, Silver Anvil 2000.

12. "Face to Face Communication at Navistar," Matha MacDonald PR, CIPRA 2000.

Chapter 10
1. "CEO speechwriters' median salary," *PR Journal*, Feb. 1990.
2. "Clout and prestige in being a speechwriter," *IABC Communication World*, Oct. 1990.
3. "The Executive Speaker Philosophy," program, www.executivespeaker.net.
4. Spalding, J., "Speech Writers in the Thick of It," *IABC Communication World*, Oct. 1990.
5. Koranda, T. J., "Writing Speeches with Impact," *PR Journal*, Sept. 1990.
6. Francis, C., "How to Stop Boring Your Audience to Death," Speech delivered to the New York chapter of the International Association of Business Communicators (IABC), Sept. 20, 2000. www.executivespeaker.net.

Chapter 11
1. "Utilities Hire Ex-Chairman of G.O.P. to Avert Suits," *The New York Times*, June 6, 2001.
2. *Public Affairs Review*, 2000 Journal of the Public Affairs Council.
3. *Creating a Digital Democracy* (Foundation for Public Affairs).
4. *Cyber Activism*, published by the Foundation for Public Affairs.
5. "Spin Doctor to the World," *Los Angeles Times Magazine*, Nov. 24, 1991.
6. "Detroit's Ace in the Hole," TomPaine.com.
7. "Experience Your America," Ogilvy PR Worldwide for National Park Foundation.
8. American Association of Political Consultants, Mission Statement.
9. Campaign 2000: Media Money, *Columbia Journalism Review*, Sept./Oct. 2000.
10. Stopping the Government Takeover of the TAV. CIPRA 2000. Burston-Marsteller PR for the Tennessee-American Water Company.
11. Public Affairs Council Services. www.pac.org.
12. Public Policy Government Affairs. www.naa.org.
13. "Spheres of Influence Grow in Washington," *The New York Times*, Oct. 16, 1999, C1.

14. "Drug Lobby Wins Big With Massive Spending Against Medicare Plan," *The Wall Street Journal*, Dec. 15, 2000.
15. "Lucrative Lobbying Jobs Await Many Leaving Government Service," *The New York Times*, Dec. 16, 2000, p. A11.

Chapter 12
1. "Getting the Message From 'Eco-Terrorist'," *The New York Times*, Jan. 8, 2001.
2. "Microsoft Faces 3 Suits Alleging Racial Bias," *Los Angeles Times*, Jan. 3, 2001.
3. AT&T Foundation. Learning Network. www.att.com.
4. IBM Corporate Community Relations. www.ibm.com.
5. Philip Morris family of companies, ad for BAM 2000 Next Wave Festival, *The New Yorker*, Oct. 9, 2000, p. 3.
6. Philip Morris family of companies for Artist Reborn Lee Krasner, *Brill's Content*, Oct. 2000.
7. Philip Morris family of companies, ad for National Network to End Domestic Violence Fund, *The New York Times*, Oct. 29, 2000.
8. University of Michigan job offering for Development Officer. www.umich.edu.
9. "Arching Into Education Scholarship Program," CIPRA 2000 for McDonald's New York Tri-State Owners.
10. "Get the Helmet," Bike Helmet Safety Campaign. Silver Anvil Award 2000. Category: Public Service. McDonald's Corp. with Golan/Harris PR International.
11. "AOL Foundation." Silver Anvil Award 2000. Category: Institutional Programs. AOL Foundation with Fleishman-Hillard PR.
12. "At $112 a night, the homeless aren't the only ones paying a high price." Ad in *The New York Times*, Nov. 24, 2000, p. C2.
13. Target's "Take Charge of Education" campaign. Target with Martin/Williams PR.
14. MasterCard International campaign, "Are You Credit Wise," CIPRA 2000.

Chapter 13
1. EPSON Stylus Color 740i Product Launch. Silver Anvil 2000 Award. Category: Marketing Consumer Products. Epson America, Inc., with Walt & Company Communications.

2. "Microsoft Exec Stays Focused." *Advertising Age*, Oct. 9, 2000, p. S24.
3. Burston-Marsteller PR Practice Profile. www.bm.com.
4. The WingspanBank.com. "Female Finance Factor." Silver Anvil 2000 Brand Development entry. WingspanBank.com with Ogilvy Public Relation Worldwide.
5. Rubin, B., "Campaign Opens Door to Safety Issue," *Public Relations Journal*, Feb. 1991, p. 28.
6. Edmondson, J., "Come Together: Why Integrated Marketing Works," *Tactics*, Jan. 2000.
7. Forbes, P. S., "Applying Strategic Management to Public Relations," *Public Relations Journal*, March 1992, p. 32.
8. Publishers Clearing House with Rogers & Cowan PR. Silver Anvil 2000. Category: Marketing Consumer Sources.
9. The National Cattlemen's Beef Association with Ketchum PR. Silver Anvil 2000. Category: Integrated Communications.
10. Marken, G. A., "Corporate Image—We All Have One, But Few Work to Protect and Project It," *Public Relations Quarterly*, Spring 1990, p. 21.
11. Ogilvy Public Relations Worldwide Corporate Practice (booklet).
12. United Airlines, ad in *The Wall Street Journal*, April 22, 1997.
13. Target ad in *The New York Times*, Nov. 12, 2000.
14. Burson-Marsteller website: www.bm.com/expertise/mergers.

Chapter 14

1. "General Electric Buying Honeywell In $45 Billion Deal," *The New York Times*, Oct. 23, 2000, p. A1.
2. "The Changing Relationship Between IR and PR," *Inside PR*, Sept. 1998.
3. Cantor, B. (1989). *Experts in Action: Inside Public Relations* (White Plains, NY: Longman).
4. "Chase Hopes Deal for Morgan Will Bring it Prestige," *The New York Times*, Sept. 14, 2000, p. C1.
5. "Fund Bolsters University Ideas," *The Los Angeles Times*, Dec. 18, 2000, p. C1.
6. Clark, C., "What Every Public Company Must Know About Disclosing Information," *The Strategist*, Fall 2000, p. 32.
7. Tribune Company, 1999 Annual Report.
8. Zschunke, S., "The Annual Report: Corporate Compass," *Reputation Management*, June 2000.

9. "Nike Annual Report Shows Company Still has Sense of Humor," *Inside PR*, August 1998.
10. "Managing the Annual Report," *Public Relations Journal*, Aug. 1992, p. 24.

Chapter 15
1. Weinraub, B., "Gatekeeper to the Stars," *The New York Times*, May 3, 1999, p. B1.
2. Seipp, C., "The puppet masters," *The American Journalism Review*, Oct. 1999, p. 22.
3. Akst, D., "Legendary Hollywood Flack Ready for Next Starring Role," *Los Angeles Times*, June 30, 1992.
4. Fearn-Banks, K. (1996). *Crisis Communications*," (Mahwah, NJ: Lawrence Erlbaum Associates).
5. Collins, S., "Hollywood's PR People," *Los Angeles Times*, Dec. 26, 1995, p. D1.

Chapter 16
1. Petersen, M., "Pushing Pills With Piles of Money," *The New York Times*, Oct. 5, 2000.
2. Hyman, D., "Pharmaceuticals: Balancing the Demands of Diverse Publics," *Public Relations Journal*, Oct. 1990, p. 22.
3. Rosenblatt, J., "Some Doctors See Scare Tactics in Device's PR," *The Wall Street Journal*, Aug. 2, 2000.
4. Full-page ad for Sudafed and Benadryl: *The New York Times*, Nov. 12, 2000, p. 25.
5. Information about American Psychological Association (APA). www.apa.org.
6. "America's Awakening" with Eli Lilly. CIPRA 2000. Eli Lilly & Co. with Chamberlain Communications Group.

Chapter 17
1. "The Columbine Tragedy." Silver Anvil 2000. Rick Kaufman for Jefferson County Public Schools.
2. Cantor, B., *Experts in Action: Inside Public Relations*, op.cit.
3. Fearn-Banks, K., *Crisis Communications: A Casebook Approach*, op.cit.
4. Lerbinger, O. (1997). *The Crisis Manager* (Mahwah, NJ: Lawrence Erlbaum Associates).
5. "Crisis Odwalla" with Edelman PR. Silver Anvil 1997.

Chapter 18

1. Freeman, L., "From the Basement to the Penthouse," *Advertising Age*, Sept. 25, 2000, p. 40.
2. Beyer, A. F., "Eight Hallmarks of a Great High-Tech Agency Hire," *Tactics*, June 2000.
3. Weiner, R., "Spotlight On: Conferencing Techniques: Audio, Video and Internet," *Tactics*, June 2000.
4. "Pitching Online Media," *Media Relations Insider*, Nov. 2000, p. 1.

Chapter 19

1. Dennis Wilcox, Survey of West Coast Employers.

Chapter 20

1. Public Relations World Congress 2000 Program Guide.
2. Public Relations Society of America (PRSA). Various materials. www.prsa.org.
3. International Association of Business Communications (IABC). Various materials. www.iabc.com.
4. The Council of Public Relations Firms. *Careers in Public Relations* (booklet). Various materials. www.prfirms.org/student.
5. The Institute for Public Relations. www.instituteforpr.org.
6. Association for Education in Journalism and Mass Communications (AEJMC). www.aejmc.org.

Chapter 22

1. Special Report: "Recruiting and retaining the most competent professionals," *The Strategist*, Fall 2000, p. 7.
2. *A Student's Guide to Public Relations Education 2000*, Council of Public Relations Firms, Princeton, NJ.
3. Milkereit, J., "Want To Be in Public Relations?," *Tactics*, March 2001, p. 15.
4. Half, R., "Is Your Resume a Joke," *Managing Your Career*, Spring 1997, p. 19.
5. *Yale Daily News Guide to Internships 2000* (New York: Kaplan and Simon & Schuster, 1999).
6. Stromp, S., "Resumes and Cover Letters," live online discussion on www.washingtonpost.com, Nov. 15, 1999.
7. Eaves, E., "Job Sites Deliver Too Much—and Too Little," *Los Angeles Times*, May 4, 2000.

8. *How to Use the Internet to Choose or Change Careers* (New York: Kaplan/*Newsweek* 2000).
9. Brust, P., "Convincing Interviewers to Bite," *Managing Your Career*, Spring 1997, p. 28.
10. Kirby, D., "Finessing Interviews: Don't Ask, Do Tell," *The New York Times*, Jan. 30, 2001, p. E2.
11. Greenberg, K., "Student Interns Get Real-life Experience, and sometimes a job," *Public Relations Journal*, Dec. 1991, p. 7.
12. Gaschen, D., with Bohle, S., "From Backpacks To Bill Gates," *Tactics*, March 2000.
13. Sweeney, K., "Dot.Com Frenzy Fuels Red-Hot Job Market," *Tactics*, March 2000.
14. Howard, C. M., "Skills You Need to Expand Your Counselor Role," *Tactics*, Oct. 2000.
15. Asher, D., "How to Earn a Promotion in 12 Months or Less," *Dow Jones Managing Your Career*, Spring 1997.
16. "The 50 Most Powerful Women in PR," *PRWEEK*, August 9, 1999, p. 16.
17. Marshall Consultants 1999 Compensation Review.
18. The IABC and PRSA Profile 2000: A Survey of the Profession.
19. Council of Public Relations Firms October 2000 Salary Survey.
20. "A Young Public Relations Professional's Day," from *Careers in Public Relations*, booklet (Council of Public Relations Firms).

Chapter 23

1. Fremes, C., "The Future Face of Public Relations," *Strategy Magazine*, revised April 19, 2001.

RECOMMENDED READING

Austin, Erica Weintraub, and Bruce E. Pinkleton. 2001. *Strategic Public Management*, Mahwah, NJ: Lawrence E. Erlbaum.

Baskin, Otis W., and Craig E. Aronoff. 1988. *Public Relations: The Profession and the Practice*, 2nd ed. Dubuque, IA: William C. Brown.

Bivins, Thomas. 1991. *Handbook for Public Relations Writing*. Lincolnwood, IL: National Textbook Company.

Cantor, Bill (Chester Burger, Ed.). 1989. *Experts in Action: Inside Public Relations*, 2nd ed. White Plains, NY: Longman.

Cormier, Robin A. 1995. *Error-Free Writing: A Lifetime Guide to Flawless Business Writing*. Alexandria, VA: EEI Press.

Council of Public Relations Firms. *A Student's Guide to Public Relations Education*. New York.

Cutlip, Scott M., Allen H. Center, and Glen M. Broom. 2000. *Effective Public Relations*, 8th ed. Upper Saddle River, NJ: Prentice Hall.

Detz, Joan. 1992. *How to Write and Give a Speech*. New York: St. Martin's Press.

Doty, Dorothy I. 1990. *Publicity and Public Relations*. Happauge, NY: Barron.

Ewen, Stuart. 1998. *PR! A Social History of Spin.* New York: Basic Books.

Fearn-Banks, Kathleen. 1996. *Crisis Communications.* Mahwah, NJ: Lawrence Erlbaum Associates.

Goodwin, Richard. 1988. *Remembering America.* Boston: Little Brown.

Grunig, 1992. James E. *Excellence in Public Relations and Communications Management.* Mahwah, NJ: Lawrence Erlbaum Associates.

Grunig, Larissa A., Elizabeth Lance Toth, and Linda Childers Hon. 2001. *Women in Public Relations.* New York: The Guilford Press.

Kelly, Kathleen S. 1998. *Effective Fund-Raising Management.* Mahwah, NJ: Lawrence Erlbaum Associates.

Koten, John A. 1997. *The Handbook of Strategic Public Relations and Integrated Communications.* New York: McGraw-Hill.

Ledingham, John A., and Stephen D. Bruning (Eds.). 2000. *Public Relations as Relationship Management.* Mahwah, NJ: Lawrence Erlbaum Associates.

Lerbinger, Otto. 1997. *The Crisis Manager.* Mahwah, NJ: Lawrence Erlbaum Associates.

Marlow, Eugene. 1996. *Electronic Public Relations.* Belmont, CA: Wadsworth.

Mitchell, Howard. 1989. *What Every Account Executive Should Know About Public Relations.* New York: American Association of Advertising Agencies.

Mogel, Leonard. 1998. *The Magazine: Everything You Need to Know to Make It in the Magazine Business,* 4th ed. Pittsburgh: GATF Press.

Mogel, Leonard. 2000. *The Newspaper: Everything You Need to Know to Make It in the Newspaper Business.* Pittsburgh: GATF Press.

Montgomery, Robert, and Peter J. Pitts. 1998. *Become Strategic or Die.* Indianapolis, IN: MZD Publishing.

Nagelschmidt, Joseph (Ed.). 1982. *Public Affairs Handbook.* New York: Amacom.

Newsom, Douglas, Alan Scott, and Judy Van Slyke Turk. 1993. *This Is PR: The Realities of Public Relations,* 5th ed. Belmont, CA: Wadsworth.

Newsweek Inc. and Kaplan Inc. 2000. *How to use the Internet to Choose or Change Careers.*

Noonan, Peggy. 1991. *What I Saw at the Revolution*. New York: Ivy Books.

Public Relations Society of America. 1999. *Careers in Public Relations: Practical Information to Help you Land Your First Public Relations Job*. New York: Public Relations Society of America.

Rayfield, Robert, J. D. Pincus, and J. E. Knipp. 1991. *Public Relations Writing: Strategies And Skills*. Dubuque, IA: William C. Brown.

Reilly, Robert T. 1987. *Public Relations in Action*, 2nd ed. Upper Saddle River, NJ: Prentice Hall.

Seitel, Fraser P. 1998. *The Practice of Public Relations*. Upper Saddle River, NJ: Prentice Hall.

Simon, Raymond, and Joseph Zappala. 1996. *Public Relations Workbook: Writing & Techniques*. Lincolnwood, IL: NTC Publishing Group.

Swift-Rosenzweig, Leslie. 2000. *What We Learned on Our Visit to The State of Corporate Public Affairs*. Public Affairs Review.

Vivian, John. 1997. *The Media of Mass Communications*, 4th ed. Boston: Allyn & Bacon.

Weiner, Richard. 1990. *Webster's New World Dictionary of Media and Communications*. New York: Simon & Schuster.

Wilcox, Dennis L., and Lawrence W. Nolte. 1990. *Public Relations Writing*. New York: Harper & Row.

Wilcox, Dennis L., Phillip H. Ault, Warren K. Agee, and Glen T. Cameron. 2000. *Public Relations, Strategies and Tactics*. Reading, MA: Addison-Wesley Educational Publishers, Inc.

Yale Daily News. 2000. *Yale Daily News Guide to Internships 2000*. New York: *Kaplan and Simon and Schuster*.

AUTHOR INDEX